Praise for Joe Mulhall and his work

'Mulhall watches the extreme right revival from the inside – as an anti-fascist infiltrator criss-crossing the global networks of modern fascism – but he brings a deep analytical focus. By the end of it we understand one thing: the threat of a second fascist era is real.'

Paul Mason, author of *Postcapitalism*

'What struck me about [*Drums in the Distance*] is that Joe Mulhall is someone who has walked the walk […] and he also offers fascinating analysis into the global Far Right movement.'

Mobeen Azhar, BBC Radio 5 Live

'Few, if any, are better placed to write a book of this breadth and scale than Joe Mulhall. Not only increasingly pertinent, the global far right needs to be understood on all levels if it is to be tamed. Many, me included, would enthusiastically embrace such a book.'

Mark Townsend, *Observer* Home Affairs editor and author of *No Return: The True Story of How Martyrs Are Made*

'Joe has had a unique view of the far right over the past decade as it transformed from a marginal subculture into one of the defining political currents of our time. He understands how these groups think and operate, and is perfectly placed to guide readers through this disturbing but vital story.'

Daniel Trilling, author of *Bloody Nasty People: The Rise of Britain's Far Right* and *Lights in the Distance: Exile and Refuge at the Borders of Europe*

T0026957

'This is an urgent missive from the global frontlines of the fight against fascism, combining a gift for storytelling with meticulous research and academic rigour.'

Nima Elbagir, CNN Senior International Correspondent

'Mulhall has been studying far-right politics since long before anyone in the United States realized that an understanding of this issue would be crucial for policymakers, local governments, corporations, civil society, journalists, and philanthropy in the 21st century. After four years of watching the rise of domestic extremism, many decision-makers now know that they need to understand what's unfolding in the United States and abroad. This book moves past the "hot takes" that have dominated the public conversation by providing in-depth empirical evidence and analysis that can truly ground the conversation and help the reader situate what's happening in the United States within a broader historical, geopolitical, and technical context.'

danah boyd, partner researcher at Microsoft Research and founder and president of the Data & Society Institute, New York

DRUMS IN THE DISTANCE

DRUMS IN THE DISTANCE

JOURNEYS INTO THE GLOBAL FAR RIGHT

JOE MULHALL

ICON

This edition published in the UK and USA in 2022 by Icon Books Ltd
Omnibus Business Centre, 39–41 North Road, London N7 9DP
email: info@iconbooks.com • www.iconbooks.com

Previously published in the UK and USA in 2021 by Icon Books Ltd

Sold in the UK, Europe and Asia
by Faber & Faber Ltd, Bloomsbury House, 74–77 Great Russell Street,
London WC1B 3DA or their agents

Distributed in the UK, Europe and Asia
by Grantham Book Services, Trent Road, Grantham NG31 7XQ

Distributed in the USA
by Publishers Group West, 1700 Fourth Street, Berkeley, CA 94710

Distributed in Canada
by Publishers Group Canada, 76 Stafford Street, Unit 300,
Toronto, Ontario M6J 2S1

Distributed in Australia and New Zealand
by Allen & Unwin Pty Ltd, PO Box 8500, 83 Alexander Street,
Crows Nest, NSW 2065

Distributed in South Africa
by Jonathan Ball, Office B4, The District, 41 Sir Lowry Road,
Woodstock 7925

Distributed in India by Penguin Books India,
7th Floor, Infinity Tower – C, DLF Cyber City, Gurgaon 122002, Haryana

ISBN: 978-178578-861-1

Text copyright © 2021 Joe Mulhall

The author has asserted his moral rights.

Certain passages in this book have previously been published
by HOPE not hate.

No part of this book may be reproduced in any form, or by any
means, without prior permission in writing from the publisher.

Typeset in Sabon by Marie Doherty

Printed and bound in Great Britain
by Clays Ltd, Elcograf S.p.A.

CONTENTS

ABOUT THE AUTHOR

Dr Joe Mulhall is one of the UK's leading experts on far-right extremism. Senior Researcher at the UK's largest anti-fascism and anti-racism organisation, HOPE not hate, he is the co-author of *The International Alt-Right* and author of *British Fascism After the Holocaust* (both published by Routledge), and has written for the *Guardian* and *New Statesman*. He appears regularly on broadcast media including the BBC *News at Ten*, Radio 4's *Today* programme, *The Moral Maze* and *Channel 4 News*, among others.

ACKNOWLEDGEMENTS

This book tells the story of the rise of the global far right – but wherever the organised politics of hatred have emerged, there are people who have risen up and fought back. My first thanks go to these countless, nameless anti-fascists, radicals and romantics for their sacrifice and struggle, which continue to provide me with hope that we can win.

More personally, my thanks go to my friends, colleagues and comrades at HOPE not hate (HNH), whose tireless work and passion inspire me every day. A special thanks must go to its founder Nick Lowles for creating the organisation that has shaped my life over the past decade. None of the stories in this book would have happened without him placing his trust in me and allowing me to turn my passion into a job. This book also touches briefly on the story of numerous colleagues, especially Patrik Hermansson, David Lawrence, Simon Murdoch and 'Titus'. None of this would have been possible without their courage and commitment and they each have a book of their own to write one day. Thanks must also go to the wider HNH family and the numerous undercover sources whose names cannot be mentioned in this book.

I am deeply indebted to my agent Kay Peddle, without whom this book would have never made it to print. Her guidance and patience are extremely appreciated. I must also thank my editor Duncan Heath and all at Icon Books for taking on this project and being such a pleasure to work with.

A book like this relies heavily on the scholarship of numerous academics, researchers and anti-fascists who have produced necessary and fascinating work. I hope my truncated overviews do not exploit or misrepresent their work. The endnotes of this book show where my countless debts lie, and I hope I represent their work fairly.

Numerous friends pop up in these pages, namely Rob Trigwell, Rob Powell and Ena Miller. Thanks for sharing those adventures with me and for checking I retold them accurately. Thanks also to Nithi Sevaguru for his kind help in India. Others have graciously taken the time to read the draft manuscript and provided invaluable feedback, especially Craig Fowlie, Duncan Stoddard and Laura Dixon. Their honest criticism and recommendations have been a great help and improved this text significantly.

As well as the history of the far right stretching back across the post-war period, this book is entwined with personal stories that cover the last decade of my life. At times this work has no doubt made me difficult to be around, and at these moments it was the unwavering support of my closest friends that got me through. A special mention must go to those who have always been there for me, many of whom I have already mentioned above. On this account, thanks must also go to, among others, Mark and Kat Neale, Rob Gordon and Charlie Field, Matthew Walker and Sian Cain, Ed Thurlow, Charlie Burness, Ali Horn, James Bowker and Steven Judge. Apologies to those there is not space to mention, but special thanks to the rest of my friends from Woking and university.

Finally I must acknowledge my family, without whose love I would not have managed. Endless love and thanks to mum, dad, Philip, Kelly and Rich. Thanks for picking up the pieces.

For my friends at HOPE not hate

INTRODUCTION

It was roughly 8.00am when I entered the Wetherspoon's pub at Stansted airport. As I waited at the packed bar, surrounded by stag and hen parties, I noticed a man to my right who stood out among the groups of twenty-somethings in fancy dress. He wore a Fred Perry polo shirt, black with champagne twin tipping detail on the collars and cuffs and an embroidered laurel wreath over his left breast. It was tucked neatly into bleached Levi's jeans, cuffs rolled halfway up his shins, held up by plain black braces with silver clips. Most striking of all were his cherry-red Dr Martens boots, matched in their high sheen only by his closely shaved head. I scanned his arms for tattoos, the usual way to distinguish a racist skinhead from the non-racist original. Over his left arm he had draped a classic maroon Merc Harrington jacket with ribbed cuffs and hem, flap-covered side pockets and the standard tartan lining, leaving just the bottom half of a crucified skinhead tattoo protruding. Inconclusive. However, as he reached out his right arm to pay for his drink, a large Odal rune tattoo came into clear view. The symbol, originally a letter in the pre-Roman runic alphabet, was adopted by the Nazis, used by some Waffen SS divisions and subsequently embraced by post-war fascists. As if further confirmation were needed, he was joined at the bar by a group of similarly dressed skinheads, one of whom – the bravest or perhaps the stupidest – was wearing a white T-shirt emblazoned with a hooded figure atop a white steed rearing up on its back legs. Above it was the unmistakable logo of the Ku Klux Klan.

I instantly knew they were going to the same place I was: Warsaw.

It was November 2018 and I was on my way to Poland with a colleague from HOPE not hate, the British anti-fascist organisation that we work for. We were to attend the Polish Independence Day demonstration, a huge event that has become a major date in the calendar of the international far right. We were to infiltrate the demonstration, photograph international attendees, and report back to London with our findings. My colleague had overslept and was in a taxi frantically winding his way to the airport so I finished my drink and made a swift exit from the bar to board the plane without him. As I entered the cowshed-like structure that passes for a departure gate at Stansted my chest tightened as I practically tripped over a group of activists from the British branch of the far-right youth movement Generation Identity (GI). By chance they didn't notice me – which was lucky as my HOPE not hate colleagues and I had spent the past year attacking them in print with a series of damaging exposés. I hid behind a newspaper and began to sweat as the realisation struck that I was to be locked in a confined space with a menagerie of racists for the next two and a half hours with no escape should one of them recognise me. I wasn't particularly worried by the pubescent GI crew but the fifteen or so inebriated skinheads were a different matter altogether. I made a last-minute decision to get on the plane regardless, boarding last but one via the rear door. My colleague dived aboard as the doors were closing and thankfully we touched down in Warsaw without incident.

The sight that greeted us as we stepped onto the tarmac was staggering. Rows of planes emptied out hordes of far-right activists from around the world alongside Polish nationalists returning for the celebrations. The events of the next 48 hours were the perfect embodiment of the nature of the contemporary international far right. Traditional nationalists representing various political parties were joined by nazis who prioritised race above nation, alongside activists from modern transnational far-right movements such as the alt-right, the Identitarians and anti-Muslim 'counter-jihadists', all reported on by right-wing alternative media outlets and livestreamed by the new breed of far-right social media influencers. Hate has gone global and this demonstration proved it.

By 10.00 the next morning the streets around the Palace of Culture and Science, the vast brick edifice that towers over central Warsaw, had already begun to pulse with red and white flags. Most of the crowd wore Polish flag armbands, the young girls had red and white flowers in their hair, the young boys' scarves and hats were proudly adorned with the Polish eagle. It looked like any other national celebration, with patriotic families and friends gathering to commemorate the centenary of the restoration of the country's sovereignty in 1918. Yet look a little closer and a more sinister picture emerged. Some wore scarves emblazoned with the white supremacist version of the Celtic cross, while others streaming out of the metro station sported Odal rune and Nazi SS Black Sun tattoos on their arms and faces, sometimes partly obscured by skull face masks and balaclavas.

The crowds began to gather in earnest from around midday at the Dmowski roundabout. As nationalist songs blared out across the closed roads, groups huddled around a green gazebo, the roof of which bore the green crooked-arm-and-sword logo of the National Radical Camp (Obóz Narodowo-Radykalny – ONR). The trestle tables were loaded with badges, stickers, T-shirts, bandannas reading 'Goodnight

Left Side' with an image of one man stamping on another, and a selection of books including what looked like a self-published Polish language version of Norman Finkelstein's notorious *The Holocaust Industry*. The men taking the money wore balaclavas, combat trousers, bomber jackets and black Dr Martens boots. The National Radical Camp is a fascist group (named after an antisemitic organisation of the 1930s) well known for being the organiser of numerous marches in Myślenice, a town in southern Poland, to mark the anniversary of the anti-Jewish riots in that city in 1936. Joining them as co-organisers of the demonstration were All-Polish Youth, a virulently homophobic far-right youth organisation whose motto is 'Youth, Faith, Nationalism'. They erected their own gazebo adjacent to that of the ONR, raised their own triangular flags – a sword on a green background – and began to distribute stickers and leaflets.

As the 2.00pm start time grew nearer, ever-larger groups of balaclava-clad men gathered and the first of countless red flares was lit. The city echoed with the sound of exploding bangers, making demonstrators jump and flinch. What started as a trickle became a flood as people burst out of every tributary road, alleyway and metro station. The police presence was inconceivably small with just the odd group of officers scattered around, albeit with pump-action shotguns and strings of cartridges across their chests. This demonstration was marshalled by the far-right organisers themselves. The roads along the route were lined by All-Polish Youth activists, faces covered, red electrical tape around their arms to identify them, some wearing military helmets and protective glasses. The ONR had a flatbed truck with a PA system over which call and response was demanded of the crowd. In the distance I could hear the faint pounding of a bass drum to keep the

4

chants in time. At far-right demonstrations you often hear the sound of drums in the distance well before you see them. Then the Polish national anthem boomed over the loudspeaker and the crowd, by this time tens of thousands strong, exploded into rapturous song, countless red flares lighting up the grey November sky. People let off fireworks that exploded over the heads of the crowd. The march was about to begin.

The week prior to the march had been an uncertain and tumultuous one for the organisers. Just days before it was due to take place the mayor of Warsaw, Hanna Gronkiewicz-Waltz, banned the demonstration, citing the likelihood of violence and hate speech. Just hours later Poland's president, Andrzej Duda of the Law and Justice party, announced that the Polish state would organise its own demonstration at the same time and along the same route as that planned by the fascists.

Negotiations ensued and a deal was struck between the Polish authorities and the far right, meaning the President and a small state contingent would march first, closely followed by the main demonstration behind. As the march was about to start, Duda climbed onto the back of a green military-style jeep, took the microphone and addressed the enormous crowd before him, now easily over 200,000. As he looked out he would have seen the massed flags of the fascist ONR, the green flags of the All-Polish Youth, a large contingent of flags of the Italian fascist group Forza Nuova and a sea of skinheads in bomber jackets. This didn't stop him.

Despite our thick heads after a night out in Warsaw, my colleague managed to climb atop a bus stop from which to film. I lacked the agility and made do with a high wall from where I deployed my long lens. Him on film, me on stills. So large was the crowd that it took three hours for the demonstrators to all file past the start point. By the time they had, the city was cloaked in darkness, illuminated only by the mass of red pyrotechnics. Alongside Polish and Italian fascists in frighteningly large numbers were a host of other international figures. The notorious British anti-Muslim activist Tommy Robinson (real name Stephen Yaxley-Lennon) had been due to speak but had cancelled several days before, though two of his associates attended the event and appeared to be working alongside the racist alt-right Canadian YouTuber Stefan Molyneux. We also spotted several British vloggers with pro-Tommy Robinson high-visibility jackets, as well as British activists James Goddard and Tracy Blackwell. Also in attendance was the American 'citizen journalist' Jack Posobiec of the alt-lite (the section of the Alternative Right preoccupied with culture rather than race).

The march flowed down towards the Poniatowski Bridge, over the wide Vistula River and past the National Stadium. Hundreds of bangers were dropped over the edge of the bridge and down into the archways, exploding with mighty cracks that reverberated up through the floor. The flares and smoke bombs covered us in ash and burned our eyes. Once over the bridge we flooded into the park behind the stadium. As far as the eye could see, there were hundreds of thousands of people waving flags.

At the centre was a large stage from which two priests led prayers, followed by more political speeches. To left and right on an embankment were the massed fascist flags of the All-Polish Youth and the National Radical Camp, an image reminiscent of Nuremberg in the 1930s. Masked men ceremoniously burned the flag of the European Union. While many of those on the march were not neo-nazis or fascists, and were there merely to celebrate the independence of their country, the presence of the far right was so ubiquitous that no one could pretend they didn't know who was running the event. Despite this, they were happy to march alongside them, listen to their speeches and join in their chants. The President himself marched just metres ahead of fascist flags, no doubt in earshot of the ONR drummer.

Apart from some small running battles between attendees and stewards to the right of the stage, the day passed in relative peace. Yet that did not make it any less terrifying. The numbers were bigger than expected, dwarfing those of the previous year, and the nonchalance with which fascists were treated – and the willingness of the President to strike a deal with them – only confirmed the increasing normalisation of the far right that we are seeing across the globe. The night finished with a firework display and more singing as the crowds slowly dispersed. Back at the Palace of Culture and Science in central Warsaw, the streets had already been cleaned and traffic once again bustled through the streets.

When I first got involved in anti-fascist politics back in 2010 it was inconceivable that just a decade later over 1.9 billion people would live in countries with radical right governments. By 2020, this included three of the five most populous countries on earth, with the United States under then-President Donald Trump, Brazil under President Jair Bolsonaro and India under Prime Minister Narendra Modi. In Europe, President Andrzej Duda and Prime Minister Mateusz Morawiecki, both of the Law and Justice party, govern Poland, while Hungary is ruled by Prime Minister Viktor Orbán of Fidesz. Meanwhile, the radical right has been in parliamentary chambers across the continent including those of Bulgaria, Estonia, Italy and Slovakia. Elsewhere, parties like the Swedish Democrats, the Austrian Freedom Party, Alternative for Germany, the Danish People's Party, Vox in Spain, Chega in Portugal and the Finns Party in Finland have all achieved success at the ballot box. Simultaneously we have seen the rise of new transnational far-right movements like the alt-right that have embraced the internet and rewritten the manual of far-right activism. Recent years have also seen a wave of tragic far-right terrorism on a scale I couldn't have imagined a decade ago.

At the time, I had just finished university and was renting an illegal sublet in a council flat near Gospel Oak station in north London. I spent my days on a camp bed in a comically tiny room with no television and dreadful internet, eating tinned peaches and listening to Dave Brubeck's *Time Out* on repeat. The boredom was punctuated by playing in what I thought at the time was the greatest band ever, inexplicably called Mad Moon Sea. Listening back to the demo tapes now, it's clear we were punishingly mediocre and only occasionally in time, which is not ideal as I was the drummer. Nowadays I am often asked, when meeting new people and telling them what I do, 'How did you get into that?' I always wish I had a dramatic and inspiring reply like, 'I read Mandela's *Long Walk to Freedom* and it changed my life', or 'I cried when watching children from different backgrounds playing together at a multi-faith bake sale'. The truth is that I fell out with the singer and was kicked out of my band, leaving me jobless, on benefits and confined to a room in which I could touch all four walls without moving. I just needed something to do and so I applied for an unpaid internship at HOPE not hate (HNH), campaigning against the far-right British National Party in Dagenham, Essex, at the upcoming general election. I obviously didn't know it then, but that decision completely changed my life. In the decade that followed I went from delivering anti-fascist leaflets door-to-door to infiltrating a heavily armed far-right US militia group, where I was handed a shotgun and sent to the Mexican border.

HOPE not hate's job is to monitor and disrupt the activities of organised hate groups and as a researcher I have infiltrated organisations on both sides of the Atlantic, attending hundreds of far-right events in the UK, Europe and North America. By being on demonstrations and inside meetings we get unparalleled information on their plans and internal workings, but we also get to spend time with activists, learning what motivates them and their hateful politics. I'd be lying if I didn't admit that there is a real buzz to this type of research, the addictive adrenaline and moreish terror of being there among the firecrackers, police charges and clandestine meetings. Later, as my undercover days came to an end, there were the long sleepless nights that came with running operations, terrified for friends and colleagues who were now taking the risk instead. There have also been moments of immense and affecting sadness, like meeting a woman, cold and shivering on a dusty concrete floor in Zakho, northern Iraq, who had just had a miscarriage while fleeing the advancing ISIS forces. Or the sense of utter uselessness one feels when being begged for help by migrants desperately trying to cross the Mediterranean from Tangier to Spain. Of course, it's not all been scary or sad. For every depressing and tragic moment in this job there is one of joy and inspiration. Being hugged by refugees excitedly taking their first steps on the beaches of Europe, hearing stories of successful resistance or the resolve displayed by young Indians demonstrating against discrimination in Chennai and New Delhi. This book weaves ten years of infiltrations and operations for HOPE not hate into the much more important story of the rise of the global far right over the past 50 years. It uses personal stories and insights as a way into understanding the scale of the problem we currently face and to shed light on the people behind it.

Over the past decade I can point to victories and proud moments when I feel I really made a difference – but the truth is that we are now losing. When I started campaigning in 2010 we set out to stop the far-right British National Party taking control of a council chamber and after one of the largest anti-fascist campaigns in British history we were remarkably successful. The years that immediately followed now feel like halcyon days when we moved from victory to victory. At one point, the threat of the organised far right was so small that I left HOPE not hate to do a PhD. At the time my anti-fascist activism was usually viewed by friends and family as earnest but unnecessary. In a post-9/11 world the usual view was that I should have been focused on Islamists rather than the irrelevant far right. Sadly, no one thinks that any more.

One of the reasons people have started to take the threat more seriously in recent years is the bloody rise of far-right terrorism. Among the worst-hit countries has been Germany, which has seen a string of terror attacks. In October 2019 a far-right terrorist killed two at a shooting in Halle, Saxony-Anhalt, with a further nine people killed in February 2020 in two shootings at Shisha bars in Hanau, Hesse. These came off the back of the extraordinary events surrounding the activities of the National Socialist Underground that included the murder of nine immigrants between 2000 and 2006, the killing of a police officer in 2007 and three bombings in Nuremberg in 1999 and Cologne in 2001 and 2004.

Sadly, Germany is by no means the only country to have been struck by far-right terrorism in the last decade.

In Norway in 2011 Anders Behring Breivik mercilessly shot 69 people on the island of Utøya and killed a further eight people with a van bomb in Oslo. In the US in June 2015, Dylann Roof, a white supremacist, murdered nine African Americans at a mass shooting at a church in Charleston, South Carolina. More recently, there were two antisemitic mass shootings, first in October 2018 at the Tree of Life synagogue in Pittsburgh, killing eleven, and then at Poway synagogue, California, in April 2019, killing one and injuring three more. These were followed in August 2019 by the slaughter of 22 more innocent people at a Walmart store in El Paso, Texas in an anti-Hispanic attack. The UK has by no means been exempt from the killings, with the murder of Member of Parliament Jo Cox in 2016 and a van attack on a mosque in Finsbury Park, north London in 2017. There would likely have been more bloodshed were it not for the brave work of nazi turned anti-fascist Robbie Mullen alongside my HNH colleagues Nick Lowles and Matthew Collins, who together stopped the murder of another MP by members of the banned nazi terrorist group National Action in 2018.

The deadliest attack in recent years came on 15 March 2019 when a far-right terrorist burst into Friday prayer at the Al Noor mosque and then the Linwood Islamic Centre in Christchurch, New Zealand, killing 51 and injuring a further 49 people. The killer, an Australian, was inspired by the actions of British terrorist Darren Osborne, Swedish school murderer Anton Lundin, US church killer Dylann Roof, and Norwegian mass murderer Anders Breivik. His manifesto showed that his ideology was derived from the ideas of British fascist Oswald Mosley and the so-called '14 Words' slogan popularised by the US white supremacist movement. He also flagged historical reference points popular among the international anti-Muslim 'counter-jihad' movement, and was motivated in large part by the key tenets of the European 'Identitarian' movement. Before his attack, he had spent time in France, Croatia, Bulgaria, Hungary, Turkey and Bosnia-Herzegovina, all of which influenced his politics. Among the victims that day, alongside Muslims from New Zealand were migrants and refugees from Pakistan, India, Malaysia, Indonesia, Turkey, Somalia, Afghanistan and Bangladesh. The Christchurch attack was a truly international tragedy perpetrated by one man but motivated by a global movement.

Many of these terror attacks were carried out by individuals not associated with traditional far-right political parties but rather part of looser, often transnational far-right movements that lack formal structure. While all these groupings have formal organisations within them, they are often post-organisational. Thousands of individuals, all over the world, offer micro-donations of time and sometimes money to collaborate towards common political goals, completely outside traditional organisational structures. These movements lack formal leaders but rather have figureheads, often drawn from an increasing selection of far-right social media 'influencers'. For most of the post-war period, 'getting active' required finding a party, joining, canvassing, knocking on doors, dishing out leaflets and attending meetings. Now, from the comfort and safety of their own homes, far-right activists can engage in politics by watching YouTube videos, visiting far-right websites, networking on forums, speaking on voice chat services like Discord, and trying to convert 'normies' on mainstream social media platforms like Twitter and Facebook. The fact that this can all be done anonymously hugely lowers the social cost of activism.

These new movements are best understood as a many-headed hydra. If one prominent activist or leader falls from grace, it is no longer a fatal hammer blow; others will simply emerge and the besmirched are discarded. Of fundamental importance is that these movements are genuinely transnational. While activists will generally be primarily preoccupied with local or national issues, they invariably contextualise them continentally or even globally. Often activists from all over the world come together for short periods to collaborate on certain issues and these loose networks act as synapses passing information around the globe. An Islamophobe in one country outraged by the serving of halal chicken in their local fast-food restaurant can post on social media and the story will spread through the network. If picked up by a 'supersharer' (an especially influential activist with a large social media following), that local story will be adopted and then distributed by like-minded Islamophobes all over the world and act as more 'evidence' and further convince them of the threat of 'Islamification'.

All this means that if we are to truly understand the contemporary far right we must change our thinking. We live in a shrinking world and are interconnected like never before. Our ability to travel, communicate and cooperate across borders would have been inconceivable just a generation ago, and while these opportunities are by no means distributed evenly, they have opened up previously impossible chances for progress and development. Yet greater interconnectivity has also produced new challenges. The tools at our disposal to build a better, fairer, more united and more collaborative world are also in the hands of those who are using them to sow division and hatred around the world. If we want to understand the dangers posed by the politics of hatred and division we can no longer just look at our street, our community or even our country; we must think beyond political parties, beyond formal organisations altogether, and beyond national borders.

This book aims to do just that by telling the story of the far right from an international perspective, outlining its different manifestations – be that political parties, street protest groups, nazi terrorists or individual actors working online – and exploring the many factors contributing to their current rise. Among the personal experiences I will draw on are my infiltration of the US militia movement and the Ku Klux Klan, as well as attending meetings of major anti-Muslim groups and extreme alt-right conferences. In the UK, I've attended literally hundreds of far-right demonstrations and got inside extreme fascist meetings. I've been to far-right events in Sweden, Denmark, Germany, Poland and the Czech Republic, and to understand the rise of Hindu nationalism I travelled to India during a period of violent anti-Muslim riots. I've also handled infiltration operations for others, including that of my colleague Patrik Hermansson who bravely spent one year undercover, the story of which became the documentary *Undercover in the Alt-Right*. Academic and journalistic research is invaluable for properly understanding the far right, but all too often they lie or moderate their politics when they know someone is watching. Sometimes it is only by getting inside these movements that you can really uncover the truth.

I've also tried to better understand the drivers behind the rise of these movements around the world. I've spent time in the communities affected by far-right politics such as Dagenham, Burnley and Stoke in the UK, and in the Rust Belt of North America, exploring the effects of deindustrialisation, globalisation and economic hardship. Yet, economics alone cannot explain the mess we are in. Cultural and social factors also play a role. The so-called 'migrant crisis' undoubtedly had an important effect on the rise of the European far right, and in 2015 I travelled to the Greek islands to witness it first-hand, spending nights on the beaches meeting refugees and migrants as they took their first steps on European soil. More recently I returned to the Mediterranean, meeting with migrants in Morocco hoping to do the same.

Finally, there is no way of telling the story of the modern far right without exploring the role of Islamist terrorism. The wave of Islamist terrorist atrocities since 9/11 and especially the spate of attacks in recent years have lit a fire under the international far right. While some have oversimplified the relationship between the far right and Islamist extremism, there undoubtedly is one. For many years, I researched the UK terrorist group Al-Muhajiroun, attending dozens of their demonstrations in London. Many of the people I met at those events, including their leader Anjem Choudary, went on to be convicted of terrorist offences. Others headed to Syria and Iraq to fight for the Islamic State and many died there. In 2014 I followed them with a trip to northern Iraq, a few months after the dramatic fall of Mosul. Together these stories, some published previously by HOPE not hate but all revised and updated, will not only add colour but will also, I hope, contribute to people's understanding of the current threat.

The variety of individuals, parties and movements discussed in this book, ranging from Donald Trump to nazi terrorists, raises the question: how can they all be called far right? Debates about terminology, whether it be 'far right' or 'fascism', have spilled a staggering amount of ink and filled much bigger books than this one. While 'far right' is a very broad term, those within it are united by a common set of core beliefs. Jean-Yves Camus and Nicolas Lebourg point out in *Far-Right Politics in Europe* that:

> Far-Right movements challenge the political system in place, both its institutions and its values (political liberalism and egalitarian humanism). They feel that society is in a state of decay, which is exacerbated by the state: accordingly, they take on what they perceive to be a redemptive mission. They constitute a countersociety and portray themselves as an alternative elite. Their internal operations rest not on democratic rules but on the emergence of 'true elites.' In their imaginary [*sic*], they link history and society to archetypal figures […] and glorify irrational, nonmaterialistic values […]. And finally, they reject the geopolitical order as it exists.[1]

Though 'far right' is a useful umbrella term, it is necessary to split it further into its constituent parts: the democratic radical right and the more extreme far right. The social scientist Cas Mudde explains that the far right 'rejects the essence of democracy, that is, popular sovereignty and majority rule', while the radical right 'accepts the essence of democracy, but opposes fundamental elements of *liberal* democracy, most notably minority rights, rule of law, and separation of powers'.[2] While that's a useful distinction, it is worth noting that even much of the radical right's acceptance of democracy is tactical or performative. Most but not all on the radical right can also currently be described as 'populist', which Mudde defines as 'a (thin) ideology that considers society to be ultimately separated into two homogeneous and antagonistic groups, the pure people and the corrupt elite, and which argues that politics should be an expression of the *volonté générale* (general will) of the people'.[3]

Another important term is the perennially difficult-to-define 'fascism', which makes up a part of the far right. But what is fascism? Even 22 years after Mussolini had seized control of Italy, George Orwell identified the difficulty of distilling a single consensually derived definition, asking: 'Why, then, cannot we have a clear and generally accepted definition of it? Alas! we shall not get one – not yet, anyway.'[4] Unfortunately, we are still some way off consensus, despite the emergence over the last twenty years of a field often called 'fascism studies' designed to achieve just that. One issue is the widespread misuse of the term. During the so-called 'Free Speech Week' events organised by the British far-right provocateur Milo Yiannopoulos in California in 2017, the campus at Berkeley echoed to the sound of anti-fascists chanting 'No Trump, no KKK, no fascist USA'. Placards, posters and leaflets littered the streets, many of which unequivocally called Trump a 'fascist'. Trump is many things. He is a racist, a misogynist, a nativist and far-right, but he is not a fascist. In the words of the historian of fascism Roger Griffin: 'You can be a total xenophobic racist male chauvinist bastard and still not be a fascist.'[5] Of course, none of this is new. As far back as 1944 Orwell lamented:

It will be seen that, as used, the word 'Fascism' is almost entirely meaningless. In conversation, of course, it is used even more wildly than in print. I have heard it applied to farmers, shopkeepers, Social Credit, corporal punishment, fox-hunting, bull-fighting, the 1922 Committee, the 1941 Committee, Kipling, Gandhi, Chiang Kai-Shek, homosexuality, Priestley's broadcasts, Youth Hostels, astrology, women, dogs and I do not know what else.[6]

However, despite the slovenly bastardisation of a deeply serious term, the word fascism has not been debased beyond usefulness for the classification of political individuals or organisations, despite what some historians argue. As Robert O. Paxton rightly states: 'The term fascism needs to be rescued from sloppy usage, not thrown out because of it. It remains indispensable. We need a generic term for what is a general phenomenon [...].'[7] Some reject the term, arguing that fascism died in 1945 with the fall of Nazi Germany, while others go even further and argue that its use should be confined to Mussolini's Italy. Gilbert Allardyce, for example, argues that 'Fascism is not a generic concept. The word fascismo has no meaning beyond Italy.'[8] However, as Graham Macklin explains in *Failed Führers*, while the 'epochal' conditions 'ceased to exist after 1945' and post-war fascism lacks 'the broader economic and existential crisis from which it derived its "significance"' during the interwar period this does not mean that post-war variants have ceased to be "fascism"'.[9]

Neither the frequent incorrect use of the term nor the diversity of the phenomenon is cause enough to discard it altogether, though all of this makes it extremely hard to define what we mean when we use the word fascism. However, the conundrum of defining a sprawling, diffuse and deeply varied historical phenomenon with a single term can be overcome by the adoption of an 'ideal type'. Of the numerous 'ideal type' definitions, the closest to have achieved a consensus is that provided by Roger Griffin, who defines 'generic fascism' as a 'genus of political ideology whose mythic core in its various permutations is a palingenetic* form of populist ultra-nationalism'.[10]

While this may all seem academic, it is not. Who we call far right or fascist is important, as it has ramifications for both the state and anti-fascists alike. Lumping everyone together with the term 'fascist' results in some seeking to combat Nigel Farage's Brexit Party with the same tactics one would use against a nazi terrorist group. How we understand and define elements of the far right is the first step to working out how to oppose them.

Many thought the march towards progress and equality was one-way, but the past decade has shown this not to be the case. Around the world we are witnessing the return of the far right, posing a genuine threat to many of the rights and freedoms we had begun to take for granted. While this has been uneven and by no means universal, there is a worrying direction of travel that can be seen in several continents simultaneously – and in many countries around the world the very pillars of liberal democracy are beginning to wobble. The differences from country to country are of course as numerous as the similarities; there is no monocausal explanation for what we are witnessing. Yet while the rise of the right in each country has its own drivers, rooted in unique histories and experiences, there are international similarities that help shed light on these troubling times. The better we understand the threat we face around the world, the better we will be able to fight back. I hope this book will contribute to that exercise of understanding.

* Palingenesis is the concept of rebirth or recreation.

1

FROM THE BRITISH NATIONAL PARTY TO BREXIT

I was standing on the opposite side of the road to a police station with an extendable paint roller in each hand. It was dark and the roads were now quiet, but our plan was already starting to feel a little underdone. At any moment a police officer could walk out of the station and ask us what we were up to – and I certainly didn't have a believable answer. A touch of night-time decorating, perhaps? Not sure that would wash. I was in front of a huge British National Party (BNP) billboard attached at ground level to the outside wall of a terraced house. 'People Like You Voting BNP' it read, with a picture of an idyllic white family. My friend, Cookie, was behind me holding a 10-litre tub of brilliant white matt emulsion paint. The plan was simple: he would throw paint on the billboard and I would use the rollers to distribute it, after which we would jump in a third friend's waiting car and make our getaway.

Conscious of the proximity of the police station, we knew we had to be quiet and fast. What could go wrong? I faced the billboard, rollers at the ready. 'On three', I whispered. 'One, two, thr—' Before I could finish, 10 litres of paint had hit me on the back of the head. I turned in disbelief to my buffoon of an accomplice. 'Sorry, it slipped', he said sheepishly. I turned to look back at the billboard. We had managed the seemingly impossible – it was completely untouched, not a drop on it. I on the other hand was covered from head to toe. Starting to panic, I turned myself into a human roller and slid my body left and right across the billboard, smearing as much paint on it as possible. My mate took the roller, ran it up and down my back and then onto the billboard. I had essentially become a paint tray. We did what we could and then ran to the waiting car.

'There is no fucking way you are getting in my car.'

'What?'

'You're not getting in my car covered in paint, no way.'

'Are you joking? There's literally a police station right there.'

'You'll ruin my seats.'

'It's already a shit car, I'm getting in.'

'Do not, get in.'

'I'm getting in.'

'Do not, get in.'

I jumped into the seat with a squelch. 'DRIVE THE FUCKING CAR!'

Our little operation hadn't got off to an ideal start, so we moved on to the next billboard while arguing about who would pay for the destroyed upholstery.

The next advertising board was an altogether harder proposition. Instead of being at ground level it was up high. To reach it we had decided on the ingenious plan of filling cheap plastic pint glasses with paint, covering the tops in masking tape and throwing them as paint bombs. We pulled up next to a vast billboard that ran alongside the A13 motorway. One side was for the BNP, the other was a UKIP sign reading '5,000 New People Settle Here Every Week: Say No

To Mass Immigration'. Cookie picked up one of the pint glasses and took aim before hurling it up at the sign. However, instead of smashing, it bounced, and I looked up to see a pint glass filled with paint heading straight for my head. Surely not. Not again. I dived out of the way just in time, the pint glass whistling past my face and smashing on the floor next to me, once again covering me in paint. I looked up at a pristine billboard and then down at my paint-spattered legs. 'I think we should call it a night.'

Throughout the post-war period, the British far right's ability to exert influence beyond the confines of the political fringe has depended on its cohesiveness and size. While it is unwise to measure the threat of the far right purely in terms of electoral strength or number of feet on the street – it only takes one right-wing extremist to bomb a pub or murder an MP – its ability to influence mainstream political debate, especially on issues like immigration and integration, has generally been tied to the relative importance and scale of political parties and street movements. Since 1945, there have been cycles of unity and division that correspond to periods of relative influence, decline and obscurity.

In 1948, 51 far-right and fascist organisations merged at a meeting in Farringdon Hall, London, forming the Union Movement (UM) under the leadership of the notorious pre-war British fascist leader Sir Oswald Mosley.[1] Though officially lasting into the 1990s the UM, which encountered fierce opposition, remained noteworthy for just a few years before fading back into obscurity. 1967 saw a second period of coalescence, with the formation of the National Front (NF) following the merger of the League of Empire Loyalists with the then British National Party and elements of both the Greater Britain Movement and the Racial Preservation Society. Though never achieving mainstream support, the NF became a household name during the 1970s and was a fixture on the political landscape, peaking in 1979 when it stood 303 candidates at the general election, only to have the rug pulled from under it by Margaret Thatcher's infamous 1978 television interview in which she said British people feared being 'swamped' by immigrants, and by the intensity of campaigning by the Anti-Nazi League. A period of splintering and decline in the 1980s followed as a result.

On 7 April 1982 a rival far-right party emerged, muscling in on the political space previously occupied by the NF. With time it grew into the most electorally successful fascist party in British history. The British National Party (BNP) was formed by John Tyndall who brought with him former activists from the NF and his splinter group, the New National Front. As well as personnel, there was a continuity of politics, with explicit racial nationalism remaining the central pillar of the party's platform.[2] So much so that in 1986 Tyndall and the editor of the BNP's newspaper were both sentenced to a year in prison for conspiracy to incite racial hatred.[3] While the BNP stood in elections throughout the 1980s it remained a party of the streets, best known for provocative and confrontational marches. At the end of the decade they launched a 'Rights for Whites' campaign that sought to exploit growing racial tensions in multicultural communities exacerbated by the economic and social turmoil unleashed on industrial towns by a decade of Margaret Thatcher's rule. Their first electoral breakthrough came in September 1993 with the shock victory of Derek Beackon as a councillor in the Isle of Dogs, a large peninsula in East London, bordered on three sides by the winding River Thames. The victory became a blueprint for the BNP, which benefited from local anger over decades of neglect following the decline of the once mighty docks, combined with a local housing crisis blamed by many on the growth of the local Bengali community.[4] Demographic change and economic decline were a potent mix and the BNP were always ready to provide easy answers to complex questions, a tactic that saw them emerge as a terrifying electoral threat from the turn of the century onwards.

In 1999 the party leadership changed hands with Nick Griffin, a long-time fascist from Barnet in north London who had joined the National Front aged just fourteen, graduated from Cambridge and had a history of extreme racism and Holocaust denial. He had joined the BNP in 1995, becoming the editor of two extreme publications, the *Rune* and subsequently *Spearhead*, where he built a reputation as a hardliner who argued that 'We need to take political people and convert them into thugs.'[5] In 1998 his extremism landed him in trouble with the law when he was convicted of inciting racial hatred and received a nine-month prison sentence, suspended for two years.[6] It is perhaps surprising then that Griffin went on to become the great moderniser of the BNP, the man who led the British far right out of the wilderness and into the European Parliament.

With one eye on the success of the modernising project undertaken in France by Jean-Marie Le Pen's Front National, Griffin sought to make the BNP a more viable electoral option by altering how it presented itself, if not its core beliefs. While this was correctly criticised by many anti-fascists as a superficial transformation, it began to pay dividends at the ballot box. Though remaining a racist, antisemitic and homophobic political project, the party began to professionalise both its image and its structures, a move encapsulated in its decision to finally drop its policy of compulsory repatriation for non-white people. Griffin understood that being labelled as antisemitic and racist was the primary hurdle to gaining mainstream success. So much so that in July 2001 the BNP even launched their 'Ethnic Liaison Committee' designed to 'organise publicity activity with non-whites who have expressed favourable sentiment towards the BNP' – all designed to break down the media image of the BNP as 'racists'.[7] Hence, in the early 2000s the BNP publicly jettisoned the more explicit elements of its traditional anti-black racism and shifted towards what they felt was a target more likely to garner public support: Islam and Muslims.

The BNP's decision to change the focus of their racism towards a different community is nothing new for the British far right. Throughout the whole post-war period the far right have sought out an Other, a target of their ire, on the back of which they hope to secure wider public support and gain entry into the mainstream of domestic politics. In the years immediately following the Second World War the British far right was still obsessed with its traditional enemy, namely Jews, a target that, in the post-Holocaust age, only served to isolate them further from the mainstream. However, as public hostility towards the arrival of non-white immigrant communities grew, large sections of the UK far right shifted their attacks onto the new arrivals.[8] By the 1970s, the far right was ready to seize any available political capital by targeting whichever community they felt would garner the widest public support. One only has to take the briefest look at how the far right reacted to the arrival of Ugandan Asians in 1972 to understand how immigration shot up the agenda between the late 1940s and the early 1970s with their realisation that it was *the* issue that could help them break out of their post-Holocaust exile. The National Front, then Britain's leading far-right party, greeted Prime Minister Edward Heath's compassionate decision to grant asylum to many Ugandan Asians with a ruthless but astute political campaign. The result of the NF's swift opportunism led to a rapid swelling of their rank-and-file membership.[9]

The next shift came in the 1980s when the primary target of the far right slowly began to move from all immigrants, with an emphasis on anti-black racism, towards a more specific anti-Muslim politics. Matthew Collins, former NF organiser turned anti-fascist, pinpointed the Salman Rushdie Affair as the moment this shift occurred: 'Salman Rushdie's book was when the far right first saw Islam and all its challenges. And that's never changed since then. It's always been about Muslims since then.'[10] While much of the British far right began to specifically target Muslims throughout the 1980s and 1990s, the shift to Islam and Muslims as the primary target was solidified by the BNP in 2001. That year saw a series of riots in northern towns with large South Asian communities – Oldham, Bradford, Harehill and Burnley – which saw ethnic tensions erupt. As spring turned to summer the BNP's rhetoric around the riots visibly shifted. When disturbances first broke out, their newspaper, *The Voice of Freedom*, talked of anti-white rampages and 'Asian gangs'. In July, they even claimed to be engaging with the Muslim community to try to reduce tensions in Oldham, and Griffin offered to encourage white Oldham residents to stop their boycott of Muslim shops.[11] They also ran an article highlighting the threat posed by 'Islamic Fundamentalism' that stated: 'It would clearly be unfair to tar all Moslems with the violent fundamentalist brush.' However, with rising public anger over the riots, the BNP clearly saw an opportunity to attract support via a broader anti-Muslim campaign as the year progressed. Their August front page declared: 'Muslim Extremists Behind The Riots!' Then came the 9/11 attacks in the USA, which only served to solidify the BNP's shift towards an out-and-out anti-Muslim party. Their magazine *Identity* ran the front-page headline 'BNP Launches Campaign Against Islam' with a picture of notorious UK-based Islamists Abu Hamza al-Masri and Omar Bakri Muhammad. Inside were articles titled 'No To Islam!', 'Islam or the West' and 'Outlaw Ritual Slaughter'. In October *The Voice of Freedom* carried an editorial by Paul Golding, later leader of Britain First, entitled 'The Enemy Within', and in December they held a demonstration outside Parliament with placards that read: 'Islam Out of Britain'.

The following years saw the BNP exploit and exacerbate rising anti-Muslim prejudice. Then in July 2005 came the London bombings, which again led to widespread demonisation of the British Muslim community. Griffin quickly saw the attacks as an opportunity and in 2006 wrote:

> This is the factor which is going to dominate politics for decades to come. This is the enemy that the public can see and understand. This is the threat that can bring us to power. This is the Big Issue on which we must concentrate in order to wake people up and make them look at what we have to offer all around.[12]

By the middle part of the decade anti-Muslim politics was firmly at the forefront of the BNP's politics – and has been ever since.

However, the adoption of Islamophobia alone does not explain the electoral rise of the BNP during the first decade of the 2000s. In 2000 the BNP won 2.87% of the votes in the party list section of the London Assembly elections, the results indicating that the BNP were benefiting from increasing disillusionment in traditional Labour heartlands. Then in May 2002 the BNP shook the political landscape, winning three council seats in Burnley in the north of England, followed by a host of seats in 2003 in areas such as Broxbourne in Hertfordshire, Heckmondwike in Yorkshire and Thurrock in Essex. The diversity of the seats the BNP were winning, including some traditional Conservative seats, proved that the causes underlying the growth of the BNP went deeper than economics alone. As always, it was a combination of factors, including increasing societal concern over rapidly rising immigration numbers under the New Labour government.[13] As Daniel Trilling put it in his study of the rise of the BNP, the electoral breakthrough 'was a protest from people who had something to lose, and felt they were in danger of losing it. Resentment appeared to be based on class as well as race.'[14] Also central was a very real feeling in these communities that they had been ignored and neglected too long by the political establishment. They felt powerless – and most importantly, hopeless. They wanted change and the BNP offered a megaphone through which they could shout about their anger.

In 1953 the Ford car plant in Dagenham employed 40,000 workers over a floor space of 4 million square feet. By the time I arrived in January 2010 it provided employment for just a few thousand and the office I worked in looked out over acres of derelict factory sheds and flattened concrete wasteland. I took the train each morning to Dagenham Heathway station and made the fifteen-minute walk down to New Road

– there was nothing new about it – where the HOPE not hate campaign office was based. We had taken over the unused top floor of a dilapidated four-storey trade union building which we shared with the local Labour Party. One whole wall was taken up by a huge HNH canvas banner that had the names of infamous fascists in grey and anti-fascist campaigns in red. Lord Haw-Haw, the Union Movement, Colin Jordan, the British Movement, the National Front in grey. Cable Street, the 43 Group, the 62 Group, Free Nelson Mandela in red. As a young intern it served as a daily reminder that the battle for Barking and Dagenham was set to be another defining moment in this historical struggle. The general election was fast approaching and the town had become the front line against the British far right. The BNP had made the community its main target. At the time, after receiving nearly 1 million votes in 2009 the BNP had two members of the European Parliament, one member of the London Assembly and dozens of councillors around the country, twelve of whom were in Barking and Dagenham, making them the most electorally successful far-right party in British history. They were now genuinely in with a chance of taking outright control of the council, an unthinkable prospect.

HOPE not hate was launched in 2004 by Nick Lowles as the campaign wing of the long-standing anti-fascist organisation Searchlight. Initially founded in 1964 by the Labour Party MPs Reg Freeson and Joan Lestor and then relaunched by Maurice Ludmer and Gerry Gable in 1975, Searchlight was both a magazine and an anti-fascist intelligence operation. It specialised in infiltrating and exposing fascist groups and was central to the demise of numerous post-war nazi organisations including the British Movement and Combat 18. Over the decades, it was involved – often amicably at first and then less so – with some of the largest anti-racist campaigns in Britain, including the Anti-Nazi League, the Campaign Against Racism and Fascism, and the militant Anti-Fascist Action. Searchlight had also been on the original steering committee of Unite Against Fascism (UAF) but resigned due to tactical differences, resulting in UAF and HNH running parallel campaigns in 2010. Lowles created HOPE not hate because many of the traditional tactics of the anti-fascist movement had become less effective in combatting the rise of the BNP. Perhaps not ideologically but certainly tactically, the far right had modernised and professionalised and too many anti-fascists were fighting new battles with old tactics. There were times when huge anti-racist rallies were held in Trafalgar Square, with stirring speeches about the need for the resurrection of campaigns of the past, while the BNP were in communities like Dagenham, Stoke and Burnley, knocking on doors and engaging with disgruntled, ignored and suffering communities. HNH was designed to go back into those same communities and speak to those same people but with a different, more hopeful message.

I worked alongside a small team of interns who reported to Sam Tarry, now the Labour MP for Ilford South, then a young, enthusiastic and energetic figure whose twin passions were campaigning and weightlifting. Above him were the Searchlight figures who quickly took on a mythical status for me. Gerry Gable was a legend of the movement with decades of daring exploits. Graeme Atkinson had built crucial anti-fascist networks in Germany in the wake of the fall of the Berlin Wall and ran the organisation's international network. Nick Lowles was not just the founder of HNH and the editor of *Searchlight* magazine, but also the man who took down Combat 18 in the UK in 1990s with remarkably daring anti-fascist intelligence work. Finally, there was the aloof and very sweary figure of Matthew Collins, the former BNP activist turned Searchlight spy.

Still very much an enthusiastic Mod at the time, I turned up on my first day in a smart three-button suit, paisley silk scarf, beautiful tasselled and feathered loafers and a pastiche Paul Weller-esque haircut. I was promptly handed a bundle of newspapers and sent out into the rain to deliver them on the council estate across the road. The atmosphere in the community was tense and partisan, making standing out a bad idea – so I quickly shelved the suit. The campaign grew exponentially as we approached polling day until it was without doubt one of the largest anti-fascist campaigns in UK history. The once derelict union office became a hub for phone canvassing, voter registration, faith community engagement and the creation and distribution of over 355,000 pieces of hyper-targeted campaign literature. Especially effective was a series of tabloid newspapers specific to each electoral ward produced by the *Daily Mirror*. Dagenham became the national focus of the election, with activists coming from all over the UK and strategists and journalists arriving to observe from around the world. At its peak we managed to deliver 92,000 newspapers in just three hours. Using innovative data techniques borrowed from the 2008 Obama presidential campaign, we identified anti-BNP voters and then worked tirelessly to make sure they could and did get out and vote. On the day of the election we managed to knock on 6,000 identified anti-BNP households across the area. Underpinning all of this was an intelligence operation gathering internal information from within the BNP to make sure our campaign knew exactly what they were planning at all times. Running alongside HNH was the re-election campaign of local Labour

MP Jon Cruddas, which also attracted unprecedented numbers of canvassers. Over in Barking was another Labour MP, Margaret Hodge, who, at the time, was not supportive of HNH and threw in her lot with UAF.

For me and the other interns the campaign primarily consisted of month after month of delivering campaign literature door to door, sometimes for twelve hours a day. The old adage, 'War is long periods of boredom punctuated by moments of sheer terror', was rather apt. It wasn't unusual to have leaflets thrown back in your face along with a racist barrage or to bump into rival activists leafletting the same streets. One day three BNP supporters were standing outside Dagenham Heathway station handing out copies of their outrageous rag, *The Barking and Dagenham Sentinel*. The station played soothing classical music over its speaker system for the pleasure of the passengers, and rather amusingly on this occasion Wagner's 'Ride of the Valkyries' rang out. A friend and I snatched their newspapers and ran for our lives as they chased us down the road. I thought we had got away with it, but several days later a white van emblazoned with BNP flags drove straight at me. It mounted the pavement, forcing me to jump into a bush before making a hasty getaway.

Key to our strategy was to chip away at the false veneer of respectability the BNP were presenting to the electorate. While Nick Griffin wore a suit and acted the politician, his supporters weren't averse to violence. During one confrontation with local Asian youths a BNP candidate called Bob Bailey was filmed kicking a young man in the head. On another occasion, we'd had a tip-off that they planned to confront our leafletters outside a station. Rather than cancelling the event it was decided that myself and Simon, another HNH activist, would be dangled as bait. We concealed microphones under our shirts, held a stack of leaflets and stood outside the tube station. Across the road a cameraman hid in the bushes with a long lens pointed at us. If it was going to happen we wanted to make sure we caught it all on camera. Thankfully on that occasion it proved to be a false alarm.

By the time the votes started to be counted on the evening of the election it was already clear the BNP were heading for a calamitous defeat. A dejected Nick Griffin walked into the count saying, 'I'm coming to pick up the bodies, we're not leaving anyone dead here.'[15] He already knew that his historic moment of victory had been snatched from his grasp. 'London is gone', he said. 'We're going to have to become a civil rights organisation for the British minority.'[16] The highlight of the night was a confrontation between Nick Lowles and Griffin in front of a scrum of journalists' cameras. 'You've won London, you've taken London from the English and you've given it to the foreigners', said Griffin.[17] Lowles' voice was giddy with victory: 'We're going to drive you out. And we've won Stoke and we've won Burnley and we've won Sandwell, we've won Solihull, we've won Bradford.' Griffin's bouncer stepped in between the two of them. 'I'm having a conversation with you, Nick', said Lowles. 'No you're not … it's over', responded the bouncer, and he was right in more ways than one.[18]

The result in Dagenham that night was disastrous for the BNP, losing all twelve of their sitting councillors, something I though impossible just months earlier. The people of Dagenham had stood up and fought back. As the sun rose over the concrete wasteland and light flooded in through the windows that ran along one wall of our office, I put the theme music from the 1969 film *Battle of Britain* on the stereo. As the marching drums rose in volume and the booming horn line echoed around the cavernous empty room, I flung my arms out like a young boy pretending to be a plane and ran around in circles.

───

The 2010 election was unquestionably a political disaster for the BNP. While their vote had actually gone up, a point Nick Griffin was keen to make, they lost all but two of the 28 council seats they were defending.[19] They had massively overstretched themselves and faced unprecedented levels of opposition from anti-fascists, local communities and other political parties. In the years that followed the BNP went into rapid decline, haemorrhaging members, then voters and subsequently seats. Despite being wiped out in 2010 they still managed to receive a remarkable 563,743 votes, but by the 2015 general election this had collapsed to just 1,667 votes.[20] While the BNP hobbles on to this day, they are an irrelevance and Griffin has been cast into the political wilderness. However, the BNP was never the sole cause of societal racism, or anti-immigrant or anti-Muslim sentiment in Britain; more often than not it was the beneficiary of it. Its decline did not mark the end of the politics of prejudice and discrimination; the BNP merely ceased to be the vessel that was exploiting it. At the same time as the BNP was imploding in 2010, a new far-right threat was already emerging, the English Defence League, of which much more later.

In the wake of Dagenham I had stayed on at HOPE not hate doing odd jobs. So secret was the organisation at the time, that come the end of the 2010 election when the team departed the temporary campaign office and returned to the main premises, I wasn't allowed to follow. In fact, I worked for HNH for a full year before I even found out where the head office was located. While the BNP were wiped out of east London they still held council seats around the country and for several years I worked for Nick Lowles on campaigns in North Wales, the Midlands and Burnley to knock off their remaining councillors. Simultaneously I began to help out the research team by attending and photographing far-right events all over the country. However, the BNP's collapse didn't mean the end of the British far right, and much of the rest of the 2010s became a fight over a referendum.

Though the BNP failed electorally, their demise by no means meant the decline of anti-immigration politics. As the second decade of the 21st century progressed, a radical right political party that had sat on the fringe of British politics for a quarter of a century finally took centre stage: the United Kingdom Independence Party (UKIP). In 2013 the Conservative Prime Minister David Cameron promised a referendum on Britain's membership of the European Union. In large part the very offer of the referendum was an admission of the growing influence of UKIP and an ill-judged attempt to reoccupy the political ground the Tories had lost to their right. The academics Matthew Goodwin and Robert Ford rightly argued that UKIP posed 'one of the most successful challenges to the established political parties in modern British history'.[21] For them UKIP was 'Far from a catch-all party or one focused on winning over disgruntled Conservatives, they have tailored a Eurosceptic, anti-immigrant appeal for disadvantaged, working-class voters who feel under threat from the changes that surround them and alienated from a seemingly unresponsive and disengaged established political class.'[22] UKIP was a very different beast to the BNP – and one that had a far more important effect on British politics than any far-right party before them had managed.

For HOPE not hate, the decision to oppose UKIP was not as obvious as it now seems in hindsight. As Lowles said at the time, referring to their then-leader Nigel Farage: 'Farage is not a fascist and UKIP is not the BNP.'[23] If UKIP weren't fascists, was it the job of anti-fascists to oppose them? Writing about this period, the historian of British anti-fascism Nigel Copsey described this question as an 'existential crisis' among anti-fascist campaigners and asked: 'Is this really anti-fascism?'[24] For us, however, it was a question of opposing organised racism and discrimination and if that required us expanding beyond the confines of fascism, then so be it. In truth, it felt like a natural progression. The far right had become mainstream and so anti-fascists were left with a choice: continue to oppose only fascists and become part of an increasingly marginal battle, or expand to oppose more mainstream manifestations of discriminatory politics. We chose the latter and it has put HNH onto a road where in recent years we have become increasingly outspoken against both Islamophobia within the Conservative Party and antisemitism within the Labour Party. From 2013 onwards, while still campaigning against the few remaining BNP councillors, the decision was taken to make UKIP our primary electoral target. This was by no means welcomed by all of our supporters. The most surprising attack came from the *Jewish Chronicle*, which in 2015 wrote an editorial titled 'Hatred not hope' that read: 'For many years this newspaper was a supporter of Hope Not Hate, an organisation that had admirable aims, and welcomed its writers in our pages. But it has now lost its claim to be taken seriously. Last year it started targeting UKIP as if it was no different to the EDL or BNP.'[25] For many, UKIP was simply not the job of anti-fascists. We disagreed.

Compared to the BNP, UKIP was a completely different scale of electoral threat. At the 2010 general election they had received 900,000 votes; they got 4.3 million votes at the 2014 European elections and then a remarkable 3.9 million at the 2015 general election.[26] From the mid-2000s onwards they had consciously courted the BNP's voters, a tactic that was accelerated after 2010 and, in part, contributed to the destruction of Nick Griffin's political dreams. In large part, UKIP's success was the result of capturing the anti-immigration vote. The coalition government at the time put the Conservative Party in an awkward position. Since the days of Enoch Powell they had always been the obvious choice for immigration controls. In 2010, with both UKIP and the BNP to their right exploiting the issue, the Tories promised radical cuts to immigration that they were unable to make good on once in government.[27] For many, this was the final proof they needed that neither of the mainstream parties could deliver on the issue they cared about most.

By time of the 2016 referendum on EU membership, Nigel Farage was one of the most recognisable political figures in the whole country and UKIP spokespeople were on practically every TV and radio show for months on end. Personally, in the early days of the referendum campaign I was undecided. Like many on the left I was wary of the undemocratic nature of the European Union's institutions. However, as the day of the vote drew nearer the debate grew ever more toxic and racist. Leading the xenophobic charge was Farage with UKIP's ugly 'Breaking Point' poster campaign that depicted huge groups of non-white migrants walking across Europe. At his side was long-time ally Arron Banks whose Leave.EU campaign disseminated a host of racist disinformation, including a malicious poster that suggested staying in the EU would result in

76 million Turkish people coming to the UK. Come referendum day I felt that a vote to leave the EU would legitimise this ugly politics.

Like many others, I woke in shock the following morning to see that we had indeed voted to leave the European Union. I shouted at my father, holding him solely responsible for what I believed to be his generation's selfishness. In truth, it is still too soon to properly explain the reasons for Brexit – that is one for the historians. However, a contested picture has begun to form. Despite many people's shock at the result, the Brexit vote had deep roots. The historian Dave Renton argues that the genesis of the Brexit vote can be traced back to Margaret Thatcher's 1988 Bruges Speech, in which she compared the EU to the Soviet Union. For Renton, 'This was the birth of British Euro-scepticism. Without the Bruges Speech, there would have been no UKIP, no referendum and no Brexit.'[28] The best work yet published on Brexit, Maria Sobolewska and Robert Ford's *Brexitland*, highlights the long-term factors rooted in political and social changes such as 'the gradual erosion of links between the traditional political parties and the electorate, the return of conflict over immigration to the top of the political agenda, the emergence of a new party (UKIP) mobilising one pole of the identity divide, and the consolidation of voters at the other pole of the identity divide behind Labour'.[29]

In the short term, the primary factors were a combination of the economic and cultural. While it's important to be clear that Brexit was not innately far-right or fundamentally racist, there is no doubt that at its core, opposition to immigration was key. As Paul Stocker explains in *English Uprising*, 'the single biggest issue propelling the Brexit vote, was immigration'.[30] 90% of people who saw immigration as a drain on the economy and 88% of those who wanted fewer immigrants voted to leave, and polling indicated that immigration had surpassed the economy as the most important deciding issue for people about to vote.[31] Polling by Michael Ashcroft released after the referendum found that 81% of Brexit voters believed multiculturalism to be a 'force for ill'.[32]

However, there were also class factors at play – and a deep feeling of anti-elitism. The remain campaign was seen by many Brexit supporters to be run by quinoa-stuffing snobs from north London, part of the political elite who for decades had ignored, or worse, looked down on working-class people from northern cities and coastal towns across Britain. As Stocker puts it, the leave vote 'was a middle finger aimed squarely at the political establishment, who for many had ceased long ago to listen to the concerns of provincial England'.[33] For such people, both the Tories and Labour had ignored their plight. The reasons that drove many to vote for the BNP were the same reasons that a significant number voted for Brexit. It's worth remembering that 64% of the leave vote was from the lowest three socio-economic groups in society.[34] So while cultural factors such as immigration and fear of societal change were no doubt central, we can't ignore the economic factors that also played a role.

In *The Rise of the Right*, Simon Winlow, Steve Hall and James Treadwell argue that the decision to vote leave was often born of despair at existing circumstances. 'When you have almost nothing to lose, when you can see nothing positive on the horizon, and when you're convinced that you have been betrayed and cast aside, "logic" and "rationality" cannot remain dominant.'[35] As they point out, for many in the toughest economic and social conditions the 'logical' thing to do was to vote for the only option that offered even the remotest opportunity of substantial change. 'The status quo had offered them absolutely nothing. The jobs that were available were of the very worst kind. No. They wanted out. They wanted change. They wanted something, anything, that wasn't this.'[36] For this reason it is unwise to separate cultural and economic factors – in truth, one is often born of the other. For many working-class leave voters, immigration and increased diversity have been indivisible from their own relative declining fortunes – brought about, in their minds, by economic competition from migrants.[37] That said, it seems likely that their decision to vote leave was not based on a laboured cost-benefit analysis of EU membership but on a visceral anger and frustration towards political elites and a desperation for change.

I sat back into the familiar contours of the moulded plastic seat and slid my hand between the front buttons of my jacket and into the inside pocket to make sure it was still there. Checking no one was watching, I removed the piece of paper and slowly unfolded it to reveal a printed picture. A man in green khaki holding a rifle with a telescopic sight affixed to the top. Behind him, hanging from a pole was the flag of the German Reich, red with a black swastika on a disc of white.

While HOPE not hate had concentrated much of its efforts on the electoral far right, we never took our eye off the more extreme elements of the British scene, and in the years since Dagenham I had increasingly been involved in research and intelligence work. My instructions were always vague but simple; intelligence operations work on a 'need-to-know basis' and in this case I didn't need to know much. I was given the picture, a time and a location and told to wait in the entrance hall of Victoria coach station, a grand and distinctive art deco building from the outside, turned dirty and dishevelled inside by years of use and neglect. On spotting the person in the picture I was to follow them unnoticed and report back locations to Matthew Collins, Head of Intelligence at HNH, who was running the operation remotely. A second pair of eyes was provided by 'Titus', a thick-set ringer for Robert De Niro who by all accounts was unusually skilled at beating up fascists, despite coming across as a giant teddy bear. He had run a militant organisation in the 1990s and having retired from direct action some years previously, was now helping HNH with security.

The target stepped off the coach and walked through the sliding double doors into the terminal. He was much smaller than I was expecting, but I recognised his wispy ginger beard from the picture. Waiting for him to pass me, I slowly closed the book I had been pretending to read, placed it in my bag, got to my feet and began to follow him. There was to be a fascist meeting that evening with activists from across the UK and Europe and he was our ticket to finding out the location. Titus and I followed him, always just out of sight, until we eventually reached the Fountains Abbey pub on the corner of Norfolk Place and Praed Street, near Paddington station in central London. It was a Victorian pub with original tile and leaded windows, black stone pillars topped with ornamental golden mouldings, benches down one side, whisky barrels topped with ashtrays down the other. I ordered a pint and took a seat in the far corner facing the door, watching as fascists I had only ever seen in pictures slowly trickled into the pub, ordered a drink and headed upstairs to the hired room. When confident that this wasn't just a redirection point, I called the location in. Instantly, Collins blew the meeting by putting it on the HOPE not hate Facebook group. Soon the pub's phone began to ring as anti-fascists called to inform them of what was happening upstairs.

Titus and I left the pub and took up our next positions. Confident the meeting would soon be shut down, we knew the fascists would be leaving the pub en masse, giving us the perfect opportunity to photograph the whole group and work out exactly who had attended. Opposite the pub was a metal fence blocking off a pedestrianised road beyond which was St Mary's Hospital. We slid underneath a large white cancer-screening truck that was parked just behind the gates and constructed our long lens camera. The meeting was shut down and the group slowly filtered out of the pub. A discussion now took place on where to head next. One attendee, bored of waiting, took a seat on the bench and pulled out a book on Nazi SS uniforms, thumbing it nonchalantly. I took rapid-fire pictures, the camera's shutter – ka-chick, ka-chick, ka-chick – the only thing giving away our position. 'He's seen us', Titus whispered.

'Who?'

'Him, there', subtly extending his index finger. 'See?'

'I don't think he has.'

I was wrong. He tapped his friend on the shoulder and pointed straight at us before slowly stepping off the kerb and into the road. We were only 20 metres from them, me lying on my stomach, Titus on one knee. 'Run!' he shouted, grabbing me by the shoulder and dragging me from under the truck. By the time I was on my feet there were half a dozen of them waiting for a gap in the traffic to cross the road. We turned and sprinted towards the hospital entrance as they started to give chase. We careered past the guards outside the accident and emergency unit and through the double doors that led to the ward, before darting right into a stairwell. Jumping three steps at a time, we climbed several storeys before composing ourselves as best we could and walking calmly into a waiting room. Hoping to blend in, we each picked up a magazine and took a seat, but we were dripping in sweat and I had a huge camera hanging from my neck so we quickly drew attention.

Seemingly out of nowhere a uniformed police officer tapped me on the shoulder and led us to a consultancy room, where we hurriedly advised him to lock the door. Titus and I both burst out at once: 'Nazis!' 'Being chased!' 'Skinheads!' Getting nowhere, I pulled out the picture of the man with the rifle and unfolded it on the table. 'He's chasing us', I said, tapping it with my finger. The police officer turned and locked the door, took a seat and asked us to explain slowly. Thankfully, the security guards at the main entrance, caught unaware by us, had managed to spring into action to stop our pursuers. We apologised profusely for storming into a hospital and the officer was remarkably understanding, likely swayed by the picture of a nazi brandishing a gun. He organised us a taxi to safety and by the time we got out on Tottenham Court Road and made it into a pub to toast our escape, HNH had already published an article celebrating the failure of the meeting and exposing the attendees.

It had been terrifying but also exhilarating. Unlike the campaign work which took months before any discernible results, this work was instant. I literally watched as we scuppered their plans and disrupted their ability to organise. By publishing their pictures we made sure that they couldn't operate in the shadows, free of social consequences. I tore the printed picture into tiny squares before flushing it down the toilet and returning to the bar. I could feel myself becoming addicted.

2

THE 'COUNTER-JIHAD' MOVEMENT AND ANTI-MUSLIM STREET PROTEST

As the clock struck eleven on the eleventh day of the eleventh month, and cars and pedestrians came to a respectful halt, chants of 'British soldiers burn in hell!' punctuated the two-minute silence. It was 2010 and I was standing in the middle of Exhibition Road in South Kensington, at the point where it meets Kensington Gore and the entrance to Hyde Park. To my left were the Victorian red brick walls of the Royal Geographical Society, to my right the slightly shabby 19th-century cream façade of the Embassy of Afghanistan. Looking down on events that day from a niche mounted in a wall alcove was Charles Sargeant Jagger's famous bronze statue of the Antarctic explorer Ernest Shackleton.

A group of roughly 35 men, most wearing a black Arab-style *thawb* – an ankle-length garment – under a hoodie and coat in the crisp November weather, stood chanting: 'British troops, murderers!', 'British soldiers, terrorists!' They held white signs: 'What are you dying for, £15K?', 'Afghanistan: The Graveyard of Empires', 'Hands Off Muslim Lands'. Some waved the flag of jihad, showing the text of the *Shahada*: 'I bear witness that there is no deity but God, and I bear witness that Muhammad is the messenger of

God.' The small demonstration was organised by Muslims Against Crusades (MAC). Officially launched in 2010, the group was actually a front for the banned terrorist organisation Al-Muhajiroun, founded by the radical Islamist cleric Omar Bakri Muhammad back in 1983. The organisation was by this point under the day-to-day leadership of Anjem Choudary, the British media's go-to Muslim extremist. It had recently re-emerged after its forerunner Islam4UK had been proscribed by the Home Secretary following a contentious protest in Wootton Bassett, the Wiltshire town where military funeral repatriations took place.

On the opposite side of the road were roughly 50 counter-protesters from the English Defence League, led on the day by the intimidating figure of Kevin Carroll. Dressed in his usual Stone Island peacoat, he is a good foot taller than his cousin and co-founder of the EDL, Tommy Robinson, who at this point was nowhere to be seen. They matched the MAC chanting with cries of 'E, E, EDL!' As usual I was with 'Titus' and the two of us were snapping away. I had only recently begun attending EDL demonstrations to take photographs for HOPE not hate, but some core EDL supporters had already started to recognise Titus and me, even if they didn't yet know who we worked for.

The police kept the two demonstrations well apart and for a while it looked like little of note would happen that day. As is so often the case, demonstration and counter-demonstration are separated by the police, making it like a football match with rival fans singing at each other, or as if two street gangs decided to do battle by forming choirs but never bothered to practise. However, demonstrations have a tangible collective temperament, with passions rising and falling as one. Often it only takes a single spark to change the whole mood. In this case it was the moment that two large red poppies were revealed by a MAC activist. The poppy is sold each year around Armistice Day to raise funds for the Royal British Legion and has been an important symbol of remembrance for those who have died at war since 1921. It holds a special place in the British national psyche, though many on the far right have gone much further and practically deified the symbol.

As chants of 'British troops, murderers' rang out, the MAC demonstrators set fire to the oversized poppies. The small group of press piled in to capture the moment, their pictures soon beamed around the world, causing outpourings of rage and upset. The EDL counter-demonstration exploded into conniptions. The fact that 1 million British Muslims support wearing a poppy, many of whom remember their own families who served in the military, was completely irrelevant at that moment.[1] Here, before the EDL's eyes, was *proof* of what they had been saying all along. Muslims were setting fire to everything they held dear, disrespecting what they were proudest of, desecrating their holy of holies.

The police held the line and kept both demonstrations behind their respective fencing. However, soon after, I looked to my right and saw Tommy Robinson, leader of the EDL, charging out of Hyde Park and across two lanes of traffic. He'd been hiding in the park to avoid the police. The MAC demonstrators were behind a waist-high fence with police all around them. Catching the officers unaware, Robinson crashed through the cordon and vaulted the fence. Arms flailing and outnumbered, he set about punching anyone in reach. The MAC activists piled in on him until police managed to drag him out. The EDL supporters' roars of approval turned to vitriolic anger as Robinson was cuffed and taken away.

One policeman needed hospital treatment for a head injury received during the clashes.

Things began to calm down once the police had escorted the MAC demonstrators back to the train station. They kept the EDL penned in to make sure the two groups couldn't clash. Titus and I were getting our last few pictures and preparing to leave when I heard someone shout, 'Where's your poppy? Why aren't you wearing a poppy?' I looked up to see Kevin Carroll pointing angrily at me. 'Where's your poppy? Eh? Where? Where?' I explained it was on a different coat but nothing seemed to placate him. Those around him soon joined in. They hated the press, seeing them as a liberal elite who unfairly labelled the EDL as far-right and protected 'Muslims' instead of 'real English' people. Special vitriol was reserved for anti-fascists, and accusations that journalists secretly worked for HOPE not hate were liberally and often incorrectly made. However, as the rest of the press had exited straight after the poppy burning, keen to file their pictures, Titus and I stood out. Not least because we were taking close-up pictures of every EDL activist there. Still hopped up on adrenaline from the previous confrontation, the EDL's mood again turned ugly. In the absence of any Muslims, the demonstrators turned their unquenched anger towards us. Just then, I heard a crackle as a police officer's lapel radio burst into life. 'You can let them out now. Over.' I quickly asked if he was indeed about to let the EDL out from behind the barriers. He was. I looked at the baying EDL crowd – 'Hey, hey, come on then, where's your poppy? Where's your fucking poppy?' – then at Titus, and we both knew it was time to leave.

We started to run, holding our cameras against our chests as they bounced around, heading for South Kensington tube station. How long would the police hold back the EDL? As we passed the campus of Imperial College London on our right we looked back one last time. They were coming. A small group had broken free and were charging down the road towards us, the police fading ever further into the background. We dived into the South Kensington subway, a 433-metre tunnel running beneath Exhibition Road back towards the tube station. The tunnel was busy with tourists leisurely strolling towards the Natural History Museum. Luck and timing were going to be everything. We had to get to the station and board a leaving train before the EDL caught us. It was no good making it all that way only to get caught on the platform. As we neared the station entrance we suddenly heard the booming sound of 'E, E, EDL!' echo off the glazed brick walls as they poured down into the tunnel after us. Titus locked arms with me. 'Head down and run together', he said as we charged towards the station, confused tourists jumping out of our way. We unlocked arms, charged through the barriers, ran down onto the platform and into a waiting train carriage. Sweat pouring off us, we looked back up the stairs, willing the train doors to close. The thought of getting stuck on a train with a group of EDL thugs out for blood was terrifying. 'E, E, EDL!' They were in the station. Then it happened – the muffled but beautiful sound of the announcer saying 'Stand clear of the closing doors' and the warning beeps as they slid shut. As the train pulled out of the station Titus and I looked at each other and laughed. We'd made it.

The international anti-Muslim movement, sometimes referred to as the 'counter-jihad movement', is a broad alliance of organisations and individuals who believe that Western civilisation is under attack from Islam. Some are more extreme than others but all generally agree that Islam is a supremacist religion, and many see little difference between violent jihadists and ordinary Muslims who live their lives quite peacefully. While there is absolutely nothing wrong with opposing jihadism or even criticising Islam, the term 'counter-jihadist' is one coined by anti-Muslim activists and actually describes a specific type of conspiratorial anti-Muslim prejudice. Most counter-jihadists believe that secular, liberal society is aiding Islam through mass immigration into Europe and policies of multiculturalism, which they believe squash any criticism of Islam. This conspiratorial notion of conscious and planned invasion is one of the key ideas that marks counter-jihadism out from more general anti-Muslim sentiment. Often activists articulate cultural nationalist ideas that spurn the narrow nationalism of the traditional far right in favour of continent-wide, or more specifically Occident-wide,* brotherhood. A mythical, usually Christian, Western culture and identity is said to be facing extinction at the hands of Islamic invasion.

For this reason counter-jihadists have often adopted imagery associated with the Crusades. Counter-jihad street demonstrations, such as those organised by the English Defence League in the UK, have often been replete with cross-emblazoned shields and images of armour-clad knights. The white supremacist Norwegian mass murderer Anders Breivik, who killed 77 people in 2011, quoted from St Bernard of Clairvaux's *In Praise of the New Knighthood* in Latin in his infamous manifesto, 'A European Declaration of Independence'. The idea of a civilisational clash is also the reason that one of the most influential counter-jihad

---

* The Occident is a term used to refer to the countries of the West, especially Europe and North America. It is used widely within the far right.

blogs, Gates of Vienna, takes its name from the 1529 Siege of Vienna by the Islamic Ottoman Empire, led by Suleiman the Magnificent. Broadly speaking, counter-jihadists believe there is a clash of civilisations between Islam and the West. While ideas around the nature of this clash vary greatly among activists, many see some sort of conflict as inevitable, with a few, including some of the most prominent bloggers and activists, believing that it is both necessary and desirable. At the most extreme fringes some argue that it will only be through civil war that new leaders will emerge and do what is required – expel Muslims from Europe and the West.

The movement's history can be traced back to the 1980s, though it crystallised in its modern form in wake of the 9/11 attacks in 2001. It was originally an internet-based movement, centred around blogs such as Atlas Shrugs, Gates of Vienna and Jihad Watch, respectively edited by Pamela Geller, Edward S. May and Robert B. Spencer. The movement's primary ideologues were writers such as Fjordman (aka Peder Nøstvold Jensen) and Bat Ye'or, who penned one of the central texts of the movement, *Eurabia*. By the second half of that decade the disparate yet like-minded activists of the scene began to formalise their networks with key meetings such as the Counter-Jihad Summits in 2007, first in Copenhagen and then in Brussels. Transnational organisations sprang up and acted as offline forums for activism that had previously been confined to the internet. The most notable was the International Civil Liberties Alliance, an international network of individuals and organisations spanning over twenty countries across Europe, the United States, Canada, India, Australia and New Zealand, run by Christine Brim and Jean-Michel Clément (aka Alain Wagner). Also important was Stop Islamisation of Nations, which served as an umbrella network of counter-jihadist organisations across Europe and the United States, including Stop Islamisation of Europe (SIOE) and Stop Islamization of America (SIOA). This was run by the infamous American Islamophobes Pamela Geller and Robert Spencer, who were barred from entering the UK in 2013 following a campaign by HOPE not hate. While these organisations never had a widespread societal impact in the UK, they did provide the ideas and specific anti-Muslim language to many of the UK's leading activists, who in turn passed that on to anti-Muslim activists at street level.

Today this first wave of international counter-jihad organisations is defunct, most having either disbanded or become inactive. Attempts to organise across borders have also largely failed, with the Defence League Network – a network of national groups created in the image of the EDL – being a prime example. Europe is now missing the transnational far-right bodies that were designed to unify it, and to all intents and purposes the counter-jihad movement, in its original form, no longer really exists. However, while the European movement is not what it once was, there are still hundreds of anti-Muslim organisations and websites that are active and continue to push the conspiratorial anti-Muslim hatred that is the heart of counter-jihad ideology. By contrast, in America the movement has gone mainstream, with key activists and organisations like ACT! for America having unprecedented access to policy-makers during the Trump administration.

In the UK, the most important counter-jihad organisation was the English Defence League, co-founded in 2009 by Tommy Robinson. It emerged following the amalgamation of a number of smaller anti-Muslim street groups, including United People of Luton (UPL) and British Citizens Against Muslim Extremists (also founded in 2009). As pointed out by the sociologist Joel Busher, the EDL 'marked a new chapter in the history of anti-minority activism in Britain'.[2] The UPL was set up by local football hooligans in response to an Al-Muhajiroun demonstration against the homecoming parade of the Royal Anglian Regiment who were returning from Afghanistan. The leaders of the UPL were invited to London and, during a meeting with future EDL financier Alan Ayling and his friends, the idea of a national organisation emerged.

For HOPE not hate, the EDL posed a very different threat to that of the BNP. Not only did the EDL not contest elections, but they were also coming from a different ideological space. Unlike the BNP, who underneath a superficial veneer of acceptability remained a far-right party with a lineage that could be directly traced back to the explicit fascist and neonazi movement of the post-war period, the EDL marked a genuine schism with the past. While Nick Griffin encouraged his core supporters to *hide* their biologically racist politics, the leadership of the EDL made much more earnest attempts to distance their movement ideologically from the fascist far right; consciously eschewing any hint of biological racism in favour of a much narrower platform concerned only with culture and Islam.[3] As George Kassimeris and Leonie Jackson argue, 'The movement rejects the BNP's conflation of Muslims, immigrants and non-whites, and does not concern itself with multiculturalism in general.'[4] Their analysis of the EDL News website found that 'Only two of 117 EDL News articles discussed immigration, and neither politicised the issue.'[5] As Hilary Pilkington rightly states in *Loud and Proud: Passion and Politics in the English Defence League*, 'This single issue focus – and absence, for example, of a more general anti-immigration stance – has been a persistent source of criticism from more traditional far-right groups.'[6] None of this means the movement wasn't far-right and often extremely racist; it's just important to note that it wasn't in the same ideological space as racial nationalist movements like the BNP. In addition to adopting a narrower, non-biologically racist platform, they also sought to consciously distance themselves from the often-vitriolic homophobia of the traditional far right. While the BNP had stickers that said 'Outlaw Homosexuality', the EDL had an LGBT Division and the series of large far-right demonstrations focused around former EDL leader Tommy Robinson in 2018 embraced some openly gay individuals as figureheads. However, while this might have ostracised them from the traditional far right, it did make their platform more palatable, tapping into the broader societal prejudice against Muslims.

In the early years, the EDL portrayed their movement as consciously anti-racist, anti-homophobia and pro-human rights. In place of the broader biologically racist and homophobic platform of the traditional far right, the EDL 'utilised rhetorical strategies such as denial of prejudice, projection of culturally racist motivations on to Muslims, positive-self and negative-other representation, and diminutives such as "we are not against all Muslims, but ..."'.[7] In early 2011 the EDL released a manifesto that followed on from the adoption of liberal rhetoric pioneered by Griffin and the BNP. Point 1 of their manifesto was 'Protecting and Promoting Human Rights', and it described the EDL as 'a human rights organisation'. Point 2 claimed that they worked to promote 'Democracy And The Rule Of Law', while the other points were 'Public Education', 'Respecting Tradition' and 'Working In Solidarity With Others Around The World'.[8] In essence, 'the EDL rearticulated Islamophobia as anti-racism and attempted to normalise it as the natural perspective of those committed to liberal freedom'.[9] The co-option of liberal, or even traditionally progressive concepts such as 'human rights', coupled with their rejection of explicit biological racism, meant the EDL, on paper at least, had the potential to resonate with a far broader audience than the traditional far right before them had been able to.

All of this means that, as the historian Nigel Copsey argued in 2010: 'we should not view [the EDL] simply through the prism of the established far right. Unlike the BNP (or the NF), the EDL is not driven by a fascist or neo-fascist ideological end-goal.'[10] However, one must be careful not to merely take the pronouncements of the EDL and its leadership at face value. There is always the danger of concentrating on the public declarations of the far right and detaching these from the reality as experienced by its adherents and victims, overlooking what might be a different end goal to that espoused, and bestowing on it an unwarranted legitimacy. While constantly claiming not to be racist or prejudiced, the reality on the ground at EDL demonstrations was regularly far detached from the lofty human rights rhetoric of their manifesto.

From roughly 2009–2012, the EDL was the most significant and infamous anti-Muslim group in Europe. Its regular demonstrations, most of which I attended, attracted thousands and made news around the world, and Tommy Robinson became a leading international far-right figure. He developed an international strategy and networks, establishing links with like-minded anti-Muslim organisations in mainland Europe and North America, including neo-conservative organisations and the anti-Islam wing of the Tea Party movement in the United States. For a period the EDL became a prominent player on the international counter-jihad scene and was lauded by supporters around the world. There was also a semi-formal network of international Defence Leagues, though most were stillborn or failed to have any real impact. Over the decade I must have attended close to 100 of these demonstrations, often with fellow HNH cameramen 'Fid' and 'Titus', first organised by the EDL and later by its leader Robinson under numerous other banners. For years, my weekends were given over to travelling the country to stand in fenced-off and barricaded town centres alongside crowds of drunk and coked-up racists, listening to the vitriolic ramblings of one Islamophobe after another. Some days it was tedious in the extreme, on others it was terrifying as demonstrations turned violent and protesters clashed with police or counter-protesters.

The EDL peaked at their homecoming demonstration in Luton on 5 February 2011, attracting 3,000 people. This made it, at the time, the largest anti-Muslim demonstration in the UK. HOPE not hate ran a huge operation on the day, with a series of camera teams directed from a command hub in a hotel overlooking the demonstration site. I spent the day jumping in and out of police lines with a camera, snapping away and trying to avoid getting punched. It was only the following day that we realised I had managed to capture our first picture of Alan Ayling, then the shadowy figure behind the rise of the early EDL. However, by the end of 2011 the EDL had already begun to decline. The causes of their slow but very definite demise were numerous. The academic Joel Busher convincingly argues that they 'found them[selves] at a tactical impasse'.[11] The repetitiveness of endless demonstrations and the dwindling emotional returns, coupled with the leadership's crackdown on violence, hooliganism and alcohol

– as well as the police decision to deny them access to town centres and move demonstrations to isolated peripheral sites – reduced the atmosphere and excitement of events. Even I started to get bored of going to them.

What followed was a downward spiral as ever-smaller demonstrations increased internal tensions and infighting, seeing many EDL activists break away to form their own groups or quit the movement entirely. The murder of off-duty soldier Lee Rigby in Woolwich, south London in May 2013 provided a brief pause in their downward trajectory, but despite their best efforts to capitalise on the tragedy they achieved little more than the swelling of social media numbers and a few larger demonstrations. The final hammer blow came in October 2013 when Robinson and his cousin and deputy Kevin Carroll stood down as leaders.[12] While the EDL continues to exist and hold small and infrequent demonstrations, the organisation is now a shadow of its former self and an irrelevance on the UK far-right scene.

At the very peak of the EDL's notoriety in 2011 a new anti-Muslim organisation emerged on the scene that would well outlive the EDL. Britain First (BF) was formed by Jim Dowson and led by Paul Golding, both formerly of the BNP. They had clearly looked at the success of the EDL and seen the power of street politics over the traditional electoral party politics of the BNP. The group began its confrontational political activities by promoting actions designed to intimidate and ignite violent responses from Muslim communities. They attracted supporters enamoured by their direct action and stunts, in particular targeting Islamist extremist Anjem Choudary's network; they also embarked on a series of 'mosque invasions' where they stormed into mosques with cameras and banners. Through directly confronting their opponents on camera, they soon attracted huge support on social media.

Despite favouring direct action, often in semi-military-style uniforms, they didn't completely do away with electoral politics. Golding stood as a BF candidate in the 2016 London mayoral elections, polling just 1.2%. During the victory speech of Labour's Sadiq Khan, Golding turned his back on the winning candidate and BF later tweeted 'ISLAMIC EXTREMISTS NOT WELCOME!' In June 2016 BF hit the headlines again after the assassination of Labour MP Jo Cox by far-right extremist Thomas Mair, who despite having no apparent connection to the group, reportedly shouted the words 'Britain First' during his attack. This led to the party sitting out the subsequent by-election for fear of a local backlash.

Golding and then-deputy leader Jayda Fransen were banned from entering Luton and, later in August 2016, from all mosques and Islamic centres in England and Wales. In November 2016, Fransen was convicted and fined by a court in Luton for abusing a Muslim woman, and also fined for wearing a political uniform. On the same day, Golding was charged with having entered premises in Wales against a court order instructing him not to do so. Golding was sentenced to eight weeks in prison in December 2016 and on his release published a video in which he stated: 'I can promise you, from the very depths of my being, you will all meet your miserable ends at the hands of the Britain First movement. Every last one of you.'[13] Despite his big talk upon release, in March 2018 Golding and Fransen were both jailed again, for eighteen weeks and 36 weeks respectively, for religiously aggravated harassment. Then in 2020 Golding was charged and convicted under the Terrorism Act for refusing to provide access to his digital devices following an arrest.

Despite regular legal problems the group managed to amass a vast following online. While always struggling to get more than a few dozen on the streets at any one time, their Facebook page had over 1.9 million likes by 2018. A brief high point came in November 2017, when President Trump retweeted three anti-Muslim videos posted by Fransen. Nonetheless, since then BF have been deplatformed by Facebook and Twitter, which has hugely reduced their reach, leaving them only with smaller platforms such as Telegram. While by no means a perfect tactic, the effect on Britain First, and Tommy Robinson, of being removed from major tech platforms is evidence enough of why deplatforming is such a useful anti-fascist tactic.

Ever since major social media platforms became ubiquitous in modern society, debate about their obligation to remove hate speech and hateful individuals has raged. For the far right, deplatforming from social media is emblematic of the wider 'war' on freedom of speech and the supposed sacrificing of their rights at the altar of political correctness. Scratch the surface, though, and it becomes evident that for many it is not a right, but merely a tactic. With their ideas long marginalised from the mainstream, they are using the notion of free speech to try to broaden the 'Overton window' (the range of ideas the public is willing to consider and potentially accept) to the point where it includes their prejudiced and hateful politics. Many who criticise deplatforming argue that the best way to defeat white supremacists or fascists is simply to expose their bankrupt arguments – often phrased as 'sunlight is the best disinfectant'. Most untenable is the oft-repeated notion that debate inevitably leads to greater understanding: 'the truth will out', in the words of Shakespeare. Another is that diversity of opinion always leads to the attainment of the truth; yet another is that the correct argument will always win if debated. It would be wonderful if these ideals were true, but such optimism ignores the possibility that ill-informed opinions will flood the debate and that 'he who shouts the loudest' will end up drowning out others. In reality the 'marketplace of ideas' can often signal little about the quality or value of the speech being sold. These arguments look even less tenable when applied to the febrile online world with its trolling and 'pile on' cultures. One also has to explain how nearly a century of 'sunlight' on far-right ideas has yet to 'disinfect' them; and it compels the question of how many more people have to die in terrorist attacks such as those in Poway, Christchurch and El Paso before someone finally manages to comprehensively debate white supremacy out of existence.

Though the philosophical arguments against deplatforming are often based on such untenable assumptions, one still has to ask whether it actually works as a tactic in the fight against hate. Many critics of the tactic make the legitimate argument that pushing extremists to marginal platforms makes it harder for civil society groups and law enforcement to monitor them. While Twitter is open, channels and discussion groups on apps like Telegram or dark web forums are often much harder to find and keep an eye on. Those on the more extreme end of the far right are already well aware of the trade-off between different types of platforms. Scholars Bennett Clifford and Helen Christy Powell have called this the 'online extremist's dilemma', which is the lack of platforms that allow extremists to both recruit 'potential new supporters' and maintain 'operational security'.[14] Many critics of deplatforming summarise this as 'forcing them underground', the idea that kicking them off open platforms makes it much harder to find and actually combat them. Understanding these criticisms is important, but so too is avoiding caricatures of the pro-deplatforming position. Few, if any, are simply arguing for the deplatforming of the far right from mainstream platforms and then ignoring them while they operate on smaller or more secret platforms. The difficulties that arise from extremists migrating to other platforms is well understood, yet the decision to continue to push for deplatforming has to be made on a cost-benefit analysis.

If we think of mainstream platforms like Facebook and Twitter as recruitment platforms where extremists can meet and engage possible new recruits, while smaller platforms like Gab and Telegram can facilitate inter-movement collaboration, discussion and even planning, I still think that the benefits of reducing extremists' ability to propagate hate and recruit people outweigh the challenges faced by monitoring them on marginal and more secure platforms. In addition – and lack of consideration for the following point is a core indictment of liberal critics of deplatforming – it starves extremists of victims to target online. Clifford and Powell suggest a strategy of 'marginalisation' that seeks to make it difficult for extremists to reach the public while also maintaining the possibility for law enforcement to continue to detect and monitor them. The aim of such a strategy is to 'force extremists into the online extremist's dilemma between broad-based messaging and internal security', thereby keeping 'extremist narratives on the periphery by denying them virality, reach and impact'.[15]

The success of this tactic is shown clearly in a report by researchers from the Royal United Services Institute (RUSI) and Swansea University, 'Following the Whack-a-Mole', which explored the impact of deplatforming on Britain First. The group had a wildly disproportionate online presence, with 1.8 million followers and 2 million likes on Facebook in March 2018, making it 'the second most-liked Facebook page within the politics and society category in the UK, after the royal family'.[16] However, its removal from Twitter in December 2017 and from Facebook in March 2018 had an enormous effect on the organisation's influence in the UK. As the report states, Facebook's decision 'successfully disrupted the group's online activity, leading them to have to start anew on Gab, a different and considerably smaller social media platform'.[17] Facebook's decision to finally act dramatically curtailed Britain First's ability to spread hate and has undoubtedly been a key factor in the movement's decline.

Another important case study is the deplatforming of EDL founder Tommy Robinson. In March 2018 he was permanently banned by Twitter, and then in February 2019 he was banned from Facebook, where he had more than 1 million followers, depriving him of his primary means of communication and of organising his supporters. Another major blow came on 2 April 2019 when YouTube finally placed some restrictions around his channel, which resulted in his views collapsing. Hundreds of thousands fewer people now see his content every month, which is a huge step forward. It may have also played into the severely reduced numbers we have seen at pro-Robinson events since. During the summer of 2018 London was witness to demonstrations in excess of 10,000 Robinson supporters. Since deplatforming, numbers have struggled to reach beyond a few hundred. The reasons for this go beyond one single cause, but Robinson's and his associates' inability to spread the word about events and animate the masses beyond core supporters has clearly played a role.

The brutal truth is that the last decade has seen far-right extremists attract audiences unthinkable for most of the post-war period, and the damage has been seen on our streets, in the polls, and in the rising death toll from far-right terrorists. Deplatforming is not straightforward, but it limits the reach of online hate, and social media companies have to do more – and do more now.

3

THE EFFECT OF ISLAMIST EXTREMISM AND THE ISLAMIC STATE

I had been told that the most dangerous part of the flight was just as you come in to land – that's when you are low enough for the missile to get you. It was the middle of the night and I had struck up a conversation with some oil workers in the departure lounge at Istanbul airport. I couldn't tell if they were just winding me up, but it certainly sounded feasible and did little to calm my nerves. I would soon find out, as in two and a half hours I was due to be touching down in Erbil, northern Iraq.

A few weeks earlier Nick Lowles and I were in the Crown and Anchor on Drummond Street in London having a drink and raging about the apparent lack of attention being paid to the Islamic State by certain parts of the British anti-fascist movement. That summer, June 2014, ISIS had made huge advances and taken control of the major Iraqi city of Mosul, with appalling consequences for the local population. Women were now required to be accompanied by a male guardian and to cover their bodies completely, while ethnic minorities were 'cleansed'. The Armenian Christians, Assyrians, Kurds, Yazidis, Turcoman, Kawliya, Mandeans and Shabaks were dispossessed, many of them murdered, assaulted or displaced.

Videos of cheering fanatics destroying ancient cultural sites or throwing gay men off buildings flooded the internet.

While some anti-fascists were outraged – and some bravely went out to fight – other parts of the movement seemed bafflingly uninterested. At the time, many were far more animated by a spate of small far-right demonstrations in Cricklewood, north London than the rapid expansion of ISIS. While I was in Iraq a group called Left Unity, founded by the film director Ken Loach, held a conference at which a motion proposed that the Islamic State could be a 'stabilising force' in the region and 'an authentic expression of [...] anti-imperialist aspirations', and that 'Unlike a continuation of the framework of western-imposed nation states, it therefore, theoretically, has progressive potential'. I had spent the day listening to tragic stories of death and torture only to get home and hear about supposed allies in Britain discussing the 'progressive potential' of the perpetrators. While the motion failed, it was exactly this sort of idiotic politics that Nick and I felt was a danger to our movement and needed to be challenged.

We had actually started researching domestic Islamism several years before. I was doing my PhD at Royal Holloway, University of London but was still working regularly for HOPE not hate, mainly attending street demonstrations by the EDL. For years I had listened to anti-Muslim speeches and spoken to far-right activists who blamed all Muslims for the crimes of the minority of extremists who made the news for their outbursts or terrorist atrocities. We had long known that one of the primary reasons that people were being attracted to the far right was in response to the actions of Islamist extremists. This idea is called 'cumulative extremism', a theory devised by the historian of fascism Roger Eatwell, who described it as 'the way in which one form of extremism can feed off and magnify other forms'.[1] I have never been convinced that this is an equal and symbiotic effect as some argue, but I have no doubt that the actions of Islamists have serious ramifications for the rise of the far right.

However, our opposition to Islamism went well beyond the fact that it can be a driver of far-right recruitment. It was about consistency as well. We knew we had to speak out against all extreme organisations preaching hatred and division. We wanted to make sure that there was a progressive voice criticising these groups and not just concede the ground to the often hysterical and discriminatory tabloid press – or worse, the far right. In 2013 we published our first major report into British Islamist extremism, *Gateway to Terror: Anjem Choudary and the Al-Muhajiroun Network*. We were nervous. This was outside our usual research area and we knew many would think it wasn't our job. For some of the more lazy elements of the anti-fascist movement we knew this would be seen as pandering to the far right. But it was the right thing to do. After all, while by no means the same, Islamist extremists and fascists do share some commonalities, not least vehement antisemitism, homophobia and misogyny. We wanted anti-fascists to be at the vanguard of the battle against Islamist extremism, shaping the fight in the interest of tolerance, equality and human rights. We knew that if we didn't do this we would be conceding the battlefield to those who wanted to use the issue for the promotion of intolerance, bigotry, racism and opposition to democratic rights.

In the run-up to the report and in the years that followed its publication, Nick and I attended numerous demonstrations organised by Britain's most famous Islamist, Anjem Choudary, and his organisation, Al-Muhajiroun (AM). One sunny Friday afternoon in 2013 we went to watch one of their events outside the Syrian Embassy in west London. Cries of 'Sharia for Syria' and 'Burn in hell Obama' rang out through a dilapidated loudhailer, disrupting the usually calm Belgrave Square. Among the swanky cars lined up outside their respective embassies stood around 45 followers, men in the middle, women and children banished to the side. The rhetoric from the speakers was extreme, with special venom directed towards Secretary-General of the UN, Ban Ki-moon, as well as the usual targets of Britain and Israel. 'The only way we will win is not with the ballot box but with bullets and bombs', said one of the speakers.

Unlike the far right who hated us and would have attacked Nick if they saw him at an event, Choudary and his supporters didn't know who we were. Often we were the only people watching so they would come over and have a chat. I even swapped numbers with Choudary who would regularly text me, sometimes to tell me about an upcoming demonstration, other times to invite me to convert to Islam. I remember one particularly strange text conversation on a Friday night when I was in a nightclub in east London and he was trying to convince me to stop drinking and join his organisation. A friend asked who I kept texting and I replied, 'The most famous terrorist in Britain'.

Al-Muhajiroun was founded by Omar Bakri Muhammad, who was born in Aleppo, Syria in 1958.[2] Outwardly a jovial and friendly character, he has dedicated his life to the propagation of his extreme Islamist views. However, it was in the wake of the 9/11 terrorist attacks in America that the profile of the group began to rocket. Unlike most of the British Muslim community, which roundly and vocally condemned the attacks, AM jumped to their defence, even publicly celebrating them. In September 2002, exactly a year after the attacks, the group held the now infamous 'Magnificent 19' conference which praised the 9/11 terrorists and included a poster strapline reading, 'September the 11th 2001, a Towering Day in World History'. Support for bin Laden became commonplace among the organisation, as its website recorded:

> We will continue to support the sincere scholars, activists and Mujahideen, such as Sheikh Usama bin Laden, as long as their word and sword are risen for the dignity of Islam, as long as their terror is targeted against the enemy of Allah and as long as their effort is to preserve the dignity of the Muslims after the apostate rulers have lost it.[3]

Inflammatory statements such as these significantly raised the public profile of the group around the world, even though it still amounted to only around 160 formal members. Despite the extreme rhetoric of the group, most commentators saw them as almost clownish figures looking for media headlines and not much else. All this was to change in the wake of the 7 July 2005 bombings that killed 52 people in London. Three of the bombers were British nationals of Pakistani descent from West Yorkshire, one was a Jamaican convert from Buckinghamshire. Mohammad Sidique Khan, the ringleader of the plot, was an AM convert and Shehzad Tanweer, an accomplice, has been described as a 'member' of AM in the UK.[4]

Importantly, members of this organisation took part in the protest in Luton against homecoming soldiers in 2009,[5] which led to the formation of the United People of Luton that was the embryo of the English Defence League, as we saw in Chapter 2. By this point, with Bakri in exile the leadership of the UK-based operation had fallen to the increasingly high-profile Anjem Choudary.[6] Clearly energised and encouraged by the mass public outrage that followed their Luton demonstration, Islam4UK (an AM front group) called a protest in early 2010 in Wootton Bassett – the town that had become an unofficial site of public mourning for returning British military fatalities. The group's plan to march through the streets holding black coffins was widely condemned by everyone from then Prime Minister Gordon Brown to the Muslim Council of Britain, which stated that 'the overwhelming majority of British Muslims want nothing to do with such extremists'.[7] The group cancelled the planned march but was quickly proscribed under counter-terrorism laws.[8]

While they were often described as little more than a collection of 'nutters' and eccentrics, Nick and I knew the truth was far more worrying and sinister. We treated AM just like we would a far-right organisation and set about mapping their organisational structures and key activists. It soon became clear that the AM network both in Britain and abroad had become a conveyor belt for terrorists and foreign jihad fighters. In 2013 we found that over 70 people from within their orbit had either been convicted of planning terrorist attacks or had actually been successful in doing so. That number is much higher today following the rise and fall of the Islamic State.

Major planned attacks involving AM-linked people include the Wootton Bassett bomb plot, in which three men, including AM activist Richard Dart, were arrested, charged and convicted for secret conversations aimed at planning an attack in 2013. The Christmas bomb plot of 2010, in which nine men planned a bombing campaign with targets including Big Ben, the London Stock Exchange, Westminster Abbey and the London Eye, had Mohammed Chowdhury at its centre. He had formal links with Al-Muhajiroun and is known to have attended demonstrations with Islam4UK and Muslims Against Crusades (another AM front group). Most of the other men in the plot also had some links with AM, from having Anjem Choudary's number in their phones to having attended AM demonstrations. Another foiled attack was the so-called fertiliser bomb plot, in the context of which British authorities found 600kg of ammonium nitrate fertiliser. The targets of the plot were said to be the Bluewater shopping centre in Essex, the Ministry of Sound nightclub in London and the domestic gas network. Five men were jailed for life in the UK, and others around the world have also faced charges. AM was intimately linked to the planned attacks. *The Observer* showed 'how al-Muhajiroun became the incubator of a global terror network that played a decisive role in radicalising the five "fertiliser bomb" plotters ... The fertiliser bomb plotters were typical of those al-Muhajiroun found and indoctrinated.'[9] In addition, both Richard Reid, the shoe bomber, and the Mike's Place suicide bombers had links with AM.* Another attack linked to AM was the murder of soldier Lee Rigby, on the streets of Woolwich on 22 May 2013. The leader of the whole terrible network was Anjem Choudary, the man I was getting texts from while I was out clubbing.

---

* Richard Reid attempted to detonate a shoe bomb while on a flight between Paris and Miami in 2001. The Mike's Place suicide attack took place in 2003 at a bar in Tel Aviv, Israel. It resulted in the death of three people and the wounding of 50 others.

Our report into AM received widespread press coverage and successfully contributed to the case that Choudary and his supporters needed to stop being treated by the press as a circus act and more like the terrorist network they truly were. We took a camera crew down to a demonstration he was holding in China Town in London. I thrust the report into his hand and put the accusations to his face: I called him a terrorist. He shrugged, rolled the report up and smiled at me. Despite this he continued to invite me to events, which Nick and I duly attended to keep track of the group's activities. However, with time, we noticed that many of the familiar faces we had seen at demonstrations were no longer coming. Then we started to see them turning up in Iraq or Syria fighting for the ever-expanding Islamic State. By the end of 2013 somewhere between 50 and 80 people within the orbit of AM in the UK had headed to Syria (including perhaps as many as fifteen from Luton alone).[10]

I organised one last meeting with Choudary, this time in a café in East London. It was 18 June 2014 and I was determined to challenge him one last time. I sat down, refused his offer of tea, and started the camera. 'You're a coward', I opened with. 'Why is that?', he calmly replied. 'You send dozens of young men to Syria and Iraq to fight and die and you just sit in London. You're a coward.' He never did go to Iraq himself, but lots of his supporters did, many dying on the battlefield. In 2015 Choudary himself was arrested and charged under Section 12 of the Terrorism Act 2000 for inviting support for the Islamic State. He was sentenced to five years and six months in prison.

They called last orders in the Crown and Anchor so Nick and I drank up and agreed that I should go to Iraq, meet victims of the Islamic State in person and produce a special magazine to continue to make the case that Islamist extremism was an anti-fascist issue. I woke up the next morning slightly dazed and presumed it had been the booze talking, only to roll over, check my phone and see a text from Nick: 'Still up for Iraq?'

I touched down at 3.00am and nervously entered the modern vaulted terminal building of Erbil international airport.

Waiting for me with arms outstretched was Rob 'Trig' Trigwell, a friend from university who had ended up working in Iraq. He was the country coordinator for an NGO called REACH Initiative, which meant he oversaw the whole of Iraq with a 1.7-million-dollar budget and a team of 84 people. Their job was to gather and distribute information on affected populations during humanitarian crises such as environmental disasters and wars. Trig kindly offered to put me up for the week and to take me around to visit refugee camps and informal settlements.

As we climbed into the waiting 4x4 I was taken aback by the balmy night air – despite being November it was still 20-odd degrees Celsius. We drove the deserted streets from the airport towards Trig's house in Ankawa, said to be one of the oldest inhabited suburbs in the world. Traditionally an Assyrian part of town, it had more recently become the principal settlement for Christians in Iraq. To my amazement, from the car window I could see an enormous gaudy blue and white statue of Mother Mary on a plinth of plastic Greek-style pillars. Her golden crowned head and outstretched arms looked down on an empty intersection surrounded by shuttered shops, including a liquor store. It was hard to believe that ISIS fighters were only 25 miles away and that just two months earlier US drones and fighter jets had been dropping 500-pound bombs to destroy rebel positions in the area, including mobile artillery that had been shelling Erbil.

We arrived at Trig's place, a large square building on a well-to-do cul-de-sac of identikit homes. We tiptoed through the sleeping house and dropped my bags in his room. 'Come and see this', he said, leading me up a set of stairs that led to the roof. By now the sun was rising and the sounds of a city slowly getting to its feet began to break the silence. Along one wall of the rooftop was a mural reading 'Solidarity'. 'It's barely dry', he said as I walked over to inspect the dozens of signatures scattered around the block letters. It was for David Haines, a colleague of Trig's who had been kidnapped by ISIS and beheaded not long before my arrival.

Through spread fingers I had watched the video of Haines in an orange jumpsuit on his knees and an ISIS fighter all in black, face covered, speaking with an English accent. 'Your evil alliance with America, which continues to strike the Muslims of Iraq and most recently bombed the Haditha dam, will only accelerate your destruction and claim the role of the obedient lap dog', he said, before sawing at Haines' neck with a kitchen knife as the video faded to black. I had no idea he worked for the same NGO as Trig, and seeing the mural made the situation startlingly real to me. I hadn't had long to prepare for the trip and though I'd felt the odd pang of nervousness I had generally been viewing it as an adventure.

Clearly I wasn't going to be able to sleep, so I looked down from the roof and watched the empty roads begin to fill with morning traffic as the call to prayer echoed across the city.

'Would you like a coffee?'

Before I could say no, the aid worker accompanying me turned and said, 'Always say yes. It's the only thing they have left to offer you.'

We were in the tent of a family of Syrian refugees living in Kawergosk, perilously close to Mosul and the front line with ISIS. To my surprise, the tent, onto which they had built a second room from wood and tarpaulin, was relatively spacious, housing a TV, cooker and fridge. To reach it I had walked down a bustling makeshift shopping street, small shacks lining a dirt road offering food, clothes, paraffin gas stoves, hairdressing, electrical goods and even currency exchange: Iraqi dinars, dollars and euros. The tent was larger and better equipped than I had imagined, but that had the opposite effect on me than I had expected. It made me feel sorrier for them than if it had just been a small white tent with the UN logo emblazoned across the side. This was now it – they were likely never going home. Just months before, they had owned a house and all the things in it, had cars and jobs, friends and lives. It had all been taken from them. This two-roomed tent was now all they possessed in the world, and the only thing they could offer me, their guest, was a coffee. The poured concrete floor on which their home now stood was no doubt progress – winter was coming and the camp sat at the bottom of a large hill, meaning any rain would flood it and wash away the mud floors – but it was also a symbol of permanence.

The trip to the camp had not gone entirely to plan. Trig was busy with work and left me in the capable hands of his colleague 'Doc', a former doctor from Baghdad whose home had been destroyed by an American plane. I had asked him to take me as close to the front line as he felt comfortable with, so we left Erbil and headed west towards Mosul. Just before reaching the Kurdish checkpoint of Aski Kalak we turned north and drove parallel to the Great Zab River, the forward position for ISIS troops. The landscape was scarred by huge trenches designed to halt the advance of armoured vehicles and the horizon to our left was dotted with the black flag of the Islamic State. To our right was the Khabat thermal power plant, a sprawl of industrial buildings with a red and white chimney. I rolled down my window, leaned out and began to film, hoping to capture nothing more than a shot of a flickering flame. As I watched the power plant shoot past on the camera display I suddenly spotted a soldier dressed in desert camouflage standing by an entrance to the plant. 'Get that camera back in!' shouted Doc. A hundred yards up the road a metal fence was pulled out onto the deserted street and we were waved down by several soldiers pointing rifles at the car.

One of them tapped the point of his gun on my window. 'Roll it down', said Doc. The gun came in just inches from my face as the soldier began to speak in what I presumed was Kurdish or maybe Arabic. I was too scared to work out which. 'They want your camera.' I passed it through the window and began to babble. 'I just wanted a picture of the flame. The flame, that flame there. I just wanted a picture.'

What had I been thinking? I was filming a major power plant just miles from the front line in an ongoing war and my only explanation was that I wanted a picture of a flame. Doc managed to talk them down, no doubt apologising for the staggering stupidity of his English passenger. They made me delete the footage but thankfully allowed me to keep the camera before removing the roadblock and waving us on our way.

As my heart rate slowly lowered and I was confident I had apologised enough to Doc, we drove over the crest of hill and for the first time the site of Kawergosk camp opened up before me. More a town than a camp, it was home to some 10,000 people who had fled across the front line. Each night more arrived under the cover of darkness. I walked its streets and marvelled at the ingenuity and invention of its inhabitants. Some had added second and sometimes even third rooms built of wood, concrete and bricks. In a matter of months, these people had managed to turn mere tents into new homes. Most people ignored me, probably bored of seeing Western journalists who never delivered the changes they promised, but others were keen to talk. Complaints ranged from a lack of privacy – parents unable to 'hug' while sharing a space with their children – through to missing favourite TV shows because 'the reception is rubbish'. However, mundane problems like these, while plentiful, were just the tip of the iceberg. Deeper fears of being stuck in this camp or one like it for months or even years were well founded; and with the first snow of winter due to appear in the air soon, new challenges would arise.

Fleeing in the hot Middle Eastern summer, most had left with just the clothes on their back, meaning that at the time I was in the camp 60% of the displaced people had no winter coats and for 90% there was less than one coat per person in their family group. The struggle to keep warm would soon be added to their list of problems. This was compounded by oil shortages in the camps, resulting from ISIS' occupation of several oil refineries in the region. Tragically, some had turned to watering down the kerosene, which had led to stoves exploding. Further north at Khamke camp I met Jallal, a Yazidi from Sinjar, who explained: 'Life in this camp is good but we are afraid of one thing ... burning. The tents are too near to each other. Five tents have set ablaze and up until now three children and one women have died.'

I heard of similar fires at other camps including Harsham, a small settlement just outside Erbil. There, a makeshift fruit and veg stand played host to a group of ten understandably angry men, all explaining how a recent fire burned down a tent in fourteen seconds. Thankfully that time the women inside escaped. Talking to this group, it became clear that ISIS' expansion had affected the lives of millions of people in ways that were not immediately obvious. Apart from the capture of refineries, sometimes hundreds of miles away, their control of arable land had pushed up prices and reduced rations in neighbouring areas. Even though the refugees had escaped, ISIS still had the power to make their lives worse.

Sadly, the group of men I met at Harsham, while facing a desperate situation, were among the lucky ones. The sprawling camps such as Kawergosk, Bagid Kandela and Chamishku were organised and run by international aid agencies; others were not. Trig and I headed further north to visit a camp called Deirabon, which sat on a plateau on the edge of a hill with a dramatic vista down to both Syria and Turkey. The camp, home to 1,200 Yazidis, was made up of large communal tents and was not managed but rather had sprung up spontaneously, seemingly left to fend for itself bar the odd delivery of water. The toilets were open pits within smelling distance of the sleeping area. The tarpaulin homes had no floor, with threadbare mattresses lying on open gravel and mud. Camp residents had received just one food delivery in the past three months, meaning they had had to scrape together what money they could to buy provisions from the local town. The diarrhoea that afflicted the camp in the summer was giving way to hypothermia as increasingly bitter winter winds whipped across the top of the hill into the exposed huddle of tents. This was a world away from the televisions and fridges I had seen at other camps. Such situations emerged because no one was able to comprehensively deal with the ongoing crisis. The huge numbers pouring across the border meant that many found sanctuary in informal settlements, derelict buildings or hastily erected camps like Deirabon.

In a one-month period just before I arrived, between 170,000 and 200,000 people fled Syria and crossed the border into Suruç, Turkey. Many then organised their own travel along the Turkish-Syrian border until they reached the town of Silopi, which sits between Iraq, Turkey and Syria. The journey took up to ten days. Some then spent another ten days in the border town waiting to be allowed across into Zakho in northern Iraq. For some, this was the end of their journey but others were then moved again, this time by the Kurdish authorities, to camps such as Gawilan further south. Of course, northern Iraq had not only had to deal with the thousands of people fleeing Syria but an ever-increasing number of internally displaced people resulting from ISIS' eastward expansion.

Their ethno-religious background often determined the final destination of those in flight. The displacement of the Shabak and Turkmen Shia, for instance, happened in two stages. Between early June and early August 2014, communities from Tal Afar fled towards Zummar and Sinjar, which were protected by Kurdish forces, while communities in Namrud and Mosul escaped towards the Nineveh Plains. However, when ISIS then expanded it triggered a wave of secondary displacement, sending internally displaced people towards the Kurdish region of northern Iraq or all the way to Shia-governed enclaves in south central Iraq, a journey made by car or plane. This process of secondary displacement also affected the Christian minorities in the Nineveh Plains. In June and July, around 50,000 Christians fled Mosul for a number of towns in the plains. When ISIS expanded again in early August, they had to move again, this time joined by a further 150,000 Christians from the Al-Hamdaniya and Tel Kaif districts. Contrary to what one might assume, people do not just flee to the nearest safe haven but rather head towards predestined locations influenced by the perception of the welcome they will receive. Christians flee to other Christian areas, Yazidis to Yazidi areas, Shia to Shia areas, etc.

Speaking to these people in refugee camps it struck me how ISIS were tearing to pieces the fabric of centuries-old communities. While it would be absurd to suggest that Iraq was previously some sort of multicultural utopia – many were persecuted by Saddam Hussein's Ba'athist regime – it had towns and cities with minority communities including Yazidis, Shia Muslims, Assyrian, Syriac, Chaldean and Armenian Christians, Druze, Mandeans and Shabaks, some of which have lived in the region for over a thousand years. The ruthless expansion of ISIS forced many of these groups to flee, turning once mixed areas into homogeneous Sunni Muslim regions. The understandable desire of minority groups to seek refuge within similar communities has meant that a once ethnically-mixed province has stratified along ethno-religious lines. Some have left the region altogether, with Christians often fleeing to Europe; while several Christian refugees I spoke with told me they had no intention of going home now, even if ISIS were defeated. They no longer felt safe. Despite often having ancient roots in the towns and cities they inhabited, trust had broken down completely. These displaced minorities had witnessed their former neighbours turn on them and saw no way of ever living peacefully among them again. Lines had been redrawn, not just on the map but among the peoples of the Middle East too.

I was at the bar of the Classy Hotel Erbil, about as 'classy' as its name would suggest. Trig was introducing me to an assortment of colleagues from various NGOs as they passed in and out to get drinks. I got the impression that the humanitarian community is an incestuous bunch forced together by circumstance, one of intense relationships forged in extreme situations and places, yet also transient as people hop between droughts, famines and wars, crossing paths in protected communal housing, refugee camp huts or hotel bars.

We took a seat and were joined by Sheri Ritsema-Anderson, a humanitarian affairs officer with the UN Office for the Coordination of Humanitarian Affairs (OCHA) based in Erbil. We had barely started talking when her phone vibrated on the table. She opened the message and fell silent mid-sentence. 'Three suspected car bombs have entered the area. Return home.' I was ready to dive under the table, but while there was some shuffling in seats, everyone seemed relatively calm. We finished our drink and walked back to the house, slightly annoyed our evening had been cut short.

The next morning we left extra early to travel north to Duhok to visit the refugee camp Domiz 1. Just 60 kilometres from Syria, it was built to house the influx of people escaping across the border. 'Little Syria' was a vast conurbation of tents and water tanks that was home to tens of thousands of people. We pulled in through the gate and headed to the administration cabin where we were handed a small glass of strongly brewed Assam black tea. While waiting for Trig to sort out my entry to the camp I looked up at the TV hanging from the wall on silent. Grainy news footage of a tangled heap of metal that used to be a car was being broadcast on repeat. Someone leaned forward and turned on the sound. A suicide bomber had tried to drive his vehicle into the governorate building, only to be mown down by guards. The bomb detonated, killing six people and injuring dozens more. It was the first attack to target the city in seven months and a hush came over the cabin as we watched the macabre footage. We had driven those very streets earlier that morning, saved by our early start.

We left the hut and headed into the camp. Trig and his colleagues had work to do. Using GPS trackers, they walked the long streets and dropped a marker at each toilet to map the camp's facilities. A bomb might have gone off and people had died but work had to go on. Bombs went off and people died every day here. That's why so many thousands were living in the tents around us.

That evening we made our way back to Erbil in our minivan, only to find checkpoints now searching vehicles entering the city. For what felt like a lifetime we queued alongside a mass of other cars, jolting slowly towards the soldiers. I couldn't help but remember last night's text. 'Three suspected car bombs in the area.' Where were the other two? Were we sitting next to one waiting to take out the checkpoint? Despite the pumping air-conditioning I began to drip with sweat as we crept forward. Eventually we passed through, and as we drove away I realised I had forgotten to breathe for some time. Trig shot me a wry smile but I was confident he had enjoyed it as little as I had.

As the trip drew to a close we made one final trip north, this time all the way up to the city of Zakho, a few miles from the Iraq/Turkey border. While there were large refugee camps housing those heading from Syria into Iraq via Turkey, the city had also become home to countless informal settlements where refugees found whatever shelter was available. We parked near what looked like a derelict concrete building, the front of which had crumbled away, now replaced by blue tarpaulins flapping in the wind. We entered the warren of corridors that led to room after room of bare concrete walls, each housing a huddled family in cramped conditions.

We were quickly beckoned to the second floor and into a room at the front of the building, opening out onto the street with a long drop to the ground. 'There is a women who's had surgery, she needs to be warm but there is nothing to heat the place.' We found her lying on the concrete floor, eyes closed, sleeping. 'What's wrong with her?' we asked. 'She was pregnant but she was so tired and too cold ... she lost her baby.' Forced to flee by ISIS while heavily pregnant, this woman had walked for who knows how long to find safety, but the effort had proved too much. In the fight to save her life she had lost her baby and now, lying on this dirty floor recuperating from surgery, there was a good chance she was going to die too. There was not much we could do beyond radioing in her location to other NGOs to see if anyone could provide medical assistance.

As we drove away I felt utterly useless and heartbroken. Over the previous two days I had seen so much human suffering. Staggered by the size of the camps and the numbers of refugees, it was hard to take it all in, but suddenly the grim reality of the situation was encapsulated in this one story of pain and death. I thought about the conference in London

I had heard about only the day before, and the idea of the 'progressive potential' of ISIS. I wanted to fly straight back and tell them the story of this dying woman.

With the sun setting I drove to the refugee camp around the corner and walked the tented streets one last time. A group of children played football on a cleared area of scrubland until their parents shouted for them to come in for dinner. Just like my mum used to do for me. Even among the endless tales of tragedy, life went on.

4

THE EUROPEAN FAR RIGHT AND THE MIGRANT CRISIS

Paris was in mourning. The nation was reeling after suffering its worst attack since the Second World War, the deadliest on European soil since the 2004 train bombings in Madrid which slaughtered 193. It was roughly a year after I had returned from Iraq. At 9.16pm on 13 November 2015 a suicide bomber blew himself up near the Stade de France, then three minutes later a second did the same. At 9.25 a gunman opened fire at Le Carillon café and Le Petit Cambodge restaurant on rue Bichat, killing fifteen more. Further slaughter followed on rue de la Fontaine-au-Roi then rue de Charonne. At 9.40 a blast tore through people on boulevard Voltaire, while at the same time mass shooting and hostage-taking began at the famous Bataclan theatre, packed that night with fans who had come to see the American band Eagles of Death Metal. In total 130 were left dead and a further 413 injured at the hands of the Islamic State of Iraq and the Levant (ISIL).

As news of these attacks was still filtering through I boarded a plane for Dresden, Germany to attend a demonstration organised by Patriotic Europeans Against the Islamisation of the Occident (PEGIDA). The group, formed in October 2014, had quickly grown to become the largest anti-Muslim street movement in the whole of Europe. In the wake of the previous terrorist attacks on the offices of the magazine *Charlie Hebdo* in Paris earlier that year, PEGIDA's weekly demonstrations had swelled to tens of thousands of people. Just weeks before my arrival some 20,000 people had filled Dresden in protest against the continuing migrant situation and Germany's welcoming humanitarian response. With the bodies still being counted in Paris I landed in Dresden, trepidatious about the approaching demonstration. I knew little about the city beyond the fact that it had been bombed flat by the Royal Air Force in February 1945. The only image I could muster in my mind's eye was the famous and heartbreaking Richard Peter photograph of the statue of Goodness looking down on a wasteland of broken buildings. For this reason I was pleasantly surprised as I walked its beautiful streets. Large parts of it are indeed scarred by ugly post-war concrete buildings, but the centre has been restored as an impressive baroque city.

As the evening of the demonstration approached I took in a few of the many bars and cafés dotted around the city centre, hoping a few strong German beers would fortify me for the coming events. Having spent years attending far-right demonstrations across the UK, I was fully expecting violence, especially in the wake of the terror attacks in Paris. I finished my drink, pulled my scarf up over the lower half of my face, and headed towards Neumarkt, the square that was the regular meeting point of PEGIDA demonstrations. To one side was a trailer with loudspeakers and a PEGIDA banner draped across it. The crowds were slowly building but something felt wrong. The usual rush of adrenaline was missing. There was a small counter-protest in the distance, but the people filtering into the square with their German flags seemed rather uninterested in them. Where were the big groups of lads swilling cans of lager and sneakily snorting cocaine under their jackets? There were some heavies doing security and a smattering of biker types but overwhelmingly the crowd was made up of very respectable-looking people, usually in couples and overwhelmingly middle-aged. Absolutely no drinking from anyone. No football-style chanting. No face coverings. No gratuitous pig's-head masks or cartoons of Allah. As a result the demo was pretty much un-policed. No pens or barriers.

I sneaked up to the balcony of a hotel that overlooked the square and looked down onto 10,000 people, well over double anything I had seen in the UK. At one point the whole crowd began to chant in unison. Thousands of German voices echoing off the surrounding buildings sent a shiver through me. It was impossible not to draw ugly historical parallels. My German isn't good enough to have understood much of the speeches, but what I did gather was the usual anti-Muslim conspiracies mixed with vocal support for Marine Le Pen in France in the wake of the attacks. Once the speeches had finished the whole crowd took a silent march around the city centre, which took roughly an hour. Again, no gratuitous chanting, throwing of cans or violence towards the police. I peeled off early to send back my report to Nick in London, detailing how much less scary it was than anything I had seen in the UK.

However, just as I was about to hit 'send' and return to my beer, a family walked past: a child sitting on her father's shoulders holding a PEGIDA sign and a German flag. It struck me how wrong I was. This was actually much more scary than the violent far-right events I had attended in England. This was normal. Seemingly acceptable. It wasn't skinheads sieg-heiling or yobs chanting football songs. It was families.

It was normal-looking people. It was women. The ideas might have been the same as anti-Muslim groups back home, their dislike of Muslims identical, but this was of a different order of magnitude. Had anger over the migrant crisis risen to such a level that what was once beyond the pale in Germany was creeping back towards the mainstream? I rewrote my report to Nick and signed it off with: 'This was different.'

I rose early, as Dresden was just the first half of the trip. The following day there was to be another anti-Muslim demonstration in Prague, and this time we had received information that the leading British far-right figure Tommy Robinson was due to attend. The train ticket was a mere €13. Coming from a country where you have to sell a kidney to afford a long train journey, I double-checked. But €13 it was, so I happily handed over my money and boarded the train. A few hours later I found myself in the shabby but still impressive art nouveau ticket hall of Prague's main station. Prague's nickname, the City of a Hundred Spires, is well deserved. Its Gothic buildings were bedecked in Czech flags to mark the anniversary of the 1989 Velvet Revolution. I checked in with Nick, dropped my bag and headed straight out to the demonstration.

Within an hour it was clear that I was woefully under-dressed, so I popped into a shop to buy one of those Russian hats with woolly earflaps. The only ones they had were emblazoned with a large plastic hammer and sickle badge, clearly marketed at Western tourists. 'Do you have any others?' I asked. 'No', came the curt response. I imagined explaining to Nick that the reason my cover was blown was because I wore a Soviet hat to a demonstration to mark the fall of communism. I bought it anyway and ripped the badge off in front of the bemused shop assistant. 'A mini Velvet Revolution of my own', I quipped, but was met with a blank stare. I thought it was funny. She didn't.

The demonstration was organised by a squat and severe-looking character called Martin Konvička, an Assistant Professor in Entomology at the South Bohemian University in České Budějovice and the founder of 'We Do Not Want Islam in the Czech Republic', later called the 'Bloc Against Islam', of which he was chairman. Back in August 2015 his followers had installed effigies in Prague of the torsos of women stoned to death, to warn of the danger of Islam. This was a much smaller gathering than the demonstration in Dresden, with all of us crowded together in a blocked-off side street with a stage at one end. I looked around and quickly spotted Tommy Robinson, accompanied by leading activists from PEGIDA in Germany, including Siegfried Daebritz and Tatjana Festerling. Also part of his group was Jamie Bartlett from the British think-tank Demos. I was shocked at first, but later found out he was following Robinson for a book he was working on.

I stood there hopping from foot to foot to keep warm and zooming in with my long lens to get pictures of Robinson and his group. The crowd waved Czech flags and also a white flag with a mosque in a red circle, crossed out like a 'no entry' sign. Others had banners attacking German Chancellor Angela Merkel and calling for her imprisonment due to her pro-migrant policies. Then a wave of excitement spread across the crowd as an elderly man took to the stage. As he hobbled forward in a long black coat, looking every inch a Soviet leader presiding over a Red Square procession of missiles, it suddenly struck me. It was Miloš Zeman, the President of the Czech Republic. I couldn't believe it. Just yards from me was Tommy Robinson, a man I had seen giving anti-Muslim rants to baying groups of EDL thugs, and now we were both watching the President of a European Union country addressing a crowd and saying practically the same things. Standing next to Zeman was Konvička, who had recently posted on Facebook: 'If it comes to worst, there will be concentration camps for Muslims FORTUNATELLY [sic]. They asked for it themselves.'[1]

This was what 'mainstreaming' looked like. No longer did you have to stand in a rainy car park in England surrounded by coked-up hooligans to hear speeches about a supposed Muslim invasion of Europe. It was now possible to hear it from a European President himself. Utterly depressed, I trudged back to my hotel and typed up my report for Nick. That night I walked the streets of Prague but it all felt less beautiful and magical than when I arrived that morning: the spires less impressive, the Gothic buildings less imposing, the Czech pilsners less delicious. The city somehow felt tainted, and a lot less welcoming.

Several months later I continued my tour of Europe and headed to Denmark. I flew into Malmö, Sweden so as to avoid getting stuck on the same flight as Tommy Robinson or any of his British supporters. It was a bitterly cold January in 2016 and the following day there was to be a far-right demonstration in Copenhagen. I took my seat on the train out of Malmö and defrosted my hands on the welcome heaters by each seat as we crossed the Øresund Bridge, made famous by the Nordic noir crime series *The Bridge*. As we began to cross the vast expanse of waterway that forms the border between the two countries, I put the programme's haunting theme tune on my iPod. As a grey Copenhagen drew ever closer the acoustic introduction gave way to majestic strings and jolting percussion, sending a shiver up my spine. Perhaps it was nerves.

The following morning, I woke early and took a quick walk in the snow-covered cobbled streets of Copenhagen. The city is an enchanting mixture of historic architecture randomly interspersed with buildings of brave and jarring modernity. Exploring would have to wait, though, as I was there to do a job. Once again, I found myself in a European capital with a long lens camera waiting for the arrival of Tommy Robinson.

Strangely, the demonstration had actually been organised from Britain, with instructions for the day posted on the event's Facebook page by Jack Buckby, the press officer of PEGIDA UK and Liberty GB. Even stranger, there were to be no Danish speakers at the event. I sat in a coffee shop overlooking the planned location for the demonstration, but as the start time approached it became clear that numbers were going to be small. In one sense this was good news, but then again small demonstrations are always harder to cover because you can't simply fade into the background. By the time the first speech started a mere 100 people had turned up.

Among the tiny audience was the leader of the Danish Defence League, Lars Grønbæk Larsen, and a contingent from the extreme right-wing Danmarks Nationale Front. Also present were a number of Swedes, including Dan Park, the 'artist' who had recently been arrested, fined and sentenced to prison for hate speech. Also over from Sweden was Ingrid Carlqvist, a 'Distinguished Senior Fellow' of the US-based Gatestone Institute and editor-in-chief of *Dispatch International*, a newspaper she founded with leading Dutch anti-Islam activist Lars Hedegaard. Just recently she had published an ugly article about what she called 'Afghan Rapefugees'. The rally passed without incident. Robinson's short speech was similar to those he gave in his old EDL days, with talk of a 'military invasion of Europe' by Muslims. As is usual with these types of demonstrations, there was a vocal and confrontational counter-demonstration by local anti-fascists. At times, this drowned out the speeches, forcing them to abandon the loud-hailer and instead opt for a microphone, a switch that took some time.

Robinson's speech was followed by a long and slow march through Copenhagen that proved rather more event-ful than the failed rally at the start. The march was flanked on both sides by anti-fascists chanting 'Refugees Welcome' and 'Where's your famous EDL?', forcing the police to use considerable force to hold them back. Then, as the march turned a corner into a narrow street, Robinson pointed to an anti-fascist screaming at him from behind the police lines and shouted, 'Come here and say that!' Agreeing to his request, the anti-fascist bolted past the police and attacked him. Demonstrators from behind Robinson jumped to his defence, followed quickly by baton-wielding police. Once order was restored the march returned to the start point for speeches by fellow British activists Paul Weston and Anne Marie Waters. Weston gave a peculiar talk mainly aimed at attacking the counter-demonstrators for being communists, followed by some strange conspiratorial claims that the UN was working to destroy all national borders and take control of the world. With so few people in the crowd he seemed to lose his enthusiasm and finished by saying, 'That's enough, I need a pint.' Waters then took the microphone and gave a speech about women's rights to a bemused-looking audience made up almost exclusively of men. Her speech reached its crescendo with an attack against the 'so-called feminists' on the counter-demonstration.

While the demonstration was a failure in terms of attend-ance, it was further evidence of the genuinely transnational nature of the European far right. Activists from the UK organ-ised an event in Denmark where they met with a prominent figure from Sweden. It was also a good reminder not to con-centrate only on the active far right. As Prague had shown me a few months previously, anti-Muslim politics had moved from the fringe to the centre. A failed far-right demonstra-tion in Copenhagen didn't mean there was no problem with Islamophobia in Denmark. The week before I arrived, the Danish government had announced plans to further tighten its immigration policy, including measures to force refugees to hand over valuables upon arrival. Then the Danish city of Randers, north-west of Copenhagen, ordered pork to be mandatory on municipal menus following a council motion proposed by the right-wing populist Danish People's Party. Similarly tough lines were being taken by governments across central Europe.

As I headed back across the Øresund Bridge, I realised that I could follow Tommy Robinson to the ends of the earth but that would only ever give me a small part of the picture. Far-right politics, especially Islamophobia, had crept into the mainstream. The gangrenous limb had begun to spread its poison through the body. For the first time since I had started this work in 2010, I genuinely felt like we were losing.

By the time the cannons fell silent across Europe in 1945 the leading architects of fascism were dead. With much of Europe turned to rubble, few families left untouched and the news-reel footage of Jewish bodies being pushed into mass graves seared into the global consciousness, most understandably thought that fascism would die with its founders. Despite all this, fascism survived the Second World War – and though changed, it survives to this day. As the theorist of totalitarianism Waldemar Gurian put it in 1946: 'The shooting war is over, but the humanitarian democratic ideology has not obtained a clear-cut triumph.'[2]

When it comes to contemporary debates about the modern far right in Europe, few think to look back to the immediate post-war period to find answers, and yet in truth, the Second World War and its aftermath significantly shaped the world we live in now. The historian Dan Stone convincingly argues that 'the further from the war we get, the more its impact is being felt and the more its meanings are being fought over ... the years since 1989 should be understood as the real post-war years'.[3] In other words, the opportunity for meaningful debate and a serious reckoning with the events of the war has only become possible since the end of the Cold War and the reunification of Europe. Prior to that the continent was divided, with each side of the Berlin Wall experiencing a different 'post-war consensus': in the West in the form of welfare-capitalist states and in the East, communist dictatorships.

While not downplaying the importance of this ideological divide, Stone offers an alternative framework through which we can understand the return of far-right politics since the fall of the Berlin Wall. He argues that the post-war consensus was entwined with a particular memory of the Second World War and that competing notions of anti-fascism were, in essence, a fire blanket suppressing the flames of far-right politics. In Eastern Europe anti-fascism became an instrumentalised tool used to suppress dissent, oppress opponents and justify the reorganisation of society. In the West it avoided becoming state dogma but rather became the intellectual basis of political and social stability, with a new consensus built around class cooperation, parliamentary democracy and welfare accepted by the right as well as the left. Thus, across the continent, as Stone argues, 'antifascism became the basis of stability in postwar Europe'.[4] As such, the end of the Cold War and the 'collapse of the political project of social democracy in the West and communism in the East went hand in hand with the death of antifascism, hence the reappearance of ideas and values which had long been assumed to be dead, or at best marginal and lunatic'.[5] The beast was merely injured, not dead, and since the end of the Cold War it has begun to reawaken.

On 9 November 1989 the Berlin Wall crumbled, followed by the Soviet Union itself in 1991. The Cold War was over, and with it what Eric Hobsbawm called the short 20th century. The world watched on as David Hasselhoff, wearing a piano-keyboard scarf and leather jacket, sang 'Looking for Freedom' at the Berlin Wall and a wave of optimism spread across the continent. Some got carried away, like political scientist Francis Fukuyama who enthusiastically declared 'the end of history' and the 'universalization of Western liberal democracy as the final form of human government'.[6] However, in the decades that have followed, a new threat to liberal democratic hegemony has emerged, not from resurrected communism, but from the radical right.

That said, fascism and far-right politics more broadly never really went away. Even as the Soviet tanks rolled into Berlin there were people across the continent plotting for the resurrection of their shattered utopia. In the East, under oppressive and undemocratic communist dictatorships, there was no place for far-right or fascist groups in the traditional sense. In the West, however, far-right political parties emerged quickly in the immediate post-war years. To summarise such a complex and varied phenomenon over such a long period is extremely difficult. German political scientist Klaus von Beyme offers a useful if unavoidably imperfect framework to try. He identifies three waves of the post-war far right that occurred between 1945 and 1955, 1955 and 1980, and 1980 and 2000. The exceptions to the three-waves hypothesis are the Iberian peninsula, where Francisco Franco survived the war unscathed and remained dictator until his death in 1975, and Portugal, where António de Oliveira Salazar remained dictator until 1968. The debate over whether Franco and Salazar were fascists is a complex one and there isn't space to explore that here. However, suffice to say that the leading historian of Franco, Paul Preston, has stated: 'Franco wasn't a fascist ... he was something much worse.'[7]

Iberia aside, von Beyme argued that the three waves ran as follows:

The first was neo-fascism (1945–55) when most far-right parties and politicians were in some way connected to the fascist regimes of the pre-war and war years. Most notable here was the Italian Social Movement (MSI) which entered parliament in 1948 despite its initials also standing for '*Mussolini Sei Immortale*' (Mussolini, You Are Immortal).[8]

The second wave was right-wing populism (1955–80). While fascist parties continued to exist, this period saw the 'rise of a variety of right-wing populist parties and politicians, which were defined by opposition to the post-war elites rather than allegiance to a defeated ideology and regime', as Cas Mudde notes.[9] The most notable of these groups was the Defence Union of Shopkeepers and Craftsmen, founded by French populist Pierre Poujade, whose supporters became known as Poujadists, numbering as many as 400,000 by 1955.[10]

The third wave was the radical right (1980–2000). This was the period that saw the first major rise of far-right politics since the war in western Europe. It was during this time, and especially from the 1990s onwards, that radical right parties began to enter European parliaments in increasing numbers. The first was the Flemish Bloc (VB) in Belgium, followed by the emergence of the Front National in France as an electoral force. A host of similar parties across the continent began to make headway, such as the Sweden Democrats (SD), the Swiss People's Party (SVP) and the Freedom Party of Austria (FPÖ) under the leadership of Jörg Haider. With the collapse of communism in 1989 the following decade also saw the re-emergence of far-right politics in eastern parts of the continent.

Following on from von Beyme's work, the social scientist Cas Mudde brought things up to date with what he has dubbed the 'Fourth Wave' of the post-war far right, running from 2000 to the present.[11] During this twenty-year period the far right in Europe has become increasingly mainstream to the point where today, radical and far-right parties are in positions of power across the continent.

The causes of this rise are diverse and complex. There is a host of long-term factors that underpin the seemingly rapid growth of the far right in Europe in the last two decades: the crumbling of the anti-fascist consensus, legacies of imperialism and colonialism, societal racism and xenophobia, and the negative ramifications of neoliberal politics and globalisation. But one crucial contributing factor is the role of the internet and social media in helping to lay the foundations for far-right growth. Ignored by many, in 2011 the think-tank Demos published a report called *The New Face of Digital Populism* which highlighted how 'Populist parties are adept at using social media to amplify their message, recruit and organise'.[12] Remarkably, to this day, many works that seek to explain the rise of the far right completely ignore the role of the internet. With time, the internet would shift from providing new opportunities for existing far-right organisations to birthing completely new types of far-right activism, a phenomenon explored later in this book.

Alongside these long-term factors, there has been a series of trigger events and phenomena that have crowbarred open the door to the mainstream in recent years. First was the wave of Islamist terror attacks, most notably 9/11 in New York but also the 2004 Madrid train bombings, the 7 July London bombings in 2005 and a series of deadly attacks in France. As well as the backlash against Islamism, an important trigger for the rise of the European far right was the financial crisis of 2008 and its fallout of economic turmoil, austerity and deprivation. The economic roots of the rise of the far right well predate 2008, however. Dave Renton has shown how the dominance of neoliberal economics from 1979 to 2008 contributed to later far-right growth because it resulted in a 'stagnation in working class living standards and especially a reduction in welfare benefits payments, which delegitimised arguments for the maintenance of the status quo', thereby giving some voters the resolution to look for more radical alternatives.[13]

Nonetheless, the huge upheaval of 2008 has accelerated some people's journey towards radical and far-right politics. Some, such as Liz Fekete, argue that 'The economics of austerity are a means to an end: any solidarity across race and class threatens a social structure that promotes radical individualism and has been reorganised to meet the demands of the market.'[14] Whether the outcomes of austerity were consciously sought as Fekete argues, it is certainly the case that the financial crisis led to the trauma of austerity and the resulting economic anxiety from which many looked to the far right for an answer. Even critics such as Roger Eatwell and Matthew Goodwin who have called this idea a 'popular myth' concede that it did 'create more room' for what they term 'national populists', and that it exacerbated 'existing divides among voters', 'contributed to a loss of support for traditional parties', and created 'record levels of political volatility in Europe'.[15] While the role of economics remains fundamental to understanding support for the European far right, it is important not to overlook more cultural explanations, chief among them the so-called 'migrant crisis'.

———

4.00am. It was only a few metres away, but while I could hear the Aegean Sea lapping against the sand, I couldn't see it. The street lamps and hotel signs across the water in the Turkish holiday resort of Bodrum did nothing to lessen the pitch dark of the beach. The only light came from a solitary flashing beacon on the small peninsula at the end of Kos island. It flashed once, paused, then flashed three times in quick succession. This was the target – the point at which the boats aim. The occasional sputtering of an outboard motor, a cough or some garbled speech in the distance was all that broke the night's silence. With such limited visibility, it was impossible to tell if the sound was coming from small refugee boats or the larger Greek and Turkish coastguard vessels that patrol the four-kilometre channel between the two countries. A rickety jeep crawled slowly along the road that runs parallel to the water and, from time to time, veered onto the beach with its lights off.

It was September 2015 and Europe was in the grip of the so-called 'refugee crisis'. The tragic fallout from the intractable and bloody Syrian civil war, the opening of the North Macedonia route for refugees and migrants, increased pragmatism by Balkan states, and Germany's vocal generosity combined to sharply increase levels of migration into Europe. The 'crisis' had gripped the media's attention, and headlines talking of 'floods' of arrivals contributed to a xenophobic backlash across the continent. The far right warned against a 'Muslim invasion' and bottom-up anti-refugee protests duly descended on city centres all over Europe.[16] The fallout from the crisis catalysed another wave of mainstreaming, with populist and far-right parties capitalising on public concerns.

After hearing about far-right attacks on refugees on Kos, HOPE not hate sent me to investigate. We knew that telling human stories alone was never going to be enough to effect real change, but at a time when much media coverage reduced refugees to statistics we felt it important to try to contribute to the humanisation of the story. I flew out with two friends, Ena and Rob, both professional journalists keen to see *the* story of 2015 first-hand.

We touched down on an island in turmoil. Checking into the very cheap and not very cheerful Captain's Hotel, we dropped our bags and made the short walk into town. At the time there was no formal refugee camp, meaning migrants were forced to build their own sites in and around the town centre. The result was at times deeply surreal, with the picturesque marina – all expensive motor yachts and holiday cruisers – right next to temporary tented villages. Holidaymakers dining alfresco sipped cocktails just metres from long lines of hungry people queuing for bread. Since the beginning of the crisis the small island had received over 35,000 refugees and migrants; more than the whole local population. At its peak, the island held 9,000 migrants at once, though tougher controls in Turkey and some improvements in registration had dropped that to around 2,000 by the time we arrived.

We walked the cobbled old town, the architecture an incongruous mixture of Aegean and Ottoman buildings alongside the newer Venetian-inspired housing, a remnant from the island's period under Italian fascist rule. The restaurants and bars were bustling, the bazaar echoing with the sound of souvenir shop owners beckoning sunburnt Englishmen inside to reveal piles of fridge magnets, keyrings and thimbles. Swept up by the holiday feeling, our guard lowered by a few cocktails, we agreed to have our picture drawn by a street-side artist. As he scribbled away he told us how the island was aching under the strain of so many refugees and how he feared for his livelihood and his children's future. As we paid I asked where the refugees actually arrived, and he pointed towards the beach. 'Every night.'

Three hours passed with no sign of a landing. We had been told most boats arrived between 4.00 and 6.00 in the morning, but had seen nothing and heard very little. As the sun crept out from beneath the horizon around 6.50am, light ran along the surface of the Aegean and up onto the beach. Visibility improved and the image of white sandy beaches that I had envisaged from the holiday brochures was quickly dashed. The stony shore was strewn with the detritus of months of migration. Slashed rubber boats, paddles and dozens of lifejackets vied with the usual assortment of bottles, cans and plastic bags. Just as we were about to give up and walk to the nearest hotel for a well-earned breakfast, a distant dot appeared on the water. It bobbed up and down until slowly, with the help of the zoom lens on my camera, the faint outline of a small boat emerged into the dawn light. As it came closer the fuzzy outline became sharper, revealing a tiny rubber dinghy crammed with eight men in buoyancy vests, desperately paddling towards the shore.

As soon as they hit land, things moved fast. The exhausted men, some in just their underpants, jumped into the surf and pulled the boat ashore. The jeep that had been patrolling hours earlier suddenly re-emerged and three men got out. Without even acknowledging the newly-arrived migrants, two detached the boat's outboard motor and carried it away, followed by the third who took the boat. Before the passengers had caught their breath the vultures had made off with their spoils. 'Do you know them?', I asked one of the new arrivals. 'No. No idea', he replied, spluttering the words out in between huge breaths. They emptied a bag of clothes onto the sand and began to change. One man sat on the shore and lit a cigarette as he looked back towards Turkey, a wry smile creeping slowly across his face. He had made it to Europe. Another hurriedly pulled out a mobile phone and called ahead to friends who had already made it to town. 'How was the journey?' I asked. 'Very tired, very tired', came the response. The outboard motor had packed in not long after setting off, leaving them with no option but to paddle the rest of the way across.

I didn't know what to say. I kept wondering what they must think of us. I'm sure they had spent months imagining what this moment would be like – and almost certainly they didn't expect to make the perilous night-time crossing only to arrive and find three British people welcoming them to

Europe with a complimentary cigarette. Luckily, Ena has a remarkable conversational style that gets people to open up instantly without seeming intrusive. They had left Pakistan ten months ago with a dream of a new life in Europe. 'Why did you leave Pakistan?' she asked. 'No work', he replied. 'No electricity.' This would cut little ice with those handing out the immigration papers in Kos town. We pointed them towards the main road and watched as they once again turned into dots on the horizon.

We turned and walked back down the beach. By now large ferries, cruise liners and tankers were visible, cluttering the narrow crossing. The unmistakable sound of an outboard motor could again be faintly heard. A small fibreglass fishing boat came into view, no more than four metres long. Unlike the other vessels along the coast this one was heading straight for the shore, a small Turkish flag fluttering off the back. As it ran aground, people started to jump into the water. One of the men returned to the boat and carried a young girl no older than seven or eight onto the beach. The girl's mother followed. There were eleven people in total, hailing from Syria, Iraq and Palestine. It had been a cramped crossing. 'We were told it would be a big boat', explained one of the Iraqi men. It seemed the people smugglers rarely delivered on their side of the bargain.

Before everyone was even out of the water the vultures again arrived on the scene, pushing past and grabbing the boat to make sure it didn't float away. A balding man with a bulbous paunch waded out and held the vessel. His accomplice was a much slighter, older man, sporting a baseball cap. He rounded on the migrants: 'Give me the key, where is the key?' The new arrivals simply ignored the Greek boat-snatcher. Some were busy making phone calls and taking excited selfies to mark their arrival in Europe. The Syrian group, a lady with her daughter and two young men of around seventeen, were much more subdued. 'Where is the key?' the local asked again, this time with a hint of frustration. One of the Iraqi men stepped forward and explained in broken English that they didn't have the key. The smugglers, who had charged everyone €2,600 (even for the child) had simply turned the boat on, pointed it in the direction of Kos and pushed it out. Had the engine cut out they would have been stranded, floating in the sea with nothing but a small paddle and the hope of being rescued by the Greek coastguard. The man grew more demanding, his voice louder. 'WHERE IS THE KEY?' One of the young Syrian boys was increasingly upset and later explained that he was convinced he was about to be assaulted, claiming he saw a gun strapped to the hip of the shouting man. I certainly didn't spot it, but the boy was clearly shaken. After just five minutes on the beach the migrants dropped their lifejackets and began the two-hour walk up the coast to Kos town to register with the police. They had made it to Europe.

'The extremists are cowards. They did nothing when there were a hundred Iraqi men. They only attacked when it was just us. Most of the aid workers were women.' Roberto Mignone, head of the United Nations Refugee Agency (UNHCR) mission on the island, was explaining the scenes that had played out at 11.00pm a few days earlier. There was a stand-off between the police, armed with batons and riot shields, and a hundred or so frustrated Iraqi refugees. Sensing the tension, Roberto had pulled a blue United Nations vest out of the thigh pocket of his cargo trousers – 'It's like my superman cape', he said – and placed himself, arms outstretched, between the police and the Iraqis. It only bought the refugees a few seconds, as the police went ahead and charged regardless, batons waving, to disperse the crowd. Watching the events unfold was a crowd of roughly 30 local thugs, too scared to properly attack the Iraqis head-on but happy to jeer from behind the police. Once the refugees had fled, the extremists turned their attention to the small group of local aid workers at the scene. 'They hate them more than the refugees. They think they're traitors', said Roberto. As the police watched, the baying crowd began pelting the aid workers with whatever they could find to hand. An ice cube brushed the side of Roberto's face just millimetres from his eye; at that distance and speed, ice is no different from a stone.

Events like this were rare but certainly not isolated. Not long before we had arrived on the island, local racists had attacked a migrant tent under the cover of darkness, kicking and punching the Iranian family inside. Another crowd attacked a group of refugees with wooden bats, shouting 'Go back to your country'. One of the rumours we heard was that some locals were waiting for the bulk of tourists to leave the island before mounting a purge of the remaining refugees. Many had fled war zones and travelled hundreds of miles, only to find themselves vulnerable and under attack on the streets of Kos. This was one of the reasons, along with poor sanitation, that the UN was so desperate to set up a properly organised camp on the island. Unfortunately, the local authority, led by an uncooperative mayor, had thwarted all attempts to do so. 'We have the tents ready in Athens but we aren't allowed to bring them over', said a UN representative. One experienced aid worker added that he had never faced such an obstructive local administration. The result was that migrants and refugees were forced to find their own shelter, with tented villages and mini shanty towns springing up.

After our night on the beach we followed the new arrivals back into Kos town to find out more about life on the island for refugees. It was morning and people had headed to the beach to wash, each taking turns with a single hosepipe. Ena struck up a conversation with Hekmat, a Syrian woman holding her young child. When asked why she had fled her home in Damascus, she replied: 'Terrible. Because of war. Everybody, everywhere, blood. Everywhere destroyed. I don't know how to explain more. Terrible.' As a moderate Muslim she was especially scared of what might await her if ISIS took control of her home. 'If they saw the tattoo on my arm they would cut it off', she shuddered. Like so many others she had made a shelter among the cluttered, cramped and uncomfortable tented village that lined the road, complaining that the bright street lights made sleeping difficult. However, not all Syrian arrivals bedded down on the streets. Some came from middle-class backgrounds and were wealthy enough to make the journey to Europe rather than having to flee to refugee camps in Iraq, Turkey or Lebanon. Many could afford to stay in local hotels. In fact, that evening Rob and I were walking through our hotel reception, heading for a swim, when we saw the woman and child we had helped off the boat that morning, checking in.

However, despite the war in Syria being a major driver behind the migrant crisis, they made up just part of the island's new inhabitants. Also well represented in Kos were Iraqis, Iranians, Afghans, migrants from numerous African countries and, in ever-increasing numbers, Pakistanis. This is where things got complicated. While a majority passing through the island were fleeing conflict or oppression, many we spoke with were economic migrants. While the Syrians were usually processed within a few days, Pakistanis could be left stranded on the island for weeks at a time. One man, who had been waiting in the sweltering summer heat for fifteen days, said he had fled violence in Kashmir. 'Every day I go to the police station', he explained. 'All Pakistanis. All day wait at the police station not give me papers. Other people go, Syrian, one day, maybe next day they get papers. Only Pakistani people is big problem ... If I have no problem why I come here to Greece?' Despite not getting papers, he was one of the lucky ones. He talked of how his friend died making the journey when his boat sank. 'There is no safety, you give $1,015 in Turkey, that's it, no safety.' Those least able to support themselves economically, often the Pakistanis or Africans, were the ones stranded on Kos for the longest. They were left to sleep on the beach with nothing more than a cardboard box for shelter. Others took refuge in what was nicknamed 'the jungle', a tree-covered area strewn with boxes, mattresses and tents huddled around fire pits. The lack of adequate sanitation meant you smelled 'the jungle' long before you saw it.

This prioritisation of some migrant groups over others meant it was not uncommon for those from other countries to claim they were Syrians, hoping to be waved into Europe, some more convincingly than others. One man, seeing my camera, rushed over to tell me of his horrific ordeal in Syria and to bemoan the slow processing of his papers in Kos. 'I thought I had arrived in heaven but it turns out I am back in hell', he raged. But something wasn't right. He spoke with a thick Eastern European accent, perhaps Albanian, and when questioned it became clear he didn't speak Arabic. The heart-wrenching story of war and struggle was no doubt true. It just wasn't his.

Despite the scenes of suffering and desperation there were moments of hope. A sixteen-year-old boy, dressed in donated Union Jack shorts, ran over to me beaming. 'I've got my papers! Yes! I have my papers and tomorrow I will go to ferry to Athens.' He was an Afghan who had lived in Iran and left his family to travel to Europe with his brother. Each day refugees like him crowded round a board pinned to a tree which listed those who were to receive papers to progress to mainland Greece via the evening ferry. Those who spotted their names were elated; those who didn't trudged off dejected, contemplating another night on the hard concrete pavement. It was a reminder that jumping off the boat and taking their first steps on European sand might have been the end of one journey but it was also the start of another. These men, women and children hadn't travelled hundreds of miles to settle for a cardboard box on the beach. They wanted to build new lives and that meant travelling on, first to mainland Greece and then, for many, further into Europe: to Germany, Scandinavia or Britain. As the sun began to set, the lucky ones, clutching their valuable papers, excitedly walked along Akti Miaouli street towards the ferry terminal. To their right the warm Aegean, to their left the crumbling medieval walls of the Castle of Nerantzia – the castle of the sour orange tree. In front of them, their future in the shape of an enormous blue and white ferry.

The scene at the terminal was chaotic, with crowds of refugees and migrants pushing towards the departure gate, some with papers, some without. In all the commotion, I was able to walk straight past the guards and into the shadow of the gaping ferry doors. People excitedly crammed onto the gangways between the harbour wall and the ferry deck. To my left, a woman, clutching her young child, was slumped in a wheelchair. Crushed in the queue, she had fainted while boarding and been disembarked. To her horror, as she came to her senses, she found herself not on her way to Athens but still at the terminal. She shrieked with desperation: 'Take me back! I have to get to Athens. I have to get to Athens. Please! Take me back!' But no amount of pleading would get her back on the boat. She had missed her chance and would have to wait for another day.

Her wailing was soon drowned out by the booming of the ship's foghorn and the grinding and whirring of the huge ferry doors closing. The freed ropes slid into the water. I looked up and saw the passengers crowding onto the open deck under a billowing Greek flag. Tomorrow, Athens beckoned, though, as many had found in Kos already, there was no guarantee of a welcome when they arrived on the mainland. They might have been in love with the idea of Europe, but many in Europe were not in love with the idea of them.

———

The migrant crisis, the role of Islamist terrorism and the fallout from the 2008 financial crisis were all reflected in the electoral fortunes of the European far right. Just how bad things had become was made clear at the 2019 European elections. The most worrying results came in France, Italy, Hungary, Poland and the UK, where Marine Le Pen's National Rally (RN), Matteo Salvini's Lega Nord (LN), Viktor Orbán's Fidesz, Jarosław Kaczyński's Law and Justice (PiS) and Nigel Farage's new Brexit Party (now named Reform UK) each came first in the polls.

Though a fraction down on its 2014 result, RN's 23.31% gave it a huge 22 seats in the European Parliament, while Lega in Italy saw a quite remarkable rise to 34.33%, giving it 28 seats. Poland and Hungary were the canaries in the coal mine and continue to be at the forefront of the problem, with Law and Justice receiving a huge 45.38% of the vote after running an ugly anti-LGBT+ campaign. Fidesz, in coalition with the Christian Democratic People's Party, gained thirteen seats with 52.33% of the vote. Sadly, none of these results came as a surprise, but that should not mean they are not shocking. Just ten years ago, at the 2009 elections, the French Front National (later renamed National Rally) received just 6.34%, and while the party has undergone dramatic changes – some would say modernisation and moderation – in this period, its rise is still meteoric; and the same goes for Lega, which received just 6.15% of the vote back in 2014. Another big winner was Vlaams Belang in Belgium, which surged by fourteen points in the Flanders region, and the party also placed second in the national vote for the federal parliament which happened simultaneously. A telling sign of the party's normalisation came just days after the elections when Belgium's King Philippe held an official meeting at the Royal Palace with the party's leader Tom Van Grieken, the first meeting between the monarchy and the far right since 1936.

One far-right populist party that did worse than predicted in 2019 was Alternative für Deutschland (AfD) in Germany, which placed fourth with 11% of the vote at the EU parliamentary elections, a smaller showing than it received at the September 2017 general election and a touch down on pre-election polls. However, this result still handed the party eleven Members of the European Parliament and was a significant rise from the 7.1% it garnered in the 2014 European elections. It has since become clear that the AfD wasn't just a short-term protest party. At the 2021 German Federal Elections they received 10.3% of the vote share, slightly down on their 2017 results. However, it was the largest party in the states of Saxony and Thuringia and has established itself as a real force in German politics. The emergence and rise of the AfD in Germany in recent years has been watched with increasing horror by anti-fascists and mainstream commentators alike. With the legacy of the Nazis and the indelible stain of the Holocaust, coupled with Germany's often admirable attempts to face up to this history, many felt the country would be immune to the contagion of right-wing populism. This has proved not to be the case.

As the decade drew to a close, the optimism of 1989 had faded and the claims of liberal democracy's total and irrevocable victory looked ever more naive. The question was no longer when the next victory would come, but whether the gains of the past two decades could be held on to at all.

5

AMERICAN MILITIAS AND THE KU KLUX KLAN

'God, guns and guts built this country.' These were pretty much the first words I heard as I entered the large Quonset hut, a prefabricated building made of corrugated steel. Eight fold-out camp beds stood in a line, most with a semi-automatic AR-15 assault rifle lying neatly on them. The flag of Alabama, a crimson cross of St Andrew on a white back-ground, hung from the ceiling; the walls were covered in maps of the local area. The hut stood in the middle of a vast U-shaped valley a few miles from the Mexican border.

I had woken early, skipped breakfast – I couldn't eat – and made the short drive east on Interstate 10 from my cockroach-infested motel just outside Tucson, Arizona, across the New Mexico state line and then south towards the border. I was exhausted. I couldn't sleep the night before because of nerves and the fact that a prostitute kept knocking on my bedroom door offering me her services. It was August and the baking heat meant the riverbeds that crisscrossed the valley floor were dry. As I drove south, the bars on my mobile phone indicating signal strength fell away until an ominous 'No ser-vice' appeared. I'd been given a mile marker on the side of the road to aim for, and then told to turn off the tarmac and onto a dirt track leading into the desert. I suddenly felt very alone and aware I was completely unable to contact anyone if things went wrong. I spotted the metal hut shimmering in the sun and headed slowly towards it, frantically running through my cover story one last time in my head. I was a sympathetic British journalist desperate to tell the world about the brave struggle of American patriots against the Mexican drug cartels and invading Muslims.

In truth, I had been sent to America by HOPE not hate to explore the rise of Donald Trump by spending time with some of his most fanatical supporters in the run-up to the 2016 election. We had seen the emergence of similar 'migrant-hunting' militias in Eastern Europe and were keen to better understand the movement. For the past few years my total focus had been on the European far right but now, in the lead-up to the election, and with the xenophobic Trump as one of the candidates, all eyes were looking across the Atlantic.

The idea was to infiltrate a militia group and expose the racism at the heart of some of these anti-immigration groups. We would then publish a special report just before the election designed to inform our European audience about what was happening in America and also hopefully provide our colleagues in the US anti-racism movement with ammunition to fight Trump. We run our operations completely independently of law enforcement, not least because some of the groups we monitor have links with them. However, preventing harm always comes before any journalistic goals, and being unable to arrest people ourselves means there are times when we report illegal activity, especially if we believe a person or group poses a physical threat. That said, over the years there have been times when our aims have clashed with those of the police, intelligence agencies and the state, resulting in heated exchanges. There have even been incidents when we have been threatened with arrest for the work we do.[1]

As I got out of the car I was approached by a mountain of a man who offered his hand and identified himself as 'Cornbread', the founder and leader of the Borderkeepers of Alabama (BOA), a heavily armed vigilante group which claimed to have 1,000 members. They make up part of America's dangerous militia movement which the Anti-Defamation League (ADL) defines as a 'right-wing extremist movement consisting of armed paramilitary groups, both formal and informal, with an anti-government, conspiracy-oriented ideology'.[2] While the militia tradition in America goes back at least as far as the heavily armed Minutemen movement of the 1960s, the first attempt to start a border militia was organised by notorious American Ku Klux Klan leader David Duke, who in October 1977 held a press conference at the US–Mexico border and announced the 'Klan Border Watch'. While Duke's project amounted to nothing, the concept of border militias 'lingered on among white supremacists, played a role in some of the movements that took off in the 1990s, and eventually led to the idea of having ordinary patriots form citizen militias', according to David Neiwert.[3]

BOA stringently denied that it was a militia, as it didn't engage in wider anti-government work and instead focused solely on the border. However, it shared much of the same ideology and cooperated in joint operations with several militias. In addition, some of their members and activists (including several with me in New Mexico) were also active within other militia groups. Some also classed themselves as 'Three Percenters', an anti-government resistance movement named after the claim that 3% of the American population engaged in armed resistance against the British during the American Revolution.

Cornbread was an imposing figure with a white Fu Manchu moustache, camouflage headband, a heavy paunch and a .45 Glock pistol strapped to his leg. He had a distinctive Alabama drawl, the lyrical, drawn-out vowel sounds never letting you forget he was a son of the American South. Yet, despite being dressed in full battle gear and armed to the teeth, his habit of addressing everyone as 'brother' or 'cuz' made him a softer and more approachable character than you would at first expect. He had set up BOA a little over a year and a half before, and I was accompanying them on their seventh trip to the border. They had driven well over 1,000 miles in convoy through Mississippi and Louisiana, then across the desolate expanses of Texas and into New Mexico. Our desert 'operation' was to last 72 hours.

While driving across West Texas they had stopped at a Waffle House and, midway through a gargantuan meal, a stranger convinced them to head to New Mexico rather than their original destination in Arizona. A local landowner had erected this Quonset hut that was part social club for bikers and part base camp for militia and 'patriot' groups on border operations in the area. Being in a valley between two dusty mountain ranges that ran down to the border made it a thoroughfare for drug smugglers and migrants on their way to the nearest interstate highway, despite Mexico being a good 40 miles away. Confusingly, many in BOA also seemed to think this made it prime territory for catching ISIS fighters supposedly flooding in from South America.

My initial thoughts were that the chances of seeing any action this far from the actual border were extremely slim, and as my cover story appeared to have passed the first hurdle of introductions my heart rate began to slow. I started to unpack my equipment and settle in for what I began to think might just be an extremely odd camping trip with some eccentric American racists. But no sooner had I torn the tags from my camouflage trousers when someone shouted 'Glass on glass!' Everyone grabbed their rifles and rushed out. 'Rocky', a Walmart employee from rural Alabama, claimed to have located an armed 'spotter' on the hill a few miles away watching our camp. I was handed the binoculars and to my complete amazement found myself looking directly at a man sitting on the hill with a Kalashnikov rifle looking straight back. Rocky floated the idea of a 'black op' to go up and 'take him out'. 'How on earth have I got myself into this situation?' I thought. I was 5,000 miles from home, dressed head to toe in camouflage and about to go to war with a Mexican cartel. I'd never even held a gun, and I presumed that even if I was a complete natural my chances in a firefight against a Mexican drug smuggler weren't good. Luckily, Cornbread shot down the idea and reminded the group that anyone breaking the law would be thrown out. Supposedly the spotter was there to report back on our location so the drug- and people-smugglers could avoid rather than confront us.

I kept watch and chain-smoked for the rest of the day, but as dusk approached and the welcome cool breeze blew through the valley it was time to begin preparing for that night's mission in earnest. They all suited up in full camouflage gear with heavy bulletproof armoured vests, a medical kit, compass, knife, flashlight and a hydration pack on their back. Each carried an AR-15 along with a pistol strapped to their leg. Glocks seemed to be the sidearm of choice. Some, such as Rocky, the youngest of the group, carried a third 'backup gun' inside their vest, while Cornbread opted for a shotgun and a belt of shells. Finally, they stuffed every remaining pouch and pocket with enough ammunition to start a small war. Most loaded their guns with hollow-point or ballistic-tipped bullets which were designed to cause maximum damage. If they ended up in a firefight they were prepared to kill.

They handed me a bulletproof vest emblazoned with an American flag that was enthusiastically received. They asked me where my gun was and I replied that, being English, I didn't own one. This left them open-mouthed in horror. The idea that I didn't own a gun was genuinely incomprehensible to them, while the thought of walking into the desert night to hunt for cartel drug smugglers empty-handed was just insane. I found myself agreeing with that.

I was pulled to one side by 'Bull', an ex-Marine turned bounty hunter with a side line in high-value security. He was an intimidating and guarded character, heavy-set with a shaved head, and the owner of a huge black armoured truck that looked military-issue. Of everyone there he was the most suspicious of my presence. After hearing about Britain's restrictive gun and knife laws he earnestly told me how 'Y'all need to take your country back!' Despite my protestations that I didn't want a gun he insisted that it would be safer for all concerned if I took one. I wasn't so sure. He filled a 4-litre jug with water, placed it on a tree stump some ten metres away and handed me a pump-action shotgun. 'Shoot that', he commanded. Remembering what I'd seen in the movies, I pulled back the pump handle that ran along the barrel and heard the shell fall into the chamber. Closing one eye, I aimed and then fired. The recoil piled into my shoulder and nearly knocked me off my feet. When I opened my eyes the water jug had disappeared, leaving nothing but a puddle. I'd be lying if I didn't admit how much I liked it. Equally, though, I had no doubt that I never wanted to find myself in a situation where I might have to use such a weapon on a human. I handed back the shotgun and said that I wouldn't be needing it. After some debate, it was agreed that I would carry a small Walther PPK handgun instead, an apt choice, they thought, as I was British and this was the gun made famous by James Bond. To keep the peace, I nervously took it but secretly swore that I would never use it unless my life was genuinely at risk.

Just as we were testing our radios and getting ready to head out into the desert I noticed that everyone was wearing metal shin pads from their ankles to just below their knees. 'What are they for?' I enquired. 'Snakes', came the response. I'd been so preoccupied with my impending death at the hands of the cartel that I hadn't given a thought to venomous snakes. It transpired that the area was swarming with the Mojave green rattlesnake, one of the world's most dangerous. 'You get a bite this far from the nearest hospital and you dead', said Cornbread unhelpfully. I hurried back into the hut to look for a spare pair of leg defenders but found none. Beginning to panic, I emptied two tubes of Pringles onto the table, sliced off the bottoms, cut down one side and wrapped them around my shins. I returned outside to howls of laughter and was told they would be of no use, but they made me feel slightly better so I kept them on. A few nights later I found myself standing in a dry riverbed, confronted by three snakes. I ran as fast as my greasy Pringles-covered legs would carry me, leaving Cornbread to prod them nonchalantly with the end of his shotgun.

By 9.00pm, we were fully kitted up and ready to head out. Having scoped out the area during the day, three groups of two men (Alpha, Bravo, Charlie) headed out in the pitch dark – some with night vision, some not – and took up locations at points that made up a triangle across the valley. The idea was that any cartel drug runners, undocumented immigrants or – as some believed – ISIS terrorists would walk into the triangle and then be pounced on and temporarily detained until the official border police arrived to take over. Back at base or 'FOB' (Forward Operating Base) was Cornbread and the operation leader, Bull. He planned and ran the actual night-time missions and clearly got a kick out of it. Like many who were ex-military or ex-law enforcement it clearly gave back some of the buzz they were missing since returning to civilian life.

I went out as part of Bravo team with Cornbread's brother 'Bama' and 'Doc', a muscular ex-policeman sporting an unzipped ammunition vest and a rifle over his shoulder, looking every inch a life-size GI Joe action figure. We found a position, took cover and waited. For hours it felt like chasing fireflies, with every tiny moving light or distant dog bark radioed in to FOB as a possible sighting. Just as I was starting to think the whole thing was an elaborate game, a garbled message came in from Alpha team over the radio. Five Mexican men were less than ten metres in front of them. According to the plan they were supposed to jump out of the darkness and 'light 'em up', dazzling them with high-power torches before effecting a citizen's arrest. But being first-timers to the desert, Alpha team failed to spring the trap and the five men walked straight past them and up onto the nearest highway, where we eventually saw cars whisk them away. When asked why they failed to act, Rocky was honest and explained: 'I pretty much buried my face in the dirt, scared.' His partner agreed: 'When you go out here and there is no moon, there's no stars and everything sets in on you and you realise these people have guns also, it becomes real ... the shit gets real.' That night's operation had failed but I no longer had any doubt that I had landed myself in an extremely dangerous situation.

———

In America the far right has often been thought to be a European problem, something that plagued the old world but never escaped the margins of US politics. However, it has been argued that the American Party of the mid-19th century 'was probably the first purely nativist party of the western world'.[4] In the US, organised far-right movements have generally emerged in reaction to challenges against systemic white supremacy. Whether it was the Civil War and the Reconstruction that followed, the movement of black communities from the south to the north and Midwest during the First World War, the civil rights movement of the 1950s and 1960s, or most recently the election of a black president, 'white supremacist movements emerged to oppose any change and recapture the status quo ante'.[5] This reactionary tradition is fundamental to understanding the US far right.

When one thinks of the American far right the first organisation that usually comes to mind is the Ku Klux Klan (KKK). Originally founded between late 1865 and the summer of 1866 by six former Confederate officers in the town of Pulaski, Tennessee, the KKK formed as a social club. The members soon found that their night-time horseplay in town caused fear among former slaves in the area. The group rapidly expanded, which resulted in a meeting in April 1867 at which the organisation's rules and structure were decided. Standing in direct opposition to the extension of black rights, the Klan engaged in a campaign of violence and murder against former slaves and black leaders. However, following law enforcement suppression and internal fighting, Nathan

Bedford Forrest, Grand Wizard of the KKK, officially disbanded the organisation in the early 1870s. In 1915 the Klan was revived by William J. Simmons in Atlanta, Georgia, following the release of *The Birth of a Nation*, D.W. Griffith's racist film that glorified the first incarnation of the KKK. This reincarnation had a wider programme than its forebear and added an extreme nativism, anti-Catholicism and anti-semitism to its traditional white supremacism. By 1921 the ranks of the Klan had swelled and some estimates placed the group's membership as high as 4–5 million, though in reality it was likely much smaller. However, at its peak it famously marched 30,000 uniformed Klansmen through the streets of Washington, DC in 1925.[6] By the end of the decade, membership had shrunk significantly as it broke into dozens of fragments, facing pressure from the law and a bad reputation for violence and extremism.

At the same time as the second incarnation of the Klan was growing in the US, across the Atlantic the rise of European fascism began to make news. The similarities were not lost on many commentators of the age. In reaction to Mussolini's rise to power in Italy, for example, the *Tampa Times* wrote: 'The klan, in fact, is the Fascisti of America and unless it is forced into the open it may very easily attain a similar power.'[7] In the words of Sarah Churchwell: 'Across the country, from Philadelphia and Iowa to Montana and Oregon, American citizens were confronted with the Klan and the Italian Fascists marching across the front pages of the news, in seeming lockstep. No one missed the comparison.'[8] However, some Americans went beyond comparisons to emulation, especially among émigré communities. Italians in the US set up groups such as the New York Fascia and the Baltimore Fascia.[9] Similarly, the rise of Nazism in Germany also found admirers across the Atlantic. In 1936 the dissolved Friends of New Germany re-formed into the infamous German-American Bund.[10] By 1939, on 20 February, just months before the outbreak of war in Europe, 20,000 American Nazis attended a vast rally at Madison Square Garden, where Nazi salutes were raised towards a towering 30-foot portrait of George Washington with swastika banners to each side. Though the group had dissolved by 1941, it remains a useful reminder that fascism has always been a transnational phenomenon and not all US far-right movements have emerged out of domestic traditions.

The next major flare-up of the American far right unsurprisingly came during the civil rights era of the 1960s, when victories against systemic and institutionalised racism again engendered a backlash. The Klan emerged once more to fight for the preservation of segregation. During this period it engaged in terrorism and murder, including the killing of four young girls in Birmingham, Alabama. In response the FBI and law enforcement agencies began to seriously monitor, infiltrate and disrupt its activities. While unable to halt progress towards greater racial equality, the KKK did survive – and does so to this day. From the 1970s onwards it has been decentralised, fragmented and hugely weakened by internal conflicts, splits and a number of damaging court cases. While it is no longer the united force it once was, it still has the ability to engage in extreme acts of violence. According to the Southern Poverty Law Center in 2019, there are still between 5,000 and 8,000 Klan members split across dozens of competing groups.[11]

While these historical legacies of racism and American fascism remain important for understanding the contemporary far right, it is the movements and organisations that emerged from the 1970s onwards that have most shaped modern US far-right extremism. As the historian of white nationalism in America, Leonard Zeskind, argues: 'The white nationalist movement of the twenty-first century grows out of the white supremacist movement of the 1970s and 1980s.'[12] Importantly, the era that followed civil rights brought about a change whereby the American far right 'built a movement around the idea of white dispossession, the notion that the country that they believed had once been the sole property of white people was no longer only theirs'.[13] This sense of loss, decline and paradoxical victimhood remains the lifeblood of the US far right and is central to understanding the rise of Donald Trump decades later.

It was so dark we could barely see our hands. The glowing cherry of a cigarette would have been seen for miles so we ducked under a bush and smoked with our heads facing the ground. It was night two and there was a determination not to repeat the embarrassing failures of the previous evening. As before the three teams set up in a triangle across the valley, surrounding a dry riverbed that appeared to be the thoroughfare from the border to the highway. This time there was no hesitation. As soon as a rustle was heard two of the team jumped out and 'lit 'em up'. With torches and guns waving they screamed for the figures to stop, but the order was ignored. A small group of about four people, maybe smugglers, possibly undocumented migrants, bolted out of the glare of the torchlight and sprinted for the highway in the distance. The whole of the BOA team set out in a 'spread pattern' with a view to forcing them towards 'Mobile 1', the name given to Bull and his truck. No sooner had the chase begun than it was over. The Borderkeepers, weighed down by decades of fried food and heavy ammunition, were no match for their agile adversaries, who disappeared into the dark only to re-emerge in the far distance getting into a waiting car that sped off.

Things then took a turn for the surreal. We spotted a car with its lights on parked in the middle of our camp. Doc cocked his gun and the team readied themselves for an ambush, presuming it was a vehicle waiting for drugs or people. I was told to get my gun out but opted for my camera instead. We approached slowly, with the whole team pointing their rifles towards the car. Someone shouted for the driver to identify himself, and instead of a Mexican accent a slow country drawl came back. It emanated from a plump American gentleman sitting in a pickup truck. My relief at not being caught in the middle of a firefight was matched by the group's excitement when they realised who it was. Sitting there, in the middle of the night, was Johnny Horton Jr, supposedly the son of the world-famous country singer, Johnny Horton, and a relatively well-known singer himself. He had turned up to donate a small dirt buggy to the group. I looked around and was confident there was very little chance of any of this lot squeezing into the tiny seat but they were elated at the offer regardless. It transpired that Horton was the commander of his own militia group called the United Constitutional Patriots headquartered in Flora Vista, New Mexico.

The next morning, we gathered around to talk with the new star in our camp. He had patently dyed pitch-black hair half visible under a baseball cap with the words 'God, Guns and Guts' emblazoned below a golden eagle, and he sang us a song that he claimed to have co-written with Johnny Cash. He then told me, with no hint of irony, that Elvis Presley was alive and living in Hawaii. I laughed, but he took out his phone, scrolled through his contacts as far as 'E' and clicked on 'Elvis'. 'You can speak to him if you want', he said, handing me the phone. Here I was, in the middle of the desert, in camouflage clothing and surrounded by an overweight army of southern racists, being offered the chance to speak to Elvis Presley on the phone. I pictured an elderly Elvis with thinning hair wearing a Hawaiian shirt pulled taut across a pot belly; very much 'fat Elvis' rather than 'comeback special'. We talked and I humoured Elvis for as long as I thought polite before swearing to keep it all a secret and handing back the phone.

Horton spent the next two days with us, not really coming out on night-time operations, but holding court around the fire; singing songs, telling stories and eating tins of small Vienna sausages. Once out of the desert and with access to the internet I was unsurprised to find that Johnny Horton didn't have a son and 'Horton Jr' was actually Larry Mitchell Hopkins. Clearly a fantasist, he seemed to be more of a tribute act than the Country Hall of Fame singer he claimed. Later, in 2019, he was arrested by the FBI on a federal complaint of being a felon in possession of firearms and ammunition. It has since been claimed that his group were training to assassinate Barack Obama, Hillary Clinton and George Soros.

If the arrival of a gun-toting country singer was surreal, what happened next was much more worrying. As we sat in the shade, hiding from the baking desert sun, chain-smoking and batting away flies, an official Border Patrol vehicle pulled into camp. With BOA being an extremely heavily armed nativist extremist group, I had naively assumed the authorities would be at pains to distance themselves from such vigilante activity. The officers who turned up, however, were genuinely pleased to see us. They talked amiably and openly expressed their gratitude for the work BOA were doing. 'Hey, we are all Americans here', one of them said. We were even told to call the local Border Patrol office and explain our plans to avoid overlapping with the activities of the official operations. A previous mission had nearly ended in calamity when BOA activists and Border Patrol officers mistook each other for armed cartel members and narrowly avoided a firefight. Both groups were screaming at each other in Spanish, during a tense armed standoff. Cornbread's claim that the BOA now worked closely with the Border Patrol while out on operations seemed, shockingly, to be true. It transpired that this was no anomaly, as a report by The Centre for New Community in Chicago revealed: 'For at least a decade, some Department of Homeland Security (DHS) union leaders and employees have been colluding with the organized anti-immigration movement.'[14]

The idea that the official Border Patrol were so friendly and willing to collaborate became increasingly disturbing to me as I learned more about the politics of the men I was with. During the long, hot days talk invariably turned to politics and every conversation eventually meandered its way towards how 'liberals' were ruining America. The vitriolic hatred for 'liberals' – a term used in its broadest possible sense to include all Democrats, some Republicans and the whole of the mainstream press – was extreme. To wide approval, 'Razor', a short, plump guy who prided himself on being something of a ladies' man, stated: 'The biggest dividing line in this country is no longer black/white, north/south or east/west. It's Republican/Democrat.' The Democrats were not merely a political party that they disagreed with, but actually all-out traitors bent on destroying America. Special anger was reserved for President Obama, or 'that n****r in the White House' as he was casually referred to. The ills of America and the world, big or small, were repeatedly placed squarely at his feet, and most had no doubt he was a Muslim.

The group were united by an acute sense of moral and national decline and a belief that white, male Christians were 'under attack'. They genuinely feared that their traditional way of life was being eroded. 'Honestly, I am really worried. We have been going downhill for a while', explained Rocky. 'For reasons I'm not sure I understand we are being told that for a long time we have been offending certain people. Whether it's subjects like homosexuality, Christian, Muslim, rights, our rights ... Why all of a sudden are we expected to tolerate things we've never tolerated before and we don't get a say so in it?', said Doc. When I asked if he felt American Christians were being persecuted, he didn't hesitate: 'Absolutely, oh, absolutely.' In a similar vein, 'Snake', ex-Navy and one of the few non-Alabamians in the group who had made the journey from Baton Rouge, Louisiana, said: 'Right now the white American male is under attack and if you are Christian you have an extra burden placed on you.' The supposed erosion of white Christian dominance was deeply painful for them and the last eight years under Obama had, they felt, brought America to a crisis point. 'Obama has sacrificed in almost eight years everything that so many people have worked for', continued Snake. 'Our country is in a dire position. We have come to a fork in the road and we must choose', said Bama.

Whatever you think about BOA, there is no doubting the commitment to their cause. They all gave up huge amounts of time and money, often taking unpaid time off work or using their one week of holiday a year, to drive thousands of miles and place themselves at real risk for what they believe is their patriotic duty. 'We are brought up to be patriots to this country, we love our country ... We believe in our Constitution and that's why we want to stand there and make sure it is enforced', Bama told me. For him, the border issue is symptomatic of a wider attack on their constitutional rights and is the front line in their imagined war. 'There is a war going on on this border', he said. 'To put it bluntly, our country is being invaded ... We are the wall, for now', reiterated Cornbread, referencing Trump's promise to build a border wall. Rocky summed up the motivation of the rest of the group: 'You've got thousands of illegals pouring in. You've got drugs. You've got sex trade. All kind of horrible things like that coming in ... Somebody has got to stand up and do something.'

However, some saw these issues as secondary to the main mission – which was (in their view) about national security. 'A lot of people associate what we are doing with illegal Mexicans', said Doc, but while he too wanted to stop Latino immigration and drug smugglers, his primary driver was combatting a supposed stream of Muslims sneaking across the Mexican border. 'We're having groups associated with ISIS crossing over the Mexican border ... You can't just take a group like Islam and invade America and expect to win.' When I asked Bama if Muslims really were crossing the southern border, he responded: 'It is a problem. There are a lot of Muslims coming across the border. We have no problem with people doing it, like I said, legally, but these guys are terrorists coming into our country to do harm to American citizens and that we cannot allow.' The narrative that terrorist suspects have been pouring across the US border was repeated by Trump during his presidency, despite the State Department issuing a report stating that there is 'no credible evidence indicating that international terrorist groups have established bases in Mexico, worked with Mexican drug cartels or sent operatives via Mexico into the United States'. Facts held no sway over these vigilantes, and conspiracy theories – whether about Muslims, liberals, Obama or the media – formed the centrepiece of their worldview.

On the final day of the trip, and with supplies of Vienna sausages running low, it was decided that a group would drive the 30 miles to the nearest town for supplies. I accompanied Snake, his brother 'Fang', Bama and Doc and steered the conversation once again towards Obama and the state of the nation. Bama reiterated his genuine fear that a second civil war was imminent and the others nodded in agreement. We pulled in to a petrol station and spread out to buy armloads of snacks and fizzy drinks. I headed to the confectionery aisle to placate my sweet tooth; America unquestionably has the best selection of diabetes-inducing nibbles anywhere in the world. As I perused the piles of Hershey Bars, Reese's Peanut Butter Cups and Milk Duds, Bama walked over, keen to elaborate on our conversation. In his view the impending civil war would have three prongs: a racial element (black vs. white), a political element (liberal vs. conservative) and a religious element (Muslims and non-believers vs. Christians). The liberals would fight alongside black people and Muslims as allies against white Christians. He leaned in close and in a half-whisper said: 'If the civil war kicks off, the first thing we're gonna do is wipe out those mosques.' Here, surrounded by kids buying candy, he was dispassionately outlining the nature of a coming race war. Until that moment, he had been nothing but charming, kind and gentle, a genuinely likable guy. Yet he thought nothing of nonchalantly talking about killing Muslims while picking out some chocolate for the drive home.

I made the decision to leave the camp a day early. I'd been with them three days and two nights and I was completely exhausted. Even though I seemed to have been accepted by the group I knew my cover story was shallow and unlikely to withstand deep interrogation. Each day, as one of the team left camp to get phone reception, I would wait for their return, terrified that they had gone to investigate me. If I was exposed as an anti-fascist I had no doubt I would be killed and left in the desert. I had no way of checking in with HOPE not hate to tell them I was safe, and I knew Nick, my boss at HNH, would be worried. The operations lasted all night and I was too scared to close my eyes during the day, so I lay awake in the heat, batting away flies. All this was compounded by the energy it takes to play a character for so long. It's exhausting, having to remember your backstory, making sure you never say the wrong thing and biting your lip and nodding during conversations about 'n****rs' and 'rapist Mexicans'. I made my excuses and planned to leave that evening. Just as my car was packed and I was saying my goodbyes, Bull pulled me to one side. He placed another water jug on the tree stump and handed me his gun, which I held tightly and fired, once again releasing a wave of exhilaration. Of all the group I felt he had warmed to me the least, but he shook my hand to indicate that I had passed his macho test. As I turned to walk off he pulled me close and whispered in my ear: 'Just remember, I'm a bounty hunter so if you fuck us over, I will find you.'

I arranged to visit several of them in Alabama later in my trip, then drove off along the dirt track and back onto the tarmac road that headed towards the highway. I'd barely made it one mile before I had to pull over. As my stomach unknotted after three days of extreme anxiety I vomited uncontrollably on the side of the road. I wiped my mouth, climbed back into the car and put Bob Seger and the Silver Bullet Band's *Greatest Hits* on the stereo. I'd made it. I joined the I10 and headed west back towards Tucson. The thundering notes of 'Hollywood Nights' – the best American driving song ever – pushed me forward as I shot down the highway towards the vast blue Arizona sky before me. Not long after crossing the state line I saw flashing blue lights in my rear-view mirror and was pulled over. The officer approached my window nervously and found me sitting there in full camouflage, sporting a BOA cap emblazoned with crossed AR-15 rifles and sick down my T-shirt and in my long beard. 'Been hunting?' he asked. 'In a way', I replied, my English accent no doubt coming as something of a surprise. I was ordered to appear at Bowie Justice Court in Cochise County but got away with a $215 fine.

I flew into Birmingham, Alabama, the dry heat of Arizona replaced by an oppressive humidity. I'd spent the past few weeks in Tucson writing up my reports on the Borderkeepers and working on another long-standing infiltration project. Roughly a year earlier, while back in London, I'd begun an infiltration of the Ku Klux Klan. It started off as a fishing exercise designed to flush out any activists in the UK. While very much an American organisation, there have been minor British imitations throughout the post-war period. I created a fake Klan group and wrote to leading activists across the US expressing an interest in affiliating formerly. Once trust was built I asked all the major US Klan groups to put me in touch with any European supporters they had so I could organise them into a functioning unit. Some, though not all, helpfully obliged with the names and addresses of a handful of their

British supporters. The project was ticking along nicely but it was time to put it back on the shelf, reassume my cover and track down my new friends in Alabama.

On the way to Bama's I made a short detour to visit the Edmund Pettus Bridge in Selma, site of Bloody Sunday. On 7 March 1965, roughly 600 civil rights marchers left Selma heading towards the state capital of Montgomery. As they crossed the steel arch bridge over the Alabama River they were brutally attacked by armed police who fired tear gas and beat them with billy clubs. The events of that day have gone down in history as one of the major incidents in the struggle for civil rights. As I walked across the bridge I couldn't think of anything I wanted to do less than go and stay at the home of a man who called Obama a n****r.

In the late afternoon I arrived at Bama's home, a bungalow surrounded by deep green, waxy Bermuda grass. The house was well kept and homely with football memorabilia scattered around. While in the desert I had explained that I didn't favour any particular team and was touched to be presented with a University of Alabama cap on arrival. 'If you're going to be in the Borderkeepers of Alabama then you need to support the Crimson Tide', Bama said. He showed me to the guest room, complete with large gun rack hung above the bed, holding rifles and shotguns. Not a drinker himself, he nevertheless produced a jam jar filled with 38-year-old genuine moonshine whiskey. 'Moonshine this old is rare enough to split a family', he said, pouring me a glass. Southern hospitality is a cliché but it also happens to be true. He then pulled out a tin and began rolling himself a joint. I was taken aback. What was the point in risking life and limb on the Mexican border to stop drug smugglers only to then smoke weed yourself? 'Ah, don't worry. This weed is American.'

As we sat there drinking and smoking together I felt torn. He had been nothing but adorable and kind to me, and yet I was lying to him and knew that when I published my story I could do him real harm. This is the hardest bit of my job, liking someone on the other side. It would be easier to pretend that it's simple; we are the good guys and they are the bad – but it's far more complex than that. Several years later, after my original exposé was published, I was walking through Jerusalem as the shops were closing and a vendor pulled down the shutters to reveal a huge Crimson Tide mural. I remember being surprised, taking a picture and thinking I would send it to Bama, only to remember that we weren't friends, we were enemies.

I wanted to understand how someone so gentle to me could be so vile about others. As the evening wore on we returned to Bama's fears of an impending civil war. For him, Barack Obama was purposely stoking the fires of racial tension and actively encouraging race riots with a view to using the resulting crisis as an excuse to declare martial law, abolish the Constitution and stay in power. This would be the trigger for a second wave of secessions by the southern states and the start of another American civil war. The idea that Obama was planning to stay in office beyond his term was commonly held among BOA activists. Despite all this, Bama claimed not to be racist and even to have close black friends. When I questioned him on how this was possible, given his views, he set about explaining how there was a difference between black people and 'n****rs' – the latter were lazy, living off state hand-outs and selling drugs. The former supposedly lived in the local area and 'knew their place'.

It was sickening to hear such explicit racism, especially coming from someone I liked. It is sometimes comforting to think of racists, fascists and violent extremists as monsters, but talking to Bama was a valuable reminder that they are, ostensibly, normal people. I went to bed that night sad, knowing that our politics meant we would never be friends and that I had a duty to expose him and his dangerous racism.

I left the next morning and headed further into the middle of nowhere to see Bama's brother Cornbread. It took me hours to find his house, as his address didn't appear on my satnav. Eventually I saw a dirt track leading steeply down into a hollowed-out area of woodland, in the middle of which stood a dilapidated trailer. Cornbread emerged with a huge grin and bellowed 'Over here, cuz!' in his undeniably endearing way. He introduced his wife, who had taken a day off work from the local car factory where she stitched seats just so she could meet me. Looking around the cramped trailer I could see what a sacrifice a day's pay was to them, and felt terrible about it. Cornbread had grown up in difficult circumstances, with a tumultuous home life and very little education, and had struggled most of his life to scrape together enough for the basics. I suddenly understood why he hated politicians so much – what had they ever done for him? We passed a pleasant evening, talking, drinking, smoking and eating fried chicken, grits and collard greens. He confided in me that what little employment he did get was usually as a labourer working for an undocumented Mexican immigrant. It was becoming clear that for Bama and Cornbread the problem was never with the Mexicans or black people they knew, it was always with the ones they had heard about.

The following morning I was woken early. 'I've managed to get you on the gun talk show on local radio', said Cornbread, thrusting a phone into my hands. 'I've told them all about you and they want to hear why you've come all the way out here to support the Borderkeepers.' My feigned shyness had little effect and I was shuffled through the door before I could think of a way to back out. I was told to walk back up the dirt track as I wouldn't get reception down in the trailer. 'I'll stay here and listen on the radio.'

Before I knew it, I was live on air, talking about my supposed enthusiasm and admiration for the work of far-right border militias. This was not part of the plan. Things then took a disastrous turn when the host explained that they had done some research based on what Cornbread had told them about me and thought they had found my social media accounts. I began to sweat uncontrollably, not helped by the punishing morning humidity. 'We're sure our listeners will want to follow your work. There's a closed account here for a Joe Mulhall that says you work for something called HOPE not hate, is that you?' My heart beat with such force it felt like it might break through my sternum. There was a long pause before I managed to blurt out 'No!' I knew I'd scrubbed my online presence before starting the project and they seemed to have no idea what HNH was, so I said I never used social media and brought the conversation to an abrupt end.

Only then did I remember that Cornbread was down in the trailer – part home, part arms and ammunition dump – listening to the whole thing. My instinct was to run but my passport, money and car keys were all there, so I had to go back. I composed myself with a few deep breaths and walked down the path to the trailer, half expecting to find Cornbread busily Googling HOPE not hate. I opened the door and nearly cried with relief to see him stirring grits on the hob and grinning, thrilled with my interview. I'd got away with it but I knew it mightn't be long before my cover was blown, so I shovelled down my breakfast, gathered my belongings and got out of there as fast as I thought possible without raising suspicion.

I headed straight to the state capital, relieved that the operation was over. I'd gathered huge amounts of information on a militia group I was convinced were dangerous. In Montgomery I went to visit friends who worked for the Southern Poverty Law Center (SPLC), a historic civil rights organisation with an impressive history of fighting and in some cases destroying hate groups. They had a glistening head office in the centre of town, a stone's throw from where Rosa Parks boarded a bus in 1955 and changed the course of history. Within walking distance is the Dexter Avenue King Memorial Baptist Church from which the Montgomery bus boycott was organised, the Greyhound bus station where Freedom Riders were attacked in 1961, and the steps of the Alabama State Capitol building where Dr Martin Luther King Jr delivered his famous 'How Long, Not Long' speech in front of 25,000 people after the Selma to Montgomery march in 1965. I wanted to burst into the SPLC office and tell them everything I had found, but I knew I couldn't. HNH's rules are very clear: I wasn't to tell a single soul until I was safely out of Alabama. That evening I made the most of the limited night out on offer in Montgomery before waking early and boarding a plane to Chicago.

I'd booked the Travelodge on East Harrison Street in downtown Chicago as it was just a three-minute walk from Buddy Guy's bar, owned by the famous blues player himself. I'd heard rumours that if in town he would often be found at the bar so I hurriedly dropped my bags and headed out. I had spent the day at the offices of a small anti-racist organisation called the Centre for New Community (CNC) with which HNH worked closely. Now out of Alabama, I was free to tell them all about my adventures in the desert. We had a few drinks together before I headed off in search of Buddy Guy. After a few hours of passable blues music but no sign of Buddy, I left and walked the five minutes to the world-famous Jazz Showcase bar, Chicago's oldest jazz club.

I woke in the morning and saw I had several missed calls from my colleague at CNC. I called back and heard a nervous voice say: 'Go onto the Southern Poverty Law Center website.' I opened my laptop, and there on the homepage was an article titled 'Meet the Borderkeepers of Alabama'. The short piece, cobbled together from social media posts, also used a picture I had taken in New Mexico that Cornbread had subsequently put on Facebook. I instantly knew that when BOA activists saw this article they would understandably assume I had been working for the SPLC the whole time. It transpired that someone at the SPLC who monitored the militia movement had heard me on the gun radio show and when I then arrived at their offices later that day had put two and two together. Ironically, we had always intended to share the information I had gathered, but our plan had been not to publish anything until I was safely out of the country and back home in the UK. I suddenly had a flashback to Bull's warning: 'Just remember, I'm a bounty hunter so if you fuck us over, I will find you.'

I called Nick Lowles in London and we both agreed I needed to go into hiding for a spell until we could work out if I was under threat. I thought about jumping on the first flight back to the UK but I was running several operations in the US that were still ongoing. I hurriedly packed, leaving my TV on, and slipped away without checking out of my hotel; then I headed to the Greyhound bus station and boarded the first available coach out of town.

About four hours later I found myself in Indianapolis, one of those identikit cities you only find in America. Having not 'gone on the run' before I wasn't quite sure what to do, so I headed to a dirty sports bar and had a few drinks to make a plan. I got talking to the barman and told him I was in town for business and looking for a quiet hotel out of the city centre where I could bed down for a week or so. Looking around at the seedy clientele in the bar I got the feeling that this wasn't the first time he'd had to recommend such a place, and he seemed to understand exactly what I wanted. 'There's an old indoor waterpark on the edge of town, the slides are all closed but I think the hotel might still be open, always empty as far as I can tell.' I left him a tip and jumped in a cab.

It was perfect, exactly the sort of place I expected someone would hide out, like in the movies. But then, maybe that made it obvious and so not perfect? I wasn't sure. Caribbean Cove Water Park had certainly ceased to be an attraction some time ago, the now faded slides all closed off and the sounds of playing children just a memory. With nothing to draw visitors, the hundreds of rooms, organised with balconies facing inwards towards a pool area covered by an enormous canopy roof, were empty. As far as I could tell I was the only person there except for the odd staff member. The first night or two were nerve-racking. Sitting in my room eating takeaway pizza, I was convinced every bump or bang I heard was Bull coming to find me. To keep busy, I threw myself back into the Ku Klux Klan infiltration project – and out of the blue I struck gold.

Back in the UK I had contacted dozens of KKK groups across America, expressing my interest in getting involved. Most either didn't respond or were understandably guarded. The one exception was Chris Barker, founder and leader of the Loyal White Knights of the KKK. His Klan bragged about being 'the most active Klan in America' and had a reputation for its extremeness. Barker was hated by other prominent Klan leaders and had previously been expelled by three other groups due to his willingness to openly ally himself with neo-nazis, something that certain Klan members disapproved of. Barker was also part of the Aryan Nationalist Alliance, an extreme and eclectic coalition of white nationalist groups, racist skinheads and Klansmen. As well as an extreme racist, Barker (aliases James Spears and Robert Jones) is also a dangerous criminal with a record spanning nearly two decades. He has been found guilty of malicious arson, possession of stolen goods and larceny, and been charged with assault with a deadly weapon and assault on a woman. He and I had been corresponding for a year and got to the point where he believed I ran a small KKK branch in London. At one point, we even discussed him coming over to visit.

Barker and his wife, Amanda, would send me newspapers, leaflets and stickers for distribution in the UK and I would send back fabricated pictures of me handing them out or gluing them to lampposts, which he received with great excitement. Some leaflets simply showed a hooded figure along with the words 'Our Race Is Our Nation', while another showed a similar figure, but backed by the Confederate flag with the words 'Help Save Our Race; Everything we cherish is under assault by ZOG' above it. (ZOG is an abbreviation of 'Zionist Occupation Government', an antisemitic term and conspiracy theory claiming that Jews secretly control world power.) However, the most extreme leaflet I was sent encouraged acts of violence against gay men. It showed two stick figures engaging in anal sex with the title 'Stop Aids: Support Gay Bashing'. Under the picture, it read: 'Homosexual Men

And Their Sexual Acts Are Disgusting and Inhuman'. Not content with violent homophobia, the leaflet finished on a racist note: 'Ban Non-White Immigration. Outlaw Haitians – Deport Mud People.'

Generally, I interacted with Barker via letter and email, though I was eventually given access to the group's closed forum where I came across some of the worst racism I have ever encountered. Jokes and memes about hanging and running over black people were commonplace. A picture of Barack Obama with a noose around his neck was especially popular. The forum had an extreme culture of violence which I took very seriously due to the group's proven track record. In late February that year, members of the Klan had held an anti-immigration demonstration in Anaheim, California at which they revealed signs reading 'White Lives Matter'. During the ensuing confrontation with counter-protesters, five people were injured and thirteen arrested. Just a few days after the fracas, Barker emailed me to brag: 'we just had a fight between our members and communist [sic] our members stabbed 3 in California.' Five KKK members were arrested following the brawl but all were later released as they were said to be acting in self-defence. Previously, in 2015, Barker had been convicted for being involved in the notorious, and frankly ridiculous, plot to build a ray gun to kill Muslims that his co-conspirator described as 'Hiroshima on a light switch'.

One evening, while in my room at Caribbean Cove Water Park, I checked the email account I used for the KKK infiltration and found a message from Barker. There was a section of the White Knights website reserved for senior members that required special login details. The level of information I was already gathering made me keen not to raise suspicion by pushing for details but here, out of the blue, was an email giving me access. I followed the link and typed in the password. I couldn't believe what I was looking at: huge amounts of sensitive information about the group, including pictures, names, addresses and contact details of hundreds of members and prospective members. I spent the rest of the night screenshotting everything, and by the time the sun rose the following morning I was able to build a true picture of the organisation's membership. Perhaps unsurprisingly, the Loyal White Knights drew its strength from the southern states, with a sizeable membership in Louisiana, Mississippi, Alabama and Georgia – and of course North Carolina, where the group was headquartered. That said, the group had members all over America, with pretty much an even spread across the Midwest and the East Coast and a healthy number in California. They also had lone members in Southern Australia, the UK and British Columbia (Canada). Looking through the pictures of the members was sickening. Hooded and robed figures holding firearms or even the hangman's noose, a symbol linked to the lynching of black people, were common. I also found a list of members who had been expelled for violations ranging from drug use to sleeping with 'a JEW Whore' or a Mexican, to watching Asian porn, or having a 'mixed child' and therefore being a 'RACE TRAITOR'.

I closed my laptop, left my room and walked out into the morning. I called Nick in London on an encrypted phone line, and we excitedly discussed the remarkable information I had acquired and hatched a plan to get it safely back to the UK. We were well aware of the widespread rumours that Barker was an FBI informant, and if that was the case we were sure the Bureau wouldn't look kindly at British anti-fascists poking around in their business. I loaded the information onto a memory stick and hid it in the bottom of a cigarette packet before carefully replacing the cigarettes and resealing the plastic.

Some months later we published the exposé alongside the story of the Borderkeepers of Alabama in a HOPE not hate special report titled *A Nation Divided*. It received a double-page spread in the *Observer* newspaper with the headline 'How British anti-racist group infiltrated the Ku Klux Klan'. In advance of our investigation being made public, I emailed all supporters of the Loyal White Knights and informed them of our plans to publish. While some responded with racist slurs, others denied their links with the group. Unsurprisingly, the responses on their closed members' forum were much more panicked as they tried to work out the scale and source of the leak. Before long, they realised that hundreds of supporters had received emails and the finger-pointing began. Barker and his wife Amanda began to deflect blame. Instead of admitting they were responsible, they claimed the whole thing was a fake, dreamed up by two disaffected ex-members, 'Chris and Jacqueline from Georgia' (who had been thrown out of the Klan for using methamphetamine). Amanda wrote on the forum: 'They are trying to scare people. Don't let them get to you. As for both of them will be banished [*sic*] and harshly dealt with.' The Grand Dragon for Georgia joined in and 'confirmed' it was these ex-members. Of course, Barker and Amanda knew the truth and were lying to their membership to save their own skins. At the same time as publicly blaming embittered meth addicts, Barker emailed me saying: 'FUCK yOU Commie scum.'

Soon after, the SPLC published an article explaining how the Loyal White Knights had been 'falling apart at the seams' due to an 'ongoing pattern of leadership difficulties and dissension in the ranks that have plagued LWK for months'.[15]

The internal tension and mistrust spilled over into violence in early December 2016, resulting in some senior members being arrested and charged with assault with a deadly weapon with intent to kill, aiding and abetting assault with a deadly weapon with intent to kill, and inflicting serious injury. While there was a range of reasons behind the group's eventual disintegration, we were confident that our infiltration had played a role.

Back in Indianapolis, I packed my bags and posted the cigarette packet back to the UK. It had been over a week since the SPLC article about the Borderkeepers had been published and we had found no indication on the group's social media that I was in danger. Nick and I decided it was safe for me to come out of hiding, though probably best to keep a low profile for a while longer.

6

THE RISE OF
PRESIDENT TRUMP

It was September 2016 and I was in the very heart of
Washington, DC. The first day of the conference had been
at the historic Omni Shoreham Hotel, famous for host-
ing inaugural balls for every president since Franklin D.
Roosevelt, as well as the hotel of choice for The Beatles on
their first American tour back in 1964. The day's proceedings had been broadcast live from the ballroom on C-SPAN
across America. On day two we moved to Capitol Hill, the
historic centre of American democracy that years later in
2021 would be the scene of an attempted coup by far-right
extremists who stormed its walls. Thanks to the sponsor-
ship of Congressman Mike Pompeo we were based in the
Congressional Auditorium, a large theatre reserved for use
by Congress that sits just off the grand Emancipation Hall,
named to recognise the contribution of enslaved labour-
ers who helped build the US Capitol. A procession of nine
Congressmen and Congresswomen and a Senator addressed
the enthusiastic audience. The crowd whooped and hollered
as they heard from their representatives. Among the speakers
was Senator Ted Cruz, formerly Donald Trump's challenger
for the Republican nomination for President.

This was the national conference of ACT! for America, a

Southern Poverty Law Center-designated hate group and one that had reached right into the heart of the American political establishment. My time undercover with the Borderkeepers of Alabama was over, as was my operation against the KKK, and it was now time to focus solely on the upcoming election. Speakers at the two-day ACT! conference included a roll-call of senior political figures. These included Congressman Lou Barletta, a representative for Pennsylvania who sat on the Committee on Homeland Security and the Subcommittee on Border and Maritime Security. Also present were Congressman Scott Perry (Committee on Foreign Affairs and the Subcommittee on Terrorism, Non-proliferation and Trade, and the Committee on Homeland Security) and Congressman Louie Gohmert from Texas (Committee on the Judiciary and the Subcommittee on the Constitution, Civil Rights and Civil Liberties). Finally there was Congressman Peter King from New York, former chairman of the House Committee on Homeland Security as well as chair of the Subcommittee on Counterterrorism and Intelligence. I couldn't believe my ears or eyes. The previous day I had been sitting in the Omni Shoreham Hotel ballroom listening to extreme and conspiratorial speeches; the next day, at the very heart of American democracy, I was watching elected and powerful politicians telling this crowd of anti-Muslim activists how proud they were to be associated with ACT!.

ACT! (American Congress for Truth) was launched in the wake of the 9/11 attacks by Brigitte Gabriel, a Lebanese Christian who is now a US citizen. She has a long track record of vocal Islamophobia. In 2007 she stated:

> [A] practicing Muslim who believes the word of the Koran to be the word of Allah ... who goes to mosque

and prays every Friday, who prays five times a day – this
practicing Muslim, who believes in the teachings of the
Koran, cannot be a loyal citizen of the United States.[1]

Since being launched, ACT! had grown to be the largest
anti-Muslim organisation in America and at the time of my
visit claimed to have 300,000 members spread across the
country in nearly 1,000 chapters. It proudly called itself
the 'NRA of National Security', a reference to the National
Rifle Association's famous lobbying power and its ability to
influence legislation and policy on issues such as gun control.
ACT!'s claim was not mere bluster or aspiration: at the conference they bragged about their role in passing 43 bills in
22 different states to 'protect America', many of which have
been the so-called 'anti-Shariah' legislation.

Amazingly, Gabriel's influence went well beyond con-
vincing members of Congress and Senators to attend ACT!
events: it extended to her being asked to address Congressmen
and women, the Pentagon, the Joint Forces Staff College,
the US Special Operations Command, the US Asymmetric
Warfare Group and the FBI. If this was an anomaly it would
be worrying enough – but Gabriel is not the only anti-
Muslim activist who has been invited to address and advise
American intelligence and law enforcement agencies. In 2009
Robert Spencer, the notorious director of the anti-Muslim
and counter-jihadist website, Jihad Watch, and co-founder
of Stop Islamisation of America (SIOA) was recruited by the
FBI to personally facilitate training. His written works have
been used during training sessions on Islam.[2] Spencer was
later banned from entering the UK (following a HOPE not
hate-led petition to the government) because of his extremism.
Similarly, disgraced former FBI agent John Guandolo, who

is the founder of an organisation called Understanding the Threat and has stated that American Muslims 'do not have a First Amendment right to do anything', has provided training courses to law enforcement agencies across the country.[3]

While the intelligence and law enforcement communities seem to have distanced themselves from some of these more extreme characters, the 2016 presidential race afforded new opportunities for anti-Muslim activists to enter the mainstream. During the race for the Republican nomination, Ted Cruz announced an advisory team that included anti-Muslim activist Frank 'Obama is a Muslim' Gaffney from the Center for Security Policy (CSP) as a foreign policy advisor. However, Cruz's defeat in the nomination by no means ended Gaffney's influence, as he also played a key role in Trump's understanding of the 'threat' of Islam and Muslims. Trump quoted Gaffney's discredited research and Gaffney is said to have been a key influence on his openly racist comments about Muslims. Other CSP-linked individuals also found their way onto Trump's advisory team. At the ACT! conference in DC that I attended, another Trump advisor spoke: Lieutenant General Mike Flynn, who advised the presidential nominee on issues of national security. Flynn had also recently been appointed to ACT!'s board of directors. In later years he became best known as one of the most high-profile supporters of the bizarre and dangerous conspiracy theory known as QAnon, which believes that 'President Trump is waging a secret war against a cabal of powerful Satanic paedophiles, alleged to be kidnapping, torturing and even cannibalising children on a vast scale'.[4]

As I sat in the Capitol Building, surrounded by well-heeled racists talking of the danger posed by Muslims, I realised what a Trump presidency would mean. It would mean that anti-Muslim extremists would be ushered into the White House and play a key role in advising the American President on issues of national security and policies towards American Muslims. This proved to be the case. In December that year, just weeks after Trump's victory, Brigitte Gabriel wrote: 'ACT! for America has a direct line to Donald Trump, and has played a fundamental role in shaping his views and suggested policies with respect to radical Islam.'[5]

'Are you here to laugh at us?'

I was perched at the bar of the VFW (Veterans of Foreign Wars) Club in Duquesne, a run-down town that sits on the Monongahela River in Allegheny County about ten miles south-east of Pittsburgh, Pennsylvania. A large camouflaged artillery piece, surrounded by dozens of American flags, adorned the front lawn outside. Inside, an imposing mural of a golden eagle, clutching a banner that read 'All Gave Some, Some Gave All', stared down across the dark and smoky bar.

The 2016 presidential election was fast approaching. On 19 July Donald Trump had been officially nominated as the Republican presidential candidate. For many around the world the news came as a shock but there was a broad consensus that he would never win the actual election. It was impossible. Unthinkable. So unlikely as to be comical. Having spent time in Alabama and seen the passion they had for Trump, I had a nagging feeling that he had a chance but, like everyone else, thought it a long shot.

The idea that anyone would come to a place like Duquesne and actually care what the local people thought was anathema to Liz, a single mother, ex-steel worker, military veteran and now commander of the VFW club. She echoed a sentiment

I have heard time and time again in the US: a feeling that people living in economically deprived places like Duquesne have long been ignored by politicians, journalists and the East Coast elites ... or even worse, laughed at.

Duquesne itself is a sad example of the ravages of deindustrialisation. At one point the steel mill was home to the 'Dorothy Six', the largest blast furnace in the world. However, after twenty years of bathing the town in her orange hue the furnace was scheduled for demolition in 1984. Despite a protracted battle by workers, unions and the local community she was never fired again and eventually pulled down in the late 1980s. All that remains of this once world-famous steel mill is a single metal memorial plaque by the side of a car park. If anyone has heard of the town today it's more likely from Bob Dylan's recent and, let's be honest, not particularly good song, 'Duquesne Whistle'. In the place where the once monstrous furnace stood is a bleak post-industrial landscape, the town shrunken and dilapidated. Like so many similar places, the fortunes of the town were tied to its main industry and with its death the town began to die too. Duquesne now has a population smaller than the number of people employed at the steel mill during its peak.

When I asked Liz what people did for work in the area she paused, shrugged, then shook her head. Shockingly, the estimated annual per capita income in Duquesne in 2013 was just $14,177 (£10,750). About 35% of the town's population live below the poverty line and that number jumps to 53% for those under the age of eighteen. I drove the semi-derelict streets and tried hard to imagine what this place must have been like in its heyday. There was a sense of melancholy in the boarded-up buildings, a distant whiff of past glory. It reminded me of Dagenham, east London, where back in

2010 I had worked on an anti-BNP campaign. Despite being 6,000 km apart, the stories of anger, sadness, abandonment and betrayal I heard in Duquesne weren't that different to the ones I had heard years earlier in Dagenham.

Sadly, the story of Duquesne is not unique. In the aftermath of the recession of the 1980s around 153,000 steel workers were made redundant across the USA. If you follow the winding Monongahela River today, the banks are intermittently scarred by vast derelict industrial buildings such as the abandoned Carrie Furnace at the Homestead Steel Works, once the site of one of the most serious disputes in US labour history. The Mon Valley now has just three remaining steel works, and even the plants that have survived employ a fraction of the workforce they did at their peak (in part due to technological advancements). Jason Crosby, a third-generation steel worker based at a plant in Christy Park, McKeesport, on the Youghiogheny River, explained to me how his plant employed 7,500 people in the early 1970s, but now provides jobs for between just 50 and 60.

David Morgan, a steel worker and trade union organiser at the Mon Valley Works–Irvin Plant, reminisced about how things have changed since he was a child:

> I remember as a little kid, all my friends, everybody, their dads worked in the steel mill. Then the 80s came and a lot of my friends moved away because the steel mills closed up. I see people now who don't even realise that steel workers are in this area because there are just so few anymore.

He told a story that can be heard throughout the Mon Valley and would no doubt resonate across the Atlantic in areas like

Teesside in the north-east of England: 'It's taken a very big downturn and now I am worried about the ones that are still left because of all the imports that are coming in, the dumping from China and what have you, it's getting worse by the year.' When I asked him if we would be seeing Pittsburgh steel being made in 50 years' time, a sadness came over him. 'Oh, I hope so, I hope so', he said, pausing and shaking his head. 'Probably five years ago I would have said absolutely, but now I'm not so sure.'

Taking a wider view, the decline of industry in the Mon Valley is not an isolated tale. Deindustrialisation and the decline of manufacturing has affected communities across the country. In 1965 the share of manufacturing employment in America was 28% but by 1994 this had dropped to just 16%. Recently there has been another wave of deindustrialisation, and it is estimated that between 2001 and 2009 a further 42,400 factories closed across the US.[6] The first decade of the 21st century saw the loss of 5.8 million manufacturing jobs due to the recessions of 2001–02 and 2008–10.[7]

Studies have shown how in addition to community decay and high crime rates, deindustrialisation and the resulting economic decline can have an impact on the physical and mental health of former workers.[8] Figures produced by the US government's National Survey on Drug Use and Health have shown that around one in six unemployed workers is addicted to alcohol or drugs.[9] Coupled with the primary cause of widespread addiction to prescribed opioid pain medication, this helps to explain the terrible stories I heard about Pennsylvania's heroin epidemic. One steel worker at the Irvin Plant who graduated in 1992 explained to me how 86 of his 224 classmates were now dead from the drug. He dubbed the nearby town of Clairton the 'capital of heroin'. Another worker at a different plant estimated that at least a quarter of his son's former school year would be using the drug in one form or another. The actual statistics are horrifying. In 2015, in a state of under 13 million people, 3,383 people died from overdosing on opioids: this is greater than the number who died of overdoses in the whole of England and Wales in 2014.[10] This current opioid epidemic has spread well beyond the urban areas that one might expect, out into smaller rural communities across the state. While the epidemic has been felt across the nation – opioid overdose nationwide has quadrupled since 2000 – it is the 'rust belt' states where the number of deaths per 100,000 of population are among the highest.[11]

While Pennsylvania has seen some success stories, it is clear that wounds opened by the decline of its steel industry have by no means healed. Many people in communities like Duquesne and the wider Mon Valley are angry about the jobs that have long disappeared, and scared about the future. Speaking to workers in June 2016 at a metal recycling facility in Monessen, Pennsylvania, just 30 miles from Steel City, Donald Trump said:

> The legacy of Pennsylvania steel workers lives in the bridges, railways and skyscrapers that make up our great American landscape.
>
> But our workers' loyalty was repaid with betrayal.
>
> Our politicians have aggressively pursued a policy of globalization – moving our jobs, our wealth and our factories to Mexico and overseas.
>
> Globalization has made the financial elite who donate to politicians very wealthy. But it has left millions of our workers with nothing but poverty and heartache.

When subsidized foreign steel is dumped into our markets, threatening our factories, the politicians do nothing.

For years, they watched on the sidelines as our jobs vanished and our communities were plunged into depression-level unemployment.

Many of these areas have still never recovered.

[...]

Under a Trump Presidency, the American worker will finally have a President who will protect them and fight for them.[12]

Without question these comments reveal a staggering level of hypocrisy: Trump-brand products have been outsourced to China, Brazil, Honduras, Europe and beyond.[13] Back in 2005 Trump even said that outsourcing was 'not always a terrible thing' and sometimes 'a necessary step'.[14] Yet none of this means that what Trump said isn't true, at least in part. Globalisation has been wonderful in so many ways, cheaper consumer goods for one, yet there have been losers: people and communities that have been left by the wayside of progress. It is with these people that Trump's message – hypocritical or not – has resonated.

When I asked Jeffery O'Kelly, a worker at the Clairton Coke Plant, the largest coke manufacturing facility in the United States, about Trump support on the shop floor he estimated that around half his colleagues would vote Republican at the 2016 election. 'I know why they are supporting Trump', he said. 'The biggest reason is that he says everything that they want to hear.' Which is? 'Mostly it's about jobs.' Back at the Irvin Plant, David Morgan echoed this point: 'The floor used to be pretty much 100% Democratic vote. There is more people now that are not Democrat any more, they are leaning towards Republican ... There is a lot of people leaning towards a Republican vote, probably more than there ever has been.'

This was an industrial community where the Democrats would have once weighed the vote rather than counted it. Unsurprisingly these newly divided loyalties had led to tensions, and reports of fist fights on the factory floor were not hard to find. The sense of betrayal and decline in the rust belt by no means completely explains the rise of Trump, but it must certainly have been a contributing factor. Many Trump supporters were tired, angry and without hope. They saw no opportunity for progress and advancement, and they had nothing to lose by trying something different. Trying Trump.

It was Thursday 1 September 2016, and I instantly knew it was going to be nothing like any political event I had seen in the UK. It was only 8.00am and already the car park was filling and the queue was forming outside the Roberts Centre in Wilmington, Ohio. Trump was in town and this group of supporters, replete with the now-famous red 'Make America Great Again' baseball caps, was getting there early, determined not to miss out. Those without a hat could buy one as they waited, along with 'Hillary For Prison' and 'Build The Wall' badges. They could also snap up a tasteful 'Hillary Sucks But Not Like Monica' T-shirt with 'Trump That Bitch!' emblazoned on the back.

Trump wasn't due to arrive until lunchtime but the rapidly gathering crowd was already excited.

An armed man in a bulletproof vest, rather oxymoronically reading 'Secret Service', came around to remind the crowd to leave all firearms, ammunition and knives in their cars. Some people laughed, but apparently someone nearer the front had carelessly forgotten to remove a magazine of bullets from his pocket. After hours of queuing, the line eventually snaked through security and into the main hall. The mood inside was more like a gig than a political rally. You could buy popcorn and snacks at the back, and the large hanging speakers blasted out the Rolling Stones' greatest hits, occasionally interrupted by an out-of-place recording of Pavarotti's 'Nessun Dorma'. The room filled up with a crowd of all shapes, sizes and ages. The only unifying characteristic was their whiteness.

The jovial festival vibe soon changed once the first speech began. After the mandatory prayer, national anthem and pledge of allegiance came the chairman of the Clinton County Republican Party. As he bellowed about the ills of Hillary, Obama and the Democrats, one man shouted 'Hang the witch' – in reference to Clinton – and when he moved on to Obama's failings a man nearer the front shouted 'Lynch him!' A few people laughed, others pulled slightly nervous faces, but no one challenged him. During former New York mayor Rudy Giuliani's speech the room echoed with the chant of 'Lock her up! Lock her up!' Someone shouted 'Hang the traitor!'

With the arrival of Trump, the anger turned to adulation as he swiftly knocked out a greatest hits speech. The biggest cheer of the day was saved for his immigration policy and his promise to build a wall on the Mexican border. Then, just like that, it was over and the Rolling Stones' 'You Can't Always Get What You Want' blared out as he walked the front row shaking hands and signing hats.

Summing up the mood of the day is difficult. There was a peculiar mix of violent anger and hatred, along with jubilation and adoration. Like the wider political discourse itself, there seemed no room for subtlety or nuance. This was a matter of black or white, good or bad, and – critically – what was 'American' or 'un-American'. It struck me that the election wouldn't be a matter of mere ideological difference that could be fought out via the ballot box. The fact that you could buy blow-up Hillary punchbags in a car park outside underlined that. The people in the Roberts Centre had the fervour of zealots fighting for the very soul of their country. After eight years of Democratic rule they truly felt America was in crisis; 'the laughing stock of the world' as they saw it. For them this was a crossroads moment: down one road lay the end of the America they loved, while down the other lay salvation.

Writing in the *Huffington Post* in July of that year, the leading American social scientist Cas Mudde argued that 'Donald Trump has brought far right politics into the mainstream of US politics. What Wallace and Buchanan were never able to achieve [...], Trump has accomplished. He is the first far right presidential candidate of one of the two major political parties in the US, at least since the end of the Second World War.'[15] By the end of his term in 2021, the full extent of this transformation was laid bare when polling showed that a staggering 45% of Republicans supported the far-right rioters who stormed the Capitol, resulting in the deaths of five people.[16] But how did the Grand Old Party (GOP) get here? How did America get here?

As always, there are long-term factors such as the deep historical reservoir of racism, racial division and xenophobia that Trump by no means created but did successfully exploit. However, in terms of the transformation of the GOP into a party that nominated Trump, one has to look at the role of the Tea Party. In 2009, during the administration of Barack

Obama, a new radical-right populist movement emerged. It was named after the 1773 Boston Tea Party, when colonists who objected to taxation without representation by the British dumped British tea into Boston harbour, an event that was a forerunner to the American Revolution. The Tea Party isn't actually a political party but rather a movement that has organised protests and supports chosen candidates in elections. That said, polling by Gallup in 2010 found that eight out of ten supporters were Republicans.[17]

At the time, prominent Democratic politicians such as the Speaker of the House of Representatives, Nancy Pelosi, wrote the Tea Party off as 'astroturf', a term used to claim that supposedly grassroots activism is actually artificial and orchestrated rather than authentic and organic. However, Ronald P. Formisano, a historian of the Tea Party, suggests a more mixed picture, claiming that it was 'created by both kinds of populism, in part by the few – the corporate lobbyists from above – but also from the passionate many expressing real grassroots populism'.[18] Whatever the case, the movement expanded rapidly and managed to 'deliver powerful electoral punches in the GOP primaries and the November 2010 general election'.[19]

According to the BBC at the time, the Tea Party had three central tenets: 'fiscal responsibility, limited government and free markets'.[20] However, there is also an ugly xenophobic element to the movement, with widespread racism, especially towards Obama, commonplace within its ranks. Some have argued that 'its outrage over the debt and deficit had another purpose: giving cover and a voice to those who wanted to attack the first black president – people who in some cases showed up at rallies waving signs with racist caricatures and references.'[21] Going further, David Neiwert has shown how the Tea Party had actually 'become a wholesale conduit for a revival of the Patriot movement and its militias'.[22] While its core desire to end big government and big spending ultimately failed, the Tea Party contributed to the transformation of the GOP into the sort of party that would nominate Donald Trump as its presidential candidate. For many activists, huge government debt was symbolic of 'politicians who were unresponsive to their concerns and an economy that wasn't benefiting most Americans', as the *New York Times* journalist Jeremy W. Peters described it. Put simply, what the Tea Party did was to 'unleash the politics of anger'.[23]

When Trump actually won the nomination, many responded incredulously, claiming he had 'hijacked' the party. In truth, as Cas Mudde has argued, while he was 'perhaps not representative of the GOP at the federal level, this is not true at the state (or local) level – particularly in the American "heartland" between the two coasts'. In fact, Mudde argues, 'Trump is in many ways a much more accurate representative of the GOP electorate than party establishment politicians'.[24] This fact goes a long way to explaining not only why he won the presidency, but also why so many commentators were shocked when it happened.

When it comes to explaining Trump's victory there is no easy answer. In November 2016, CNN published an article entitled, 'How did Trump win? Here are 24 theories' – and it's not hard to find dozens more.[25] One thing is clear: any theory that offers a monocausal explanation like 'racism' or 'economics' is clearly oversimplifying things. As with discussions about the rise of the far right in Europe, the debate over the cause of Trump's victory centres around economic explanations versus cultural ones. And as in Europe, the truth is not binary but a complex combination of both.

However, the political scientist Matt Grossman reviewed an array of early academic studies on Trump's electorate and found that, while there was widespread disagreement, attitudes to race, gender and cultural change outweighed the importance of economic circumstances as an explanation.[26] The median income of Trump supporters was higher than the median income of Clinton voters. In the words of Dave Renton: 'This was not the millions-strong army of poor and working-class white voters on which the liberal press has fixated.'[27] Similarly, Diana Mutz has shown the importance of people's concerns over the rise of a 'majority-minority America' as a key factor.[28] As she put it, 'Those who felt that the hierarchy was being upended – with whites discriminated against more than Muslims, and men discriminated against more than women – were most likely to support Trump.'[29] This is certainly backed up by my experiences with BOA in Alabama. The supposed discrimination against white, male Christians was their primary explanation for why they supported Trump.

However, it is patently not true that white men are the most persecuted people in America. There is no tenable evidence for this position. As such, one of the primary reasons that people supported Trump was false – but to explain why they felt it was true, one has to look to relative economic decline, both real and perceived. It's easy to dismiss the arguments of Trump supporters but it is impossible to combat people's sense of decline, and fear of further decline, with mere statistics about economic differences between different racial groups. Trump didn't care whether white Christian men are actually the most persecuted group in America, he simply accepted that many believed that to be the case and spoke to their fears. Many voters lamented the loss of a supposedly halcyon past of universal economic prosperity – and for many, unchallenged white hegemony – and while a myth, it was a very powerful one. Trump promised to return America to a mythical past of plenty. It was a hugely powerful and emotional offer and not one that Clinton matched. That's why he won.

7

INSIDE THE INTERNATIONAL ALT-RIGHT

I sat on the steps of the District Hotel, just fifteen minutes' walk from the White House, on a crisp October evening. I needed to decompress after a stressful day so I called a friend who was in town. We made the short walk over to the Lucky Bar on Connecticut Avenue, a dingy place suited to those of us interested in English football. It wasn't long before my phone buzzed – Nick in London was asking when my intelligence report would be ready. I finished my drink and headed back to my hotel to get writing.

I had spent the day in the Polaris Suite at the Ronald Reagan Building, a neo-classical edifice, architecturally interchangeable with countless other buildings along Pennsylvania Avenue. It was the 2013 Leadership Conference of the American white supremacist think-tank, the National Policy Institute (NPI). The conference – entitled 'After the Fall: The Future of Identity' – was organised by Richard Spencer, the figurehead of the alt-right. (The alt-right is defined below on p. 170.) Back in April that year I had infiltrated a meeting of a far-right discussion group called the Bloomsbury Forum at a hotel in Hammersmith, west London. The great and the good of the British fascist scene gathered in a small windowless room to hear a speech by the infamous US racist Jared Taylor of American Renaissance. That was my first encounter with what would later become more widely known as the alt-right. The meeting had reiterated the importance of transatlantic networks to the movement, and contributed to HOPE not hate's decision to send me to Washington, DC.

Spencer gave a brief introduction and was followed by the Italian-Swiss author Piero San Giorgio, whose apocalyptic predictions of post-peak-oil environmental and social breakdown started as an ecological warning and ended with a call for a return to rural self-sufficiency. Sam Dickson, who describes himself as a 'racial communitarian', was next. He gave a hate-filled speech that was riddled with historical falsehoods and wilful misrepresentations, ending with a call for racial unity and a declaration that Abraham Lincoln's Gettysburg Address was 'a monstrous thing': 'all men are created equal', apparently not. Contributions from John Morgan, then of Arktos, the alt-right's leading publishing house, and Andy Nowicki, co-editor of the website Alternative Right followed. So far, so normal, for this sort of crowd.

Things started to heat up with a speech by novelist and writer Alex Kurtagić that called for a 'moral critique of egalitarianism based on traditionalism' and described a world of equality as a 'world without meaning'. This was followed by the insufferable French 'journalist' Roman Bernard, whose speech was littered with references to 'queers' and 'blacks'. Not to be outdone, the most offensive rant of the conference came from Jack Donovan, who called for a 'resurgence of tribalism, honour, and manly virtue'; code for racism, sexism and homophobia. Donovan defines himself as an 'androphile', which he describes as men like himself who are sexually attracted to other men but who simultaneously reject 'The highly vocal and visible queer fringe [that] publicly celebrates extreme promiscuity, sadomasochism, transvestitism, transsexuality and flamboyant effeminacy'.[1] His speech, which attacked women's liberation and LGBT+ rights and talked of race as 'blood and heritage', also called for people to create white-only communities.

I watched the shocked faces of the hotel staff, most of whom were black, as they listened to these racist speeches. Every fibre of my being wanted to apologise or just find a way to let them know that I wasn't like the others, that I didn't agree with them. But I couldn't, so I sat there nodding and applauding, feeling increasingly ashamed. Clapping along with me were some of the most notorious figures in the international far right, including Jared Taylor, Matt Parrott, then the Director of the Traditionalist Youth Network and a leading member of the American Freedom Party, and Kevin MacDonald, the neo-Nazi movement's antisemitic academic of choice.

The day drew to a close with speeches by two key European figures. The first was the Croatian Tomislav Sunić, a player in the European New Right (ENR) and author of the influential *Against Democracy and Equality*. This was followed by the keynote speech from Alain de Benoist, the French far-right philosopher who established the right-wing think-tank GRECE (Groupement de recherche et d'études pour la civilisation européenne – Research and Study Group for European Civilisation) in the late 1960s and is the primary intellectual force behind the ENR. His philosophical musings on the nature of identity, presented in broken English with a heavy accent, brought the day to a close on a subdued note. What I didn't realise at the time was the significance of de Benoist being there. In essence the ideological core of the alt-right emerged when elements of ENR thought were blended with, and adopted by, the American far right. It was only a few years later, when formulating a definition of the alt-right with my colleagues at HOPE not hate, that I realised I had watched part of this happening with my own eyes.

In the intelligence report I wrote that night I noted how the conference attendees genuinely seemed to believe that their time had come. 'After the Fall' was a reference to the imminent collapse of liberal democracy, something that felt delusional to me just down the road from Obama's Oval Office. I labelled it fascist hubris, merely another example in a long tradition of the extreme right predicting collapse and rebirth. I concluded my report:

> While the conference shows increasing links being formed between European and North American 'theorists', the question remains of how much influence these talking shops actually have on the ideas and ideology of the far right.

After the fall? What fall?, I thought.

Four years later, in 2017, I was at a secret rendezvous point outside Södra train station in Stockholm. It was late February and bitterly cold in the icy wind blowing off the Baltic Sea. The easternmost bay of Lake Mälaren on which Stockholm's Old Town sits was still frozen over. I was there to attend the Identitarian Ideas Conference, organised by leading Swedish far-right figure Daniel Friberg. It was *the* major European event in the alt-right calendar. Around me stood far-right activists from the UK, America, Canada, Australia, Estonia, Finland, Germany, Poland and the Netherlands, as well as a handful of local Swedes from the Nordic Youth, the 'media outlet' Motgift and the extreme Nordic Resistance Movement. To avoid the event being shut down by counter-protesters, the venue was kept a secret. Attendees were simply told to meet outside the train station and await further instructions. I was co-running an operation with colleagues at Expo, our Swedish sister organisation. Set up in the mid-1990s by Stieg Larsson, later the author of the wildly successful *Millennium* trilogy of crime novels, *Expo* magazine, now under the editorship of Daniel Poohl, monitors the Scandinavian far right with unrivalled effectiveness. I was to attend the event, leaking the location of the venue to Expo so their camera teams could find a secure location from which to take photographs.

Hiding from the cold, we huddled together in the ticket hall of the station waiting for instructions. I'd presumed we were to board a train, but it transpired that the venue was actually a nondescript conference hall a short walk away. Once inside I headed straight to the toilet and texted the address to Expo, who took up a position overlooking the front entrance. With a long lens, they were able to clearly capture everyone as they entered and exited the building. Notable attendees that day were the Swedish anti-Muslim activist Ingrid Carlqvist; Henrik Palmgren from the alt-right media platform Red Ice; Magnus Söderman, the former chief ideologue of the openly Nazi Swedish Resistance Movement; Ruuben Kaalep, leader of the youth movement of the Estonian Blue Awakening, and the American white nationalist blogger Paul Ramsey (aka RamZPaul). There was also a small group of attendees from the UK, including Stead Steadman from the far-right London Forum and the infamous Scottish YouTuber Colin Robertson (aka Millennial Woes). I'd been watching his videos for several years as he had risen to prominence within the international scene so I was intrigued to meet him. In person he was an amiable but shabby figure. Overlooking proceedings that day was the conference organiser Daniel Friberg, a heavy-set Swede with a menacing air about him.

The day was panning out as these conferences so often do, with a procession of poorly delivered speeches to an uninterested audience of increasingly inebriated racists. Until, that is, the arrival of Jason Jorjani. He usually wears a turtleneck sweater under a cheap suit, reminding me of the sort of pretentious teenager who walks around with a copy of Nietzsche just visible in his jacket pocket but who has never actually read it. Standing at the podium, Jorjani declared:

> Something momentous took place this winter of 2016–2017, and I'm not talking about the inauguration of President Trump. I'm referring to a development that was catalysed by the rise of Trump but in the long run will prove to be even more significant for the redemption and revitalisation of our world. The three most substantial and influential institutions of the alternative right, or new right movement came together to form a centralised power structure.[2]

The new venture saw the amalgamation of Arktos Media Ltd, the web media group Red Ice Creations, and the National Policy Institute (NPI) think-tank led by Richard Spencer. The new group, christened the Alt-Right Corporation, had a single board and an office in Washington, DC. Jorjani argued that this represented:

> nothing less than the integration of all of the [...] European right-wing schools of thought [i.e. the New Right (Nouvelle Droite), Archeofuturism, Identitarianism, and Aleksandr Dugin's Fourth Political Theory] with the North American vanguard movement most responsible for the electoral victory of President Trump.[3]

With remarkable pomposity, Jorjani genuinely seemed to believe that the alt-right was the determining factor in Trump's election – and also that the launch of his new organisation was more important. Despite the absurdity of both claims, the launch of the Alt-Right Corporation was indeed a crucial moment in the development of the movement. It further illustrated the extent of the convergence between the American far right and the European New Right (as well as its noted philosophical tributaries) and signalled an ambition to build a more formalised structure at the heart of a diffuse and decentralised movement.

I hurried out of the conference hall into the Stockholm night and made straight for Expo's offices. By the time I arrived they had already downloaded the pictures and begun to identify attendees. The operation had been a complete success. However, as we headed out for celebration drinks I thought back to 2013 and the intelligence report I wrote following the NPI conference in Washington, and how I had scoffed at the alt-right's confidence: 'After what fall?' In the intervening years, I had watched Marine Le Pen's Front National storm to victory, Hungary's Jobbik finish second, and Greece's neo-Nazi Golden Dawn get 9.4% of the vote in the 2014 European Parliamentary elections. Then came the rise of the alt-right and the previously unthinkable election victory of Donald Trump and Brexit in 2016. The pillars of liberal democracy that felt so unshakable back then had indeed begun to tremble. When writing up my intelligence report I noted how this latest conference was called 'Rising From the Ruins' – but this time I wasn't so quick to label it mere hubris.

The International Alternative Right is not what it once was. At its peak it was the most dynamic and worrying international far-right threat. Today it is more of a fragmented network than a cohesive movement. However, most of the key figures are still active and many continue to collaborate. Generally speaking, the alt-right is an international set of groups and individuals, operating primarily online though with offline outlets, whose core belief is that 'white identity' is under attack from pro-multicultural liberal elites and so-called 'social justice warriors' (SJWs) who allegedly use 'political correctness' to undermine Western civilisation and the rights of white males.

Put simply, the Alternative Right is a far-right, anti-globalist grouping that offers a radical 'alternative' to traditional/establishment conservatism. It is a many-headed hydra, an amorphous and mainly online political movement composed of a vast array of blogs, vlogs, websites and podcasts with no single leader and only a few offline organisations of note, none of which fully control the movement's direction. The eclectic and disparate nature of its constituent parts makes for large areas of disagreement yet, together, they are united around a core set of beliefs. All its adherents reject what they believe to be the left-wing, liberal democratic cultural hegemony in Western society and the rights derived from it. They reject what leading alt-right figure Jared Taylor has called the 'dangerous myth' of equality – which, in practice, means opposition to, *inter alia*, the rights of women, LGBT+ persons and ethnic and religious minorities; or, if not these rights, at the very least the movements themselves that seek to advance those rights, such as feminism.[4]

Due to the broadness of this definition it is necessary to subdivide the Alternative Right into two distinct branches:

the 'alt-right' and the 'alt-lite'. While both reject left/
liberal democratic hegemony and the rights, freedoms and/
or affiliated movements associated with it, and both are concerned with the same set of issues – the left, globalisation,
gender, the West, equality, and so on – they view these issues
through fundamentally different lenses. While both are
deeply critical of the conception of equality derived from
the liberal consensus, the core concern of the alt-right is the
threat it supposedly poses to the existence of white people,
and so they advocate for the protection of their 'race', usually through the creation of white ethno-states. As such, race
forms the basis of its worldview. As Richard Spencer, alt-right
figurehead, has claimed: 'almost every issue, political issue,
cultural issue, sports, everything, almost everything – is based
in race.'[5]

In contrast, the alt-lite perceives the liberal consensus as
a threat to traditional Western culture and so is in favour of
a Western chauvinist nationalism. Doubtless, both strands
express an interest in the topic that forms the basis of the
other's worldview. The alt-lite bemoans notions such as 'white
guilt' and 'white privilege', while the alt-right frequently talks
of pan-European civilisation and venerates classical Western
culture. The difference comes down to the significance each
places on these concepts. Gavin McInnes, a once prominent
figure in the alt-lite, summed this up when he stated:

> Both sides have in common Western Chauvinism, they're
> not embarrassed about Whiteness [...], they don't think
> diversity is the be all and end all, but [the alt-lite] cares
> about Western Chauvinism and ideas. [The alt-right] says
> 'whites have to be a part of this', [the alt-lite] is inclusive
> and wants everyone to be friends as long as you accept

the Western world as the best and refuse to apologise for creating the modern world.[6]

While the Alternative Right was a distinct far-right movement, it is not an aberration conjured into existence in the last decade, nor was it born of fundamentally novel far-right ideas. Rather its distinctiveness is derived from the fact that it is a conglomeration of existing political and social movements that when fused together, created something new and different. It is, at its core, a convergence of three broad groups: the European New Right and Identitarian movement, the American Alternative Right, and 'online antagonistic communities' (all described in more detail below). Each of these has its own history, structures, groupings and ideas and in some cases continues to operate quite independently of the Alternative Right; but when the three overlap and interact they produce what can be understood as the Alternative Right.

The leading Swedish alt-right figure Daniel Friberg once explained to an ABC News reporter that the alt-right 'is basically a global phenomenon, the American alt-right is heavily inspired by the New Right from France and Germany and Belgium especially'.[7] The European New Right (ENR) is, broadly speaking, a current of thought derived from the ideas of the far-right philosopher Alain de Benoist and his GRECE movement that was founded in France in 1968, along with subsequent strains of thought/activism such Guillaume Faye's Archeofuturism,* Aleksandr Dugin's Eurasianism,** and the

* A term coined by Faye to describe the combination of futuristic technology and science with traditional or 'archaic' values.
** Eurasianism is the concept that Russian civilisation belongs to the geopolitical concept of Eurasia.

European Identitarian movement which is discussed at length in the next chapter. The ENR sits comfortably within the far right and its ideas are best understood as a quest for the recovery of a mythical European identity. It fundamentally rejects the ideals of the Enlightenment and of Christianity, and fights back against 'materialist' and modern ideologies from liberalism to socialism. Instead, it posits a pan-European nationalism and a world of ethnically homogeneous communities.[8] Despite the explicit anti-Americanism of much of the ENR, the ideological core of the Alternative Right emerged when elements of ENR thought were adopted by the American far right, as we saw above. (By the American far right I mean the US-based radical or non-conservative right wing, including nazi and white supremacist individuals and groups, anti-government militias, and elements of the Ku Klux Klan.)

However, the blend of ENR ideas with the American far right can only be considered the Alternative Right when it is also merged with what can be termed 'online antagonistic communities'. These are defined as reactionary online groups built around various interests, but who all engage in exclusionary, antagonistic behaviour (be it through trolling, creating offensive symbolism, or just espousing and voicing hatred and contempt). These groups are found on all sides of the political spectrum or can be completely non-political, but when this behaviour is adopted by those within the Alternative Right their antagonism is directed at what they perceive as the left/liberal political and social hegemony.

In addition there is a plethora of smaller movements, cultures and communities, elements of which have contributed in varying degrees to the Alternative Right. Though many of them have continued to exist separately from the Alternative

Right as broader ideological movements, they maintained large areas of crossover in terms of ideas and cooperation when the movement was at its peak, acting, for some, as gateways into it. The three most significant are the Manosphere and the Neoreactionary and right-libertarian movements. According to Simon Murdoch, the Manosphere is:

> a loose collection of websites, forums, blogs and vlogs concerned with men's issues and masculinity, oriented around an opposition to feminism and, within parts, embrace of extreme misogyny. The prevailing interpretation within the manosphere is that feminism is about promoting misandry (contempt or prejudice of men) rather than gender equality. This perception is central to understanding the manosphere, for whilst many of its interests and ideas are inherently sexist, anti-feminist and misogynistic, others, such as concerns about male suicide, are not themselves expressions of these. Rather, they are viewed in the manosphere through a lens which places the blame for such issues at the feet of women, feminism and progressive politics.[9]

Patrik Hermansson has explained how 'The Alternative Right and libertarians cross paths time and time again. [...] While many in the Alternative Right have publicly renounced libertarianism, often with the motivation that it is too lax on immigration and socially "deviant" behaviour, some have openly identified with it.'[10] The hardest to define of these three gateways into the Alternative Right is the often strange, impenetrable and esoteric Neoreactionary movement. Broadly speaking, Neoreaction is a far-right, anti-democratic movement that rejects Enlightenment principles and seeks to meld a regressive return to a monarchical past with a fetishised post-human future. In addition to these are numerous movements whose ideas have been of interest to elements within the Alternative Right, such as the right-wing nationalist conservativism known in America as paleoconservatism, survivalism and even right-wing national anarchism.[11]

One misconception is that the Alternative Right is either completely novel or nothing more than a cynical rebranding exercise for the traditional far right. As is often the case, the truth is somewhere in the middle. This movement is indeed replete with individuals and organisations whose far-right activism long predates the adoption of the term alt-right, such as Jared Taylor and Greg Johnson in the United States, and many have indeed adopted it in an attempt to launder their image. However, the Alternative Right, while an amorphous conglomerate of disparate and sometimes even contradictory beliefs, can and should be understood as a distinct, modern, international far-right movement. This requires using the term 'alt-right' in a narrower sense than many do at present, and rejecting its use as a catch-all term for any modern far-right activist or individual.

There are a number of individuals who either did, or still do, self-define as alt-right, such as the editor of the website The Daily Stormer, Andrew Anglin, who many would argue are nothing other than traditional neo-nazis. However, this doesn't make the two categories mutually exclusive. While it is true that not everyone in the alt-right is a nazi, not every nazi is part of the alt-right, though some are. Anglin, for example, is part of the alt-right, partly because he self-identifies as such, but more importantly because of the nature of his nazi activism – the means by which he does politics, the method by which he propagates his ideology, is all alt-right in nature.

Like the alt-right more generally, his ideas lack novelty, but his activism does not.

One key element to understanding the alt-right is its genuinely transnational nature. Many of its core activists conceptualise their struggle beyond the borders of their nation-state: the alt-right is concerned with a transnational white 'nation' and the alt-lite a transnational mythical West or Occident. That said, like numerous other transnational far-right movements, there remains a tension between this and more traditional nation-state nationalism. While Richard Spencer has said he is 'ambivalent about America',[12] and alt-lite vlogger Paul Joseph Watson talks much more about 'the West' than Britain or the USA,[13] the mobilising factors for Alternative Right activists often remain national or even hyper-local. This, of course, is not a signifier of novelty – numerous earlier transnational far-right movements operated similarly, be that Colin Jordan's World Union of National Socialists in the 1960s or the post-9/11 anti-Muslim counter-jihad movement, to name just two.[14]

It was October 2016 and the first time I had been back to the campus of the London School of Economics since I had graduated some years earlier. Tucked away behind the Royal Courts of Justice is a warren of buildings between Kingsway and Aldwych that make up the university. I took a seat in the George IV pub and looked out of the window to the nondescript red-brick building that housed the Cañada Blanch Centre, where I had spent a year transfixed by Professor Paul Preston's lectures on the Spanish Civil War. We had bonded over a shared love of Everton Football Club and a shared hatred of Francisco Franco. The George IV is a proper pub with wooden floors and a decorative plaster ceiling stained yellow by decades of smoking. I was there to meet a friend of a friend.

For some years, I had known Anna-Sofia Quensel, an expert on the Scandinavian far right. She was an intriguing character who would nonchalantly mention her time among the IRA or her loose links to the Baader Meinhof Gang in the 1970s in between anecdotes about playing Pokémon with her grandchildren. A friend of hers, a young anti-fascist called Patrik Hermansson, was moving to London to study and she asked if I would meet with him. We sat opposite each other with all the usual awkwardness of a blind date. Slight with blond hair, square jaw, pale skin and rosy cheeks, conventionally handsome and dressed all in black, he was the most Scandinavian-looking person I had ever seen; the Aryan archetype. He had worked in Sweden with Expo as a photographer and expressed an interest in doing the same for HOPE not hate while in London. There were far-right demonstrations happening most weekends so I thanked him for the offer, assured him I would check how we could best use him, finished my drink and left. As I walked back to Holborn tube station, I called Nick and told him I had an idea.

With hindsight, I could pretend that from that first meeting I knew Patrik was special, the sort of person who could rapidly gain access to some of the most influential far-right figures in the world; that he would be so successful that the story would be made into a documentary screened on TV around the world. Of course, in truth, I had no idea. Patrik certainly seemed sharp and intelligent and had a quiet confidence that made me like him, but the initial plan was merely to ask if he might be interested in attending one upcoming far-right event.

My time doing infiltration work was coming to an end. While some remarkable people go undercover and stay there for years or even decades, I had merely jumped briefly in and out of groups for very short periods, exposed them and moved on. At the same time, I had attended countless far-right demonstrations, often with a camera, meaning I was increasingly recognised among the UK far right. This was compounded by me publishing academically and journalistically under my own name. All this made it unwise and unsafe for me to continue this sort of work, meaning the next logical step was for me to start recruiting others and running the operations. Though I never told him at the time, Patrik was the first person I properly set out to recruit and run. My only other experience in this area came via a colleague, an infectiously likeable person who was also an unusually talented undercover source, and who I looked after more as a collaborator than a formal handler. Though never admitted publicly, their brave work over the next year proved vital to the success of Patrik's project.

A few days later I rang and invited Patrik for another drink. We talked at length, first the usual pleasantries about how he was finding London, the LSE and his course. I had spent the week doing background checks and already spoken with our partners at Expo to ensure he was 'kosher', but I probed more deeply into his politics, history of activism and knowledge about the modern far right. We moved on to how public his anti-fascist work had been in Sweden and what his online footprint looked like. There is no point trying to recruit someone to go undercover who is well known to be left-wing. Most importantly, though, I silently judged his temperament and nature. Is he a bigmouth? Can he keep a secret? Does he have the nerve? Is he stable? Can he lie? Can he lie well?

Is he lying now? We went outside for a cigarette, and trying my hardest to sound casual I asked if he might be interested in going to an upcoming meeting for me. 'I can sort it all out for you, you'd just need to go along, listen and report back.' There was no point thinking beyond the first hurdle or making grand plans, as many understandably quickly decide this sort of work isn't for them. 'Yeah, I'll do it', he said, without realising he had changed both of our lives.

For some time, I had been looking for someone to get deep inside the London Forum, a fascist group that organised regular meetings. It attracted figures from across the far right to listen to talks delivered by some of the biggest names in the international scene. Importantly, at a time when the British extreme right was splintered and divided there was a danger that the Forum could help bring about a new unity, something we were keen to disrupt. It was run by Jeremy Bedford-Turner, a disgraced soldier turned notorious fascist whom I had met previously on several occasions. Back in September 2013 I had accompanied him to a meeting at the Tramshed Community Centre in Bethnal Green to commemorate the twentieth anniversary of the election of Derek Beackon as the BNP's first-ever councillor. I had met the group next to the half-built Bethnal Green Tube Disaster Memorial and, struggling for conversation, mentioned how it was about time we remembered those who had died in the single largest loss of civilian life during the Second World War. I had completely misjudged the crowd. Thinking I would ingratiate myself with patriotism, I had unwittingly betrayed my lack of support for the Luftwaffe.

The initial idea was for Patrik to get inside the London Forum and find the schisms and pressure points on which we could push. At that point, the limited information I had on the group all came via the work of another source, who had been attending their meetings for some time. The slow drip-feed of information they were providing was invaluable and we didn't want to compromise it by pushing too hard. With Patrik, however, I knew we had just one year before he finished his course and returned home, making the higher-risk strategy of an intense operation, targeted directly at the group's leadership, a chance worth taking. We built a backstory, manufactured a believable online persona – Patrik Hermansson became Erik Hellberg – and made our approach. Over the next six months he worked his way to the very heart of the Forum, building a close relationship with the organisation's key players.

Stead Steadman was a comical figure. Almost always dressed in a khaki shirt, khaki shorts and hiking boots, whatever the weather, he looked like an instructor in the Hitler Youth. His absurd appearance had led us to write him off, but Patrik became convinced that he was the key to the whole group. He was the organiser, the networker, the keeper of the black book of addresses that held the names and details of some of the most notorious fascists in the world. Patrik struck up a friendship and became Steadman's Swedish teacher, meeting him at the Nordic Baker in Soho to practise. So trusted did he become that he was even invited to join the team that vetted new members, giving us unprecedented access to the inner workings of the group and a real say in who could and couldn't join. With each new success, the scope of the operation was expanded until we decided to use Steadman's contacts to gain access to as many major players in the international alt-right as possible.

My admiration for Patrik's bravery and determination grew with every meeting. He agreed to everything I asked him to do, however dangerous or outlandish. When I suggested he wear a secret camera and record all his meetings he nodded like I had asked him to get me some peanuts during his round. Each of his intelligence reports was packed with more valuable information than the last. We soon moved beyond the source/handler relationship and began to become friends, bonded by our common mission and common trust. In our own little way, we felt like we were fighting to change the world. However, that made things much harder for me, as I was now asking a friend to take ever-increasing risks with his own safety. It became impossible to distance myself from the operation, to separate work from life. The higher he climbed the better the information – but the more the danger and the less I slept as a result.

By manufacturing a fake university thesis exploring left-wing suppression of the far right we could fast-track the project and encourage Steadman to make introductions to key alt-right figures for Patrik to 'interview'. We soon acquired hundreds of hours of secret footage of conversations, giving us an unprecedented understanding of the internal workings of the alt-right – still then a much-misunderstood movement. We also gathered reams of gossip related to internal fights and power struggles that were useful for stoking division. Alongside running this project, I and my HNH colleagues David Lawrence and Simon Murdoch were simultaneously producing a major report into the alt-right that set out to properly define and map it. Patrik's information guided every element of it, allowing us to marry our open-source research with his first-hand knowledge.

Once secure within the London Forum, Patrik began to move between groups in the UK, attending ludicrous meetings of the Extremist Club to hear bad poetry and worse politics, and partaking in racist pagan ceremonies where they drank from horns and worshipped Nordic gods. We then decided that to get to the heart of the movement he would have to head across the Atlantic to the home of the alt-right. In the US he gave a speech about the dangers of anti-fascist infiltration at an alt-right meeting in Seattle, and attended a barbecue at the home of the infamous Nazi ceramicist Charles Krafft – famous for his Hitler teapots. In August 2017, strapped up with a secret camera, he travelled to Charlottesville, Virginia, and attended the Unite the Right rally. Surrounded by heavily-armed extremists waving swastika flags and chanting 'Jews will not replace us', he saw first-hand the deadly consequences of fascism when Heather Heyer, an anti-fascist counter-protester, was mown down by a car in front of him. When he told me he was just metres away I nearly threw up. By this stage, we had already begun discussions with a production company about making a documentary, and I was desperate to bring the project to an end and pull Patrik out.

Beyond defining what the Alternative Right is, it is worth exploring the movement's brief history.

Generally accepted as a significant catalyst in the development of the Alternative Right was so-called Gamergate, ostensibly an effort to protect the male safe space of gaming from the perceived onslaught of feminist values. This was triggered in August 2014 after a spurned boyfriend alleged that his ex-girlfriend – a female game developer – had been unfaithful. Denizens of the manosphere and the online message boards 4chan and 8chan (which have long harboured far-right elements) then unleashed a torrent of abuse, including rape and death threats, against female game developers and critics.[15] For many, Gamergate became symbolic of a broader fightback against 'political correctness' and the left more generally. By reporting favourably on the movement, figures like the British alt-lite social media personality and one-time Breitbart News Network journalist Milo Yiannopoulos were able to greatly increase their own profiles in the ensuing scandal. The experience of engaging in coordinated online campaigning against their supposed antagonists encouraged the emerging Alternative Right as a whole.

However, it was Donald Trump's presidential campaign, launched in June 2015, that provided the momentum that brought the disparate parts of the Alternative Right together and elevated them onto the international stage. Trump had outsider status, a haphazard and unorthodox approach, extreme immigration stances, and – most importantly – was wildly politically incorrect. Moreover, he was running against Hillary Clinton, who was viewed as embodying the liberal, 'feminist' establishment. All this made Trump a magnet for the alt-lite and alt-right, both of which saw him as a means of disrupting the Republican establishment and liberal consensus. The difference was that while the alt-lite may have held a genuine belief that Trump's anti-immigration, anti-Muslim stances closely allied with its own politics, the alt-right regarded him more as a means to shift the 'Overton window' (the boundaries of acceptable debate) far to the right, with the ultimate goal of normalising race-based politics. Through Trump, the white nationalist alt-right entered a symbiotic relationship with figures on the more moderate online right wing, with commentators such as the British conspiracy vlogger Paul Joseph Watson and Breitbart News' Milo Yiannopoulos using many of the same inflammatory, mocking insults and images to attack the left and the establishment right.

Breitbart News Network, known for its vitriolic attacks on liberal groups, immigrants and mainstream conservatives alike, became the engine room for far-right pro-Trump propaganda.[16] In March 2016, Breitbart published 'An Establishment Conservative's Guide to the Alt-Right' by Yiannopoulos and Allum Bokhari, which, while disavowing openly nazi elements, also downplayed much of the movement's racism as mere trolling.[17] In July 2016, Steve Bannon, then executive chairman of Breitbart News and chief strategist to Donald Trump, told *Mother Jones* that Breitbart was 'the platform for the alt-right'.[18] The oft-repeated philosophy 'don't punch right' – i.e. do not attack more extreme elements with whom you share a common purpose – gave the racist alt-right cover. With the obvious exception of the nazi alt-right site, The Daily Stormer, which was generally deeply antagonistic to alt-lite figures, the racists largely tolerated these moderate figures while it remained expedient, despite obvious ideological differences (Yiannopoulos, for example, is an openly gay man who claims Jewish heritage). Richard Spencer, leading alt-right figurehead, told the *Daily Beast* in August 2016 that Breitbart acted as a 'gateway to alt-right ideas and writers'.[19]

Following Trump's victory, confrontation emerged between the alt-lite and alt-right on 21 November 2016, when Spencer's National Policy Institute staged its annual conference, featuring leading far/alt-right figures such as Jared Taylor,[20] Kevin MacDonald[21] and Peter Brimelow[22] – forebears of the racist alt-right – as speakers. Footage was released by *The Atlantic* showing Spencer delivering a speech laden with antisemitism and ending histrionically with the words 'Hail Trump, hail our people, hail victory!', leading several members of the audience to throw Nazi salutes.[23] This sparked worldwide negative press attention and more moderate figures quickly distanced themselves. Trump supporters who found themselves uncomfortable staring the openly racist alt-right in the face began abandoning the term en masse.

The beginning of the end for the cohering alt-right came on 12 August 2017 at the Unite the Right rally in Charlottesville, Virginia. Announced in the context of escalating violence at alt-right events, Unite the Right was intended to be the moment that the primarily online-based movement demonstrated that its various factions and figures could stand in solidarity for white nationalism, wielding power on the streets against all opposition. As events transpired, Unite the Right was defined by ferocious violence that resulted in dozens of injuries, culminating in the death of Heather Heyer after James Fields, a self-described neo-nazi, drove a car into a crowd of counter-protesters. In 2019, at a US District Court in Charlottesville, Fields pleaded guilty to 28 federal counts of hate crime acts causing bodily injury and involving an attempt to kill, and one count of a hate crime act that resulted in death.[24] Later, in November 2021, a jury awarded more than $25 million in damages against key far-right organisers of the rally. While the alt-right has long attempted to portray itself as a fresh alternative to stale, thuggish, traditional American white supremacism, in the wake of Charlottesville media outlets across the globe were adorned with images of leading alt-right figures alongside Nazi flags, Klansmen and shield-and-helmet-clad activists with makeshift weapons. The scope of negative coverage was magnified by President Trump's failure to adequately condemn the white supremacists, even describing some of the protesters as 'very fine people'.[25]

Charlottesville was a hubristic attempt to capitalise on the momentum of Trump's election, but instead gave the alt-right its most infamous moment. While some alt-right figures attempted to claim the abortive event as a victory, Charlottesville significantly intensified negative attention on the alt-right. In the aftermath it has found itself operating in a more hostile environment, and one that became even harder after the widespread crackdowns following the storming of the Capitol Building in 2021, which numerous prominent alt-right figures took part in. The alt-right will forever be associated with the events of Charlottesville, and while the demonstration brought worldwide attention, it also marked the moment that the movement went into sharp decline. The years that have followed have been marked by infighting and splits, paradoxically meaning that 'Unite the Right' was the catalyst for the disintegration of many of the already tenuous links that held this 'movement' together.

Charlottesville does not represent the wholesale collapse of the alt-right in America and abroad, but it nevertheless resulted in significant tactical shifts and altered the nature of the movement. While the alt-right undoubtedly endured a long and bruising few years following Charlottesville, the miserable attendance at Unite the Right 2 in 2018 did not signify the death of the movement, but rather a change in tack. The still active contingent of the alt-right has moved away from the streets and continued to host private conferences, bringing together the biggest American and European names in the alt-right and providing networking opportunities and fostering a sense of community. Speeches are subsequently uploaded to YouTube and other sites, continuing to radicalise a new generation of young far-right activists. The alt-right trolls still plague social media, the alt-right content producers still pump out endless hours of videos and podcasts, alt-right writers still publish reams of articles and alt-right organisers still hold conferences around the world with well-known figures travelling to speak at them. Just because the alt-right does not collectively identify or seek to demonstrate together as they did in Charlottesville, does not mean that the alt-right does not exist. The movement was always a decentralised, distributed network, and it is merely more decentralised once again.

———

The biggest intelligence score of the whole Patrik infiltration came in May 2017 at a memorial dinner for the late British fascist Jonathan Bowden. Patrik had been tipped off by Steadman that one of the guests at the event would be none other than the leading US alt-right figure Greg Johnson. Editor-in-chief of the white supremacist imprint Counter-Currents Publishing, Johnson was a ghost. Despite being one of the key players in the US far right for years, no one had ever managed to secure a picture of him, allowing him to carry out his ugly politics in the shadows. Anti-fascists had been trying to track him down but he had remained elusive, speaking only at closed meetings and always having his face blurred in pictures and videos. I even heard a story that someone got hold of his old school yearbook only to find his picture had been removed. Upon discovering he was to be in London we mounted a full operation to ensure we caught him on film. Through Steadman we knew the meeting was to take place at the Mandeville Hotel, just off Wigmore Street in swanky Marylebone. Patrik was wired up with a tiny camera strapped to his chest, while another colleague, Rosie Carter, posed as a tourist and sat in the lobby reading a book and messaging me information.

I took up a position down the road outside a juice bar with a long lens camera hidden under a coat and pointed towards the hotel's entrance. I was soon clocked by Johnson's thuggish security guards, who walked over and took a seat at my table. Feigning surprise that two men in black suits had sat down and started asking questions, I told them I was just waiting for my girlfriend to finish work. We talked for a few minutes until I thought I had convinced them of my story, but as they stood up and walked past the hidden camera the lens made a whirring sound as its autofocus sprang into action. They stared at the camera, then at me, and we made eye contact for just longer than comfortable before I grabbed the camera and made a run for it. I darted down the road into Selfridges department store, where I lost them in the maze of escalators. Thankfully Patrik had more luck and captured crystal-clear images of Johnson which we later published with glee. It was a huge scoop for HOPE not hate and achieved one of our core goals for the whole project: to let the international far right know that the UK was no longer a safe place for them to do business.

We blew the lid on the whole operation on 19 September 2017. Patrik, Nick and I travelled to the US to negotiate a deal with the *New York Times*, who were understandably interested in Patrik's secret footage of Jason Jorjani in New York boasting about his links to the Trump administration. We agreed that they would publish an article about the whole infiltration and we would simultaneously release our much larger report: *The International Alternative Right: From Charlottesville to the White House*. Patrik's boyfriend flew out to New York to support him at what must have been a terrifying time for both of them. I remember him climbing into a taxi with Patrik and me on Flatbush Avenue in Brooklyn and asking us not to talk about what was going to happen. He didn't want to think about it. It was only then

I truly realised the toll that the project must have taken on Patrik's loved ones as well as on him. I had no doubt his partner must have hated me because of what I asked Patrik to do, and I didn't blame him for it.

As expected, the story exploded on publication, with news outlets all over the world picking it up. Importantly, it had the desired effect within the far right. Fingers were pointed, schisms emerged and major splits occurred. The London Forum hasn't had a meeting since, meaning the number of major far-right figures coming to the UK has reduced. The documentary we were making hit choppy water and passed across the desk of numerous well-known directors before finally, and thankfully, being picked up by SVT in Sweden and given to the documentary film-maker Bosse Lindquist. It aired on primetime TV slots around the world, from Germany to Japan, before eventually being released on streaming services.

Of course, all this came at a cost. While Patrik now works for HOPE not hate as a researcher, he still lives with the shadow of danger over his life. Some months after publication we did a special event at the Frontline Club in London, and it was only because of another undercover source that we found out fascists were planning to attack it. When they did turn up we had security in place to get him to safety, but it was a useful reminder of the cost to Patrik's life. If fascism didn't die with the revelation of the gas chambers we knew we certainly weren't going to kill it with an article in the *New York Times* or with a film documentary. But we did land a punch, push back just a little bit – and best of all, we did it together.

8

IDENTITARIANS AT SEA AND ON LAND

'It's in Djibouti!'

'What's in Djibouti?'

'The *C-Star*. It's in Djibouti!'

'Where's Djibouti?'

'I don't know.'

'Anyone?' I said, looking at the blank faces across the office.

On 26 June 2017, Defend Europe announced that they had secured a ship. Their plan was to sail into the Mediterranean and hinder refugee rescue missions. For several years, increasing numbers of people had been heading to Europe either overland via south-eastern Europe or by making the perilous journey across the sea from North Africa to Italy or Spain. Fleeing the bloody civil war in Syria and the ongoing conflicts in Afghanistan and Iraq, refugees clambered into all manner of boats and inflatable rafts and headed north for safety. Each week the newspapers were full of alarmist headlines of invasion and passing references to the ever-increasing death toll as overcrowded boats sank with tragic regularity.

In May that year, my colleague Simon Murdoch, a bookish, youthful man who cuts his own hair with surprisingly impressive results, noticed that three members of the European far-right movement Generation Identity (GI), accompanied by the Canadian alt-lite journalist Lauren Southern, had been detained by the Italian coastguard. They had been stopped after a failed attempt to block the *Aquarius*, a vessel operated by the NGO SOS Mediterranée with an onboard medical team from Médecins Sans Frontières, from leaving the port of Catania in Sicily and travelling towards Libya on a rescue mission. Southern published a video in which GI fired a flare towards the *Aquarius* as she proudly declared: 'If the politicians won't stop the boats, then we'll stop the boats!' At HOPE not hate we spend our days looking at nasty people doing bad things, but there was something about the sight of far-right activists openly trying to hinder the rescue of desperate and dying migrants that made an uncommon anger spread through the research team. For the next four months, it became an obsession for us as we fought desperately to disrupt their plans.

In the weeks that followed the stunt in Sicily we watched as it developed into a campaign called 'Defend Europe', made up of Identitarian activists from across the continent. They began to fundraise to charter a ship to follow search-and-rescue vessels, document their activities and 'confront' them by blockading them on the seas. Their aim was to force the NGO ships to alter their routes and drain their financial and organisational resources, as well as inspire others to support the mission. Their plans were greeted with widespread enthusiasm from the international far right and money began to pour in, especially from North America. A crowdfunding campaign quickly raised nearly €100,000, with international figures such as David Duke, former Grand Wizard of the Ku Klux Klan, tweeting to his 40,000 Twitter followers: 'Defend Europe Identitarian SAR has a ship, now needs money to

get to the Mediterranean. Donate now! #DefendEurope.'
Similarly, the world's leading neo-nazi website, The Daily
Stormer, published an article stating:

> This is a great initiative ... These parasites need to be
> inculcated with a deep fear of making the trip across the
> Mediterranean sea. Right now, the Negroes believe that
> Europeans will come and pick them up to bring them
> to our countries ... Godspeed, men. Your ancestors are
> proud.

Defend Europe showed just how international the contemporary far right had become – and the danger they posed when
collaborating across borders.

A funk set in as each day we turned up at the office and
helplessly watched their fundraiser climb ever higher. We had
to find their ship. If we couldn't find it we couldn't stop it.
Then on 26 June we had our first break when they triumphantly declared they had secured the services of a vessel and
put a picture online. However, we couldn't find the vessel on
any register; it was a ghost. The breakthrough came when
we realised the image had been doctored – the colour of the
ship had been changed and it had been given a fake name,
with a view to trolling those of us on the trail. The original
picture showed a ship called *Heqet*, the name of an ancient
Egyptian goddess who was depicted as a frog. This could
have been a reference to an in-joke popular within alt-right
circles, known as 'Kek' or the 'Cult of Kek', which is a satiri-
cal religion centred on the worship of an ancient Egyptian
deity depicted as a frog; or perhaps it referred to the infamous
Pepe the Frog meme favoured by the less amusing members of
the alt-right. In reality the ship was a Finnish-made research

vessel named *Suunta*, later renamed the *C-Star*. At 40 metres long and 422 tonnes it was a proper ship, much larger than I had envisaged. It was a world away from the small raft used by Lauren Southern in Sicily back in May. This actually had the capacity to stop rescue ships, and a shiver of concern ran through the NGO community. With only a hazy idea of Defend Europe's plans, workers in the refugee sector in the Med began to contact us asking for help. Were they going to ram their ships? Might they attack their workers? What would happen if they actually came into contact with refugees? We didn't have answers. What started as a far-right pipedream had become a reality. A reality that could genuinely put the lives of refugees at risk.

Once we had the name of the ship we could really start digging. Using satellite technology we soon tracked it down. 'It's in Djibouti!' cried Simon. A wave of excitement followed by relief spread through the team when we realised the ship wasn't yet in the Mediterranean but rather in East Africa. We had a chance to slow it down.

The World Shipping Directory showed that it was managed by a UK-based company that provided 'guard vessels, chase vessels, survey vessels and offshore maintenance and accommodation vessels'. The owner of the ship transpired to be a Mr Sven Tomas Egerstrom, whose Swedish records showed he had been convicted of fraud in 2002 and sentenced to prison for two and a half years. The nagging question of 'What sort of person rents out a vessel to the far right?' had finally been answered. When we contacted him to ask whether he was comfortable with his boat being used in such a manner, he simply replied: 'We don't take political places or stance in a commercial business for any grounds. [...] I don't see any problem with the vessel being in the area conducting legal research.' Clearly not everyone was as angry about this issue as I was.

This became even clearer when on 17 July the controversial British 'journalist' Katie Hopkins tweeted: 'Looking forward to meeting the crew of the *C-Star* in Catania tomorrow. Setting out to defend the Med. All this week @MailOnline.' She also retweeted the Defend Europe Twitter account among other clearly supportive gestures. It now seemed that she was actually going to accompany Martin Sellner, Defend Europe's leader, and his fellow Identitarians on their mission and report it live on the website of the *Daily Mail*, one of Britain's biggest-selling newspapers. Hopkins had form in this area: several years earlier she had penned a vile newspaper article which included a section that read: 'NO, I don't care. Show me pictures of coffins, show me bodies floating in water, play violins and show me skinny people looking sad. I still don't care'; and 'Bring on the gunships, force migrants back to their shores and burn the boats'.

As soon as we knew Hopkins was on her way to Sicily we swung into action. I wrote an article for the *Guardian* calling out the *Daily Mail*, we launched a public petition, and behind the scenes we pulled together a private letter signed by a host of influential individuals and organisations that was sent to the editor of the *Mail*. Thankfully the response was swift, and the first article Hopkins penned from Catania soon disappeared from their websites, before she herself was returned to the UK. It was an extremely close shave. The most dangerous thing we could do was allow the far right to become normalised, and the thought of a major British newspaper providing positive media coverage to this mission would have been a disaster. This went beyond merely disagreeing with the opinions of Hopkins. It was really about the Mail Online – and any other media outlet that decided to offer a positive take on Defend Europe – playing a role in the mainstreaming of explicitly far-right and extremist people, organisations and narratives.

Rumours had started to circulate that the boat was ready to leave port, enter the Red Sea and head north towards the Suez Canal. As soon as the satellite tracker showed movement, we knew we had to change tack. I was keen to get a ship of our own and confront them; anti-fascism on the high seas! Fortunately, I was talked down and it was rightly explained to me that the last thing rescue NGOs needed was two groups of amateur ship handlers facing off and getting in the way of their life-saving work. Instead we hatched a plan. We knew that every day that passed without the *C-Star* being active off the coast of Libya was another day of funds wasted for Defend Europe. If we could just slow them down enough to drain their resources we could limit their potential to cause trouble and the number of days they could afford to stay active.

Compounding our fear was the prospect that the *C-Star* might have been carrying armed personnel. Daniel Fiss, leader of the German branch of GI, told a German website that the group would hire security staff ready to 'take action' against potentially armed human traffickers. Our concern grew when on 12 July the tracking satellite showed the *C-Star* meeting with another ship called the *Jupiter*, a vessel known to carry armed personnel. While we had no hard evidence, we worried that we were facing the prospect of a far-right ship in the Mediterranean with armed people on board. We contacted the Egyptian Embassy in London and the port authorities at Suez and raised our concerns about them allowing the *C-Star* through the canal. Unsure if our calls and letters had had any effect, we watched as the small yellow boat-shaped icon on our screens crept towards the canal. Every few hours Simon or I refreshed the screen as it passed Port Sudan, then Mecca and Jeddah, before sliding into the narrow passage of water that separates the Sinai Peninsula from mainland Egypt. Then it stopped. It was near the canal entrance but it wasn't moving. We refreshed the page again and again with no movement. What had happened? Had it worked? Nearly a week passed with the *C-Star* stalled in the Gulf of Suez.

We started to call the port authority and slowly began to get scraps of information in broken English. Unconfirmed accounts indicated that the ship might have been halted in dramatic circumstances, with the Egyptian navy surrounding the vessel and taking over responsibility. Eventually an employee at the Suez Canal Authority confirmed that the detaining of the ship had nothing to do with them but rather 'it was arrested by the security authorities', as it was 'a matter of security due to the lack of documentation and papers'. It was an embarrassing blow for Defend Europe, and we knew that every day that passed further stretched their resources. To our enormous delight, Martin Sellner released a video alongside the rest of the *C-Star*'s crew, waiting in Italy to board the vessel, blaming HOPE not hate for the delays. Our joy was short-lived, though, as the small yellow icon started to move north once more. We had slowed it down but we hadn't stopped it. Fully expecting the boat to make its way to Italy to pick up the Defend Europe crew, we dispatched Simon to Catania to monitor events from on the ground.

A man not built for the heat, Simon arrived in a sweltering Catania, a resplendent city of striking Catanese baroque architecture in the shadow of Mount Etna, scarred by centuries of earthquakes and eruptions. His job was to engage with the local resistance building on the ground and with other international NGOs such as the US non-profit organisation Avaaz, with a view to stopping the docking of the approaching *C-Star*. He tracked down Sellner and the others to some rented accommodation on Via Gagliani and began phoning in updates. Back in London I sat in the office and watched with dismay as the ship passed Port Said and finally entered the Mediterranean. By now, Defend Europe was big news. I spent my days speaking with journalists, appearing on radio and TV and frantically calling port authorities, the International Maritime Organization and the European Maritime Agency to try to find ways of slowing or stopping the *C-Star*. I was by no means alone: anti-fascists from across Europe, alongside migrant and refugee NGOs, were doing all they could. We were working closely with a group called Sleeping Giants who were at the forefront of the campaign to pressurise fundraising platforms to remove Defend Europe's webpages, with increasing success.

Rather than heading straight across the Mediterranean towards Italy, the ship tracked north towards Cyprus, possibly to take on much-needed supplies after its period of detention in Egypt. All attention turned towards the Cyprus Joint Rescue Coordination Center which, to my great excitement, confirmed that if the vessel entered Cypriot waters they would do all they could to stop it. Aware of the welcome they were likely to receive, the ship headed instead to the northern side of the island and the Turkish-controlled port of Famagusta. Using social media I found anti-racist activists in the area who fed back information in real time as the ship came into view of the dockside. Things then moved fast. Garbled messages and badly translated local news reports started to come in.

The ship's captain and his deputy had been arrested and the vessel was evacuated. In the most beautiful twist of fate, it emerged that the ship heading to Italy to begin a far-right mission to stop migration was allegedly carrying refugees hoping to reach Italy themselves. When I contacted the local police, they confirmed that: 'The crew members, the captain and the owner of the ship were arrested and they appeared before court today and the court decided on detention for one day.' They also acknowledged that they were aware of our research on Defend Europe and asked us to send on further information to help with their investigations.

It transpired that the owner and senior officers had been held for alleged 'people smuggling', after 21 South Asian men were found on board. Faika Pasa, a local human rights activist, spoke with some of the disembarked refugees: 'Some said they had paid €10,000 to smuggling rings to get on the ship and be taken to Italy. [...] Five have since requested asylum. The other fifteen have now flown back to Sri Lanka.' It was an embarrassing blow to Defend Europe and a moment of enormous relief. More good news came from Simon, whose work alongside countless others in Sicily had come to fruition when Enzo Bianco, the mayor of Catania, urged authorities in the port to deny docking rights to the *C-Star*.

Finally, on 31 July, after weeks of costly delays, Defend Europe activists finally managed to board the *C-Star* and begin their mission in earnest. Having spent over a month claiming they would triumphantly set sail from Catania – even summoning international press to the city for a supposed launch on 19 July – international and domestic pressure from NGOs, anti-racist organisations and politicians had forced them into a humiliating change of plan. Instead of the choreographed launch in front of the world's press, Defend Europe activists were forced to secretly scurry to Cyprus and board the ship there.

Over the next few weeks the *C-Star* headed towards the search and rescue zone off the Libyan coast and began to film NGO ships in the region. However, supplies soon began to run dry and they made for Tunisia to refuel and resupply. On hearing that the *C-Star* was heading towards the port of Zarzis, local fishermen organised and successfully blocked the ship, forcing them to look elsewhere for their much-needed supplies. Their inability to refuel became a real problem, and for some time they floated off Tunisia motionless. Documents later leaked to us suggest that the *C-Star* likely refuelled and took on supplies at the Ashtart Terminal, an oil terminal off the coast of Tunisia, before heading back towards the Libyan coast. However, on 11 August it suffered a 'minor technical problem' and authorities ordered the NGO, Sea-Eye, to go and rescue the stranded vessel.

By this point we were looking for the final nail in the coffin and in the end we got them on a technicality. The *C-Star* was an old and battered vessel and we realised that it might be possible to get the ship classified as unsafe. We spoke to numerous maritime experts who studied hundreds of images and raised serious concerns regarding its seaworthiness. Using their evidence we drew up a formal complaint and successfully requested an immediate inspection known as a Port State Control Inspection. It worked, and the *C-Star* was classified as 'Priority 1' – meaning the next time it entered any European port it would be stopped and inspected again. With all European ports no longer an option for supplies or fuel, the *C-Star* floated aimlessly. The final straw came on 17 August when an alliance of NGOs, both local and international, including HOPE not hate, managed to get the *C-Star* banned from all Maltese ports. Later that day Defend Europe announced the end of their mission. Despite their videos hailing it as a great success, they had managed to achieve none of their stated goals and had interfered with no rescue boats and put no lives at risk.

This short battle was a glimpse into the future of what fascism and anti-fascism will increasingly look like. The Identitarians behind Defend Europe were an international network of activists drawn from across Europe, raising support and money from far-right people all over the world. For us it was clear that effective anti-fascism no longer simply required us to know the enemy in our street or community or even our country. If we were to fight back effectively we had to think globally. It also showed us how the battlefield had fundamentally changed, and the tools required were new. While traditional anti-fascist campaigns – rooted in local communities, on the streets and through the ballot box – remained, a new front had opened. This wasn't about producing newspapers, leaflets or placards, it was about using satellites, pressurising multinational tech companies, shaping media narratives, and building new levels of international cooperation and support on social media.

Despite Defend Europe failing in its stated aims, this episode had hugely raised the profile of Identitarianism and gained them respect within the international far right. It soon transpired that among those watching adoringly were a group of young activists in the UK, and before long we would be facing GI a little closer to home.

In the autumn of 2012 a video was published online. A succession of young faces, captured in monochrome close-ups, took turns to speak slowly over a dramatic backing track of rising strings. They bemoaned the 'total failure of coexistence and forced mixing of the races', lamented society's 'rejection of tradition', rejected the 'global village' and the 'family of man', claimed their heritage from their 'land', their 'blood', their 'identity', and promised to 'march on the streets', paint slogans on the walls, and fly their 'lambda flags high'. As the strings reached a crescendo, a bearded figure looked straight into the camera and said in French: 'Don't think this is simply a manifesto. It is a declaration of war.' With that, Génération Identitaire (Generation Identity) was launched.

Seven years later, on 15 March 2019, a man armed with two semi-automatic rifles, two shotguns and a lever-action firearm entered the Al Noor mosque and the Linwood Islamic Centre in Christchurch, New Zealand during Friday prayers. The declaration of war made online had been acted on, and the result was 51 dead Muslims. The killer's manifesto was openly rooted in Identitarian ideology. Its very title – 'The Great Replacement' – is the central, alarmist idea perpetu-ated by groups like GI, and one of the manifesto's core demands – 'ethnic autonomy' – likewise corresponds to the Identitarian desire for 'ethnopluralism' (the idea that ethnic groups should live separately to 'preserve' them). Since the attack, it has emerged that the killer was not just inspired by Identitarian ideas, but had actually been in touch with GI's de facto leader Martin Sellner, and had donated signifi-cant sums to GI's branches in Austria and France. The Royal Commission of Enquiry in New Zealand found that the killer had made at least sixteen donations to international far-right groups and people since 2017, including a total of £2,500 to numerous branches of Generation Identity.[1] Later that same year another far-right activist burst into a synagogue in Halle, Germany, and fatally shot two people. During his court case the accused repeatedly mentioned the Identitarian conspiracy theory, the 'Great Replacement', and admitted to being inspired by the Christchurch attack and to having been in contact with GI before his own attack.[2] While Generation Identity and Identitarianism more generally isn't a terrorist ideology, its apocalyptic worldview that white people must act before they become extinct has inspired some to take extreme and violent action.

In many ways the Identitarian movement is a thoroughly modern one, making use of new technology and social media to spread its ideas and influence political debates. Identitarian activism as we think of it today found its earliest incarnation in 2003 with the creation of the Bloc Identitaire (BI) in France. BI (which turned into a party and then an association, 'Les Identitaires') helped nurture the country's Identitarian movement and, especially, the now independent youth organisation, Génération Identitaire, launched in 2012. However, what started as a French far-right youth movement spread across Europe, building a formal network of branches that today is just one part, albeit the largest, of a global and varied Identitarian scene. The movement has now found adherents in Russia, South America and Australia, and has growing influence in North America among the remnants of the alt-right. In 2019, Simon Murdoch and I released the report *From Banners to Bullets*, in which we profiled Identitarian organisations in 23 countries. Generation Identity was the most significant network with 63 regional branches in nine countries.[3]

Many of the ideas that make up the bedrock of this international grouping have in fact been around for over half a century and can be traced back to a European far-right movement known as the European New Right (ENR). As we saw in Chapter 7, the ENR emerged from the ideas of the French far-right philosopher Alain de Benoist and his GRECE organisation (Research and Study Group for European Civilisation), founded in 1968. De Benoist set out to create a right-wing movement that would be both modern and intellectual, operating via articulate publications and discussion groups.[4] The ENR claims to be an alternative to social democracy and conservative liberalism, a 'laboratory of ideas', a 'school of thought', a 'community of spirit' and a 'space of resistance against the system' that has transcended the existing left–right political schema.[5] Such claims can be dismissed, as scholars have clearly shown the movement's direct ideological parallels with classical fascism and the historical continuity from then, through post-war fascism, up to the emergence of the ENR in 1968. In reality, the ENR is certainly far-right, advocating for a Europe-wide form of nationalism and a world beyond that of ethnically homogeneous communities. It is anti-liberalism and anti-socialism and fundamentally rejects the ideals of the 18th-century Enlightenment and Christianity, instead harking back to a pagan past and mythical European identity.

GRECE came to be known as the French New Right (Nouvelle Droite) and in 1999 de Benoist and Charles Champetier published a synthesis of their first 30 years of thought as a *Manifesto for a European Renaissance*. In it, the duo talk of the 'Crisis of Modernity' and examine 'the main enemy', liberalism. In essence, de Benoist and Champetier argue that globalisation, liberalism and hypermodernism have led to the 'eradication of collective identities and traditional cultures'[6] and bemoan the 'unprecedented menace of homogenisation'[7] wrought by immigration, which – in blanket fashion – is held to be an 'undeniably negative phenomenon'.[8] In place of liberal multiculturalism, they call for 'ethnopluralism': the idea that different ethnic groups are equal but ought to live in separation from one another, as we saw above. This is coupled with the 'right to difference': 'The right of every people, ethnos, culture, nation, group, or community to live according to its own norms and traditions, irrespective of ideology or globalist homogenization',[9] as Guillaume Faye puts it. Furthermore, this right carries the assumption of 'cultural differentialism': the idea that there are 'lasting differences among and between cultures'.[10] It is these ideas that make up many of the core tenets of Identitarian ideology.

However, despite being the offspring of the ENR, Identitarianism is by no means identical. One major area of divergence is around the importance placed on race. While also being a racist movement, the ENR and de Benoist himself have excoriated the excesses of 'Identitarian tribalism' and deplored how Identitarians assign 'ethnic factors the role that Karl Marx assigned to economic factors'.[11] De Benoist's failure to place race front and centre is perhaps one of the reasons that many in the Identitarian movement have found greater affinity with the work of his one-time GRECE ally, Guillaume Faye, who was, in the later years of his life, much more open to overt racism. The divergence from de Benoist is best seen in Faye's adaptation of the Nouvelle Droite motto of 'Cause of peoples' to 'Cause of *our* people' and his criticism of de Benoist and his ENR colleagues for 'howling with the wolves against racism'.[12]

For many years the people and groups espousing these ideas 'perceived themselves as the rear guard of a dying world';[13] what Julius Evola described as 'men among the ruins'.[14] Yet over the last decade confidence has grown within the movement, and according to Philippe Vardon, a founder of the Identitarian movement in France: 'Far from being the last expression of a world in its death throes, [Identitarians] are the first pangs of a new birth.'[15] The 2013 book, *Die Identitäre Generation: Eine Kriegserklärung an die 68er* (*Generation Identity: A Declaration of War Against the '68ers*) by the Austrian Markus Willinger, is understood as the manifesto of the Identitäre Bewegung Österreich, the Austrian branch of the Identitarian movement. In it Willinger declares:

> A new political current is sweeping through Europe. It has one goal, one symbol, and one thought: Identity. [...] This book is no simple manifesto. It is a declaration of war. A declaration of war against everything that makes Europe sick and drives it to ruin, against the false ideology of the '68ers. This is us declaring war on you.[16]

While it would be easy to dismiss Willinger's manifesto as nothing more than an angry young man stamping his feet, *Generation Identity* is certainly an accessible articulation of the often dense and arcane ideas espoused by the likes of de Benoist. It is a reaction against the protests of 1968 and the radicals who fought for progress in France and beyond, and against the left's perceived cultural hegemony. Willinger rails against political elites who 'disgust us'; condemns the increasing acceptance of LGBT+ people in society – what he calls 'the union of nothingness' – and instead calls for a return to traditional gender roles as 'Women want to be conquered'.[17] He also rejects multiculturalism outright, stating that 'we don't want Mehmed and Mustafa to become Europeans', and, like de Benoist, argues instead for ethnopluralism.[18]

Worryingly, Identitarianism has gone far beyond Willinger's tirade and the once marginalised opinions of the wider network of Identitarian sympathisers discussed by ignored 'think-tanks' in the back rooms of pubs or in conference centres booked under fake names. It has become the bedrock of an international movement making headlines around the world, and the ideology remains one of the most influential within the global far right. However, since the extensive links between the European Identitarian movement and the far-right terrorist in Christchurch have been revealed, the movement has come under unprecedented scrutiny. First it experienced widespread social media bans and now it faces actual bans in numerous countries. In February 2021, for example, the French government announced that it had triggered procedures to close down the French branch of Generation Identity in response to their ongoing anti-migrant activity and possible contravention of a law banning incitement to discrimination.[19] While a welcome move that may curtail the efforts of GI, the ideas of Identitarianism cannot be banned and their influence will continue to inspire dangerous far-right activism.

In July 2017, at the height of the Defend Europe campaign, a Facebook page for Generation Identity Great Britain and the Republic of Ireland was launched, billing itself as the 'newest branch of the pan-European Identitarian movement'. While the ideas of the Nouvelle Droite had enjoyed moments of influence within the British far right, most notably on the National Front, it wasn't until the appearance of that Facebook page that Identitarianism had ever properly reared its head in the UK. Defend Europe had failed but its daring exploits and slick social media campaign had impressed a new wave of young racists. Later that month we picked up the first offline activity when a young Liverpudlian called Jordan Diamond travelled to London to meet Austrian and Norwegian Identitarians to discuss the development of Generation Identity in the UK. The international network was excited by the prospect of a new British branch, not least as a bridge into the anglophone world. Also in July, a group of Scottish activists attempted to hold a meeting in Glasgow but were met by fierce opposition from local anti-fascists.

Early GI activity across the UK was generally limited to putting up stickers or posing for photos in front of the group's yellow and black lambda flag. Then in October 2017, a source who was inside a far-right discussion group called the Traditional Britain Group informed us that Martin Sellner was due to speak at their next meeting. Simultaneously, my boss Nick Lowles was working with a documentary film crew and had managed to get people inside the fledgling GI branch. At the same time, Julie Ebner, a friend who also researched the far right, had gained access to the group to do research on an upcoming book. By the time Sellner touched down in London, it seemed that practically half of GI's UK activists were passing information to us in one way or another.

Following his speech, Sellner decamped to a restaurant where he met with former BNP leader Nick Griffin to talk about building GI in the UK. The following day, GI activists including Sellner and Jonathan Rudolph from GI in Germany reconvened at a large rented flat in Beaufort Gardens in Norbury, south-west London, to receive guidance from Sellner and to plan a stunt to accompany their formal public launch. They were to drop a huge Generation Identity banner off Westminster Bridge in full view of the Houses of Parliament. After the day's training they duly went and practised dropping their banner off a road bridge in preparation. Early the next morning, to no fanfare and very little press interest, they unfurled a large yellow and black banner reading 'Defend London: Stop Islamisation', marking the official launch of GI in the UK and Ireland.

Their excitement was short-lived. On 9 November, ITV aired the documentary 'Undercover: Inside Britain's New Far Right' with extensive footage of Martin Sellner during his time in London. Worst of all, he had been caught on camera using racist epithets, an embarrassment for a movement that strenuously tries to present a respectable and non-racist image. Having been plucked from obscurity and flung onto the nation's TV screens, the two joint leaders of the UK branch, Jordan Diamond and Sebastian Seccombe, soon stood down and eventually faded away from the movement. In disarray, GI UK was stillborn and fell silent for the rest of 2017. The following year, however, it began to re-emerge from the ashes with alarming speed. In January alone we tracked fifteen actions by GI, ranging from stickering and study circles to leafleting sessions. The rapid upturn in GI activity in the UK coincided with the emergence of a diminutive Norwegian called Tore Rasmussen. We knew little about him beyond the fact that he was the UK and Scandinavia manager of the Identitarian clothing brand Phalanx Europa, co-owned by Austrian GI leaders Martin Sellner and Patrick Lenart. Finding out more about his dark past would later prove to be the key to bringing down GI UK once more.

In April 2018 they attempted their first proper demonstration in London's Hyde Park, finally giving me an opportunity to see them with my own eyes. They were a distinctly average bunch of slightly awkward men in their late teens and early twenties giving tedious speeches about immigration levels. But it was their averageness that worried me. The British far right had long failed to attract young people – and if they did, they certainly wouldn't be called average-looking. This wasn't a bunch of tattooed and shaven-headed lads; they looked like geography teachers in training, all chinos and fluffy facial hair.

One figure was noticeably ordinary by far-right standards. With a neat blue shirt, tidy side-parted hair and a youthful face, Tom Dupré stood out from his pubescent peers. He gave a short speech on the day, addressing the small crowd in a well-spoken southern accent. I watched his interactions with the other GI activists closely and it was evident he was their figurehead, if not already their formal leader. When I returned to the office the following Monday, David and I gathered around Simon's computer as was customary, and slowly flicked through the pictures. 'Him', I said, pointing at the image of Dupré. 'I want to know who he is, everything about him.' In the weeks that followed we started to build up a picture of his activism, which included the ugly stunt of distributing 'warm pork suppers' to homeless people; the addition of pork to exclude any hungry Muslims. Each new fact we found made him stand out from most of the far-right people we were used to investigating. He had attended a good school before studying experimental psychology at the University of Bristol, and it transpired that he was now an Assistant Relationship Manager for Standard Chartered Bank in the City of London. Young, intelligent, well-spoken, with a very good job. Not your average fascist.

One of the most difficult parts of this job is making decisions you know will have a negative effect on the lives of the people we oppose. That sounds obvious, as it is often what we actively set out to do. But doing harm to anyone, however despicable and dangerous their politics, is never easy. They remain humans, and anyone who forgets that shouldn't be doing this job. Simon, David and I had a meeting to discuss our plan of attack and took a decision to try to get Dupré fired from his job at the bank. The danger of this tactic is that it removes options from the individual in question and can leave them no choice but to commit more fully to the far right, pushing them deeper in and closing possible exits for them. Our rationale was that the biggest risk we face with the modern far right is that it becomes normal, acceptable, like any other set of political beliefs. It is not, and we can never let it become so. Getting Dupré fired would be a reminder to far-right activists that what they do is not seen as acceptable. It acts as a warning to other young people considering getting involved that there will be a negative social cost to signing up. Their activism makes the lives of other people worse, and we can't ever allow it to continue in the shadows.

I wrote a letter to Standard Chartered outlining Dupré's egregious politics and informed them that we would be publishing an article that named them as his employer. For a few days nothing happened, so I decided to up the pressure. I rang Andrew Gilligan at *The Times* and offered him the story, which he enthusiastically accepted. I knew that a phone call from him would always hold more weight than an article by me, and that proved to be the case. A few days later his article appeared: 'The "hipster fascists" who anti-racism campaigners say are breathing new life into the far right'. Dupré was suspended pending an investigation and subsequently dismissed. I had got what I wanted.

In the short term, getting fired didn't stop Dupré or Generation Identity. During the first half of 2018, GI were the most active far-right group in the UK, with constant leaf-letting sessions, banner drops, and study groups across the country. In April they organised an international conference in the UK which was due to be attended by the leaders of the

European network. To coincide with the event we launched a new report, *A New Threat?: Generation Identity UK and Ireland*. Simultaneously we lobbied the Home Office to refuse entry to the visiting fascists, with success. Abel Bodi, co-leader of GI Hungary, was refused entry, as were Martin Sellner, his partner Brittany Pettibone and Lauren Southern. Amusingly, we received reports that Sellner was reading our report on his phone while in the queue for passport control at Luton airport, just moments before he was stopped by border officials. A ramshackle conference continued despite the no-shows but militant anti-fascists turned up at the venue and shut it down, resulting in bloody clashes on the streets of Sevenoaks. I was there to photograph the event but had to make a swift getaway in the car of a friendly journalist when I started to draw unwanted attention from the conference attendees.

The final nail in Dupré's tenure as GI leader came in August that year. By that point we had fully mapped the UK scene and knew practically every activist across the country. Simon had infiltrated the group and was attending numerous events and supplying me with a steady stream of useful information. It was his first undercover operation and it made me unusually nervous. Despite Dupré being the leader, Simon had identified Tore Rasmussen as the real power behind the throne and the contact to the wider European network. We began an investigation that soon turned dark. We contacted colleagues in Norway and the response that came back was shocking. Despite his jolly demeanour Rasmussen had been active in the Norwegian nazi group Vigrid in the late 1990s and early 2000s, and the Norwegian watchdog group Monitor described him as a 'well-known nazi' in 2001. It had been reported that Rasmussen was one of a group of nazis in Norway handing out flyers bearing the call to 'save the white race', with further information about hearing American nazi William Pierce 'talk about the Jews'. Rasmussen also used to attend matches of the Oslo football club Vålerenga alongside figures active in the Norwegian extreme right. Vigrid leader Tore Tvedt had relatively recently stated that he was 'proud' of Rasmussen, referring to him as his 'lieutenant'.

When questioned in Norwegian-language interviews, Rasmussen had briefly mentioned his nazi involvement, but it was very clear that he had downplayed the extent of it, and also the violent aspects of the movement. For all Generation Identity's extremeness, they had worked hard to cultivate a respectable image and an exposé like this would cause huge embarrassment.

As luck would have it, in August the leading figures of GI from all across Europe were to meet at a training camp in the village of Saint-Didier-en-Velay in France, giving us the perfect time to drop the story and cause maximum damage. I rang Mark Townsend at *The Observer*, a fine journalist with a track record of taking on the far right. He was happy to run the story so we packaged up the evidence and sent it over. As Generation Identity gathered for a weekend of ideological lectures and physical training, Mark sent the dossier of evidence to Dupré and asked him for a comment. What happened next was beyond what we could have hoped for. Mark rang me excitedly: 'He's left! He's stood down and left GI!' The following morning, I woke early and ran to the corner shop to buy the paper, and there it was in beautiful black and white across two whole pages. Dupré was quoted:

'I've just left; obviously, this information will cause may-
hem at the camp. I've spoken to a couple of people and
they are extremely concerned. If you're talking about

Islam and immigration, you need a complete brick wall to keep out your racists, your Nazis. If anything gets through, the whole project is a waste of time. I'm appalled. I've resigned. My personal view is that others will leave [the group].'

Dupré's departure was a hammer blow to the UK branch and another huge setback in the eyes of the network's European leaders. In the wake of Rasmussen's exposure, he announced that he was moving from Ireland back to Norway. By this point the great hope placed in the UK branch as a bridge-head to the English-speaking world had been shattered by our work and GI's days in the UK were numbered.

The movement attempted to continue under the leader-ship of the comically underqualified Benjamin Jones, but no sooner had they got back to their knees when Simon was con-tacted by a young journalist called Ben van der Merwe who had infiltrated the group on his own and was hoping for guid-ance. We met at the Windsor Castle, a pub on a back street behind Victoria station. Simon and I sounded him out and began to formulate a plan. It was only a short infiltration but he attended their national conference for us, the result being another bundle of damaging information. As well as revealing the attendance of numerous extreme characters, he found that two GI activists were serving members of the Royal Navy and one was imminently to become a sonar engineer on a nuclear submarine. As soon as we heard that, we knew there was no option but to pull the plug on the infiltration early and go public. There was no way we could let a fascist work on a nuclear submarine. Mark Townsend published another art-icle and GI was once again shamed in the national press. The recriminations that resulted from the infiltration forced the

European leaders of GI to expel the British branch from the network, and despite a short-lived rebrand the group officially disbanded in early 2020. Later that year, a handful of the key activists launched a tiny group called Identity England which has failed to make any impact on the UK far-right scene, while others went on to join the fascist group Patriotic Alternative.

In my ten years at HOPE not hate I've never seen such a complete destruction of a whole far-right organisation as we managed with Generation Identity UK. There was barely a meeting or closed chat group we didn't infiltrate, meaning that every plan they made we could thwart. For a brief period, they looked like they might be the new hope of the British far right, attracting young people into an ageing movement, but they never really had a chance. The whole of the research team played their role in this nearly two-year operation, but for Simon and me it was something of an obsession. GI were our age and it felt like this was our battle. Thankfully it was a battle we won.

MODI'S INDIA
AND HINDU NATIONALISM

As I walked along the narrow shop-lined streets, motorised
auto rickshaws dextrously weaved around each other like
a school of fish. I looked up and saw a road sign hanging
overhead: 'Jew Town'. To my left was another, a rusted white
metal sign teetering atop a pole, at the base of which was
a stall selling beaded necklaces, leather satchels and hemp
bum-bags emblazoned with marijuana leaves. The sign read
'Jew Cemetery' in red lettering with an arrow pointing away
from the street. Intrigued, I walked through a covered market
before emerging once more into the glaring heat of southern
India.

To my surprise, I found myself standing in front of a
synagogue. Built in 1568, it was reportedly the oldest active
synagogue in the whole of the Commonwealth. The plain
white outer walls gave no hint of its colourful and eclectic
interior. The floor was covered in Chinese hand-painted blue
tiles, laid in 1762 and no two the same. A small section was
covered by a hand-knotted rug gifted by the last emperor of
Ethiopia, Haile Selassie. In the middle of the room was the
bimah, the raised platform from which the Torah is read, surrounded by brass pillars, while from the ceiling hung a series
of mismatched Belgian glass chandeliers. The synagogue's

decor mirrored the surrounding area, shaped by centuries of trade and waves of immigration. Within a short walk is the Church of Saint Francis, the oldest European church in India and one-time resting place of the Portuguese explorer Vasco da Gama, and the Dutch Palace, surrounded by temples dedicated to Lord Krishna and Lord Siva.

I had arrived in Kochi the previous day after a short stopover at Abu Dhabi airport. It had been a slightly dystopian experience, surrounded by mask-wearing shop assistants spraying cologne at bloated businessmen. It was March 2020 and the coronavirus crisis was just beginning in earnest. I headed straight to the old town of Kochi and checked into the rather decadent surroundings of the Malabar House. It was the first day of the month so alcohol was banned, leaving me with no option but to retire to bed early to watch TV.

It was supposed to be the first night of a three-month research trip around India. I had arrived at a time of heightened tensions, and the blood wasn't yet dry. Just a week before, Delhi had erupted in violent Hindu–Muslim riots, the worst seen for some time. The violence began over Prime Minister Narendra Modi's new citizenship law which offers amnesty to non-Muslim undocumented immigrants from Pakistan, Bangladesh and Afghanistan. By excluding Muslims, the bill violates the secular principles enshrined in the Indian constitution, which prohibits religious discrimination. The law is linked to another controversial Modi initiative, the National Register of Citizens, which critics argue could leave millions of Indian Muslims stateless. Horrendous stories of beatings, lynchings and people being burned alive in Delhi were being reported around the world. While there were undoubtedly examples of Muslim-led violence, it was the Muslim community that suffered worst. Of the estimated

53 people who died the majority were Muslims, many shot or hacked to death on the streets of north-east Delhi.

I turned on the TV and flicked through the channels. The first English channel I landed on was Republic TV, a show called *The Debate* with Arnab Goswami. I had long thought American news channels were unwatchable with their endless split screen 'debates', but this was an order of magnitude worse. The screen was divided into no fewer than ten talking heads, all shouting over each other. It was like Fox News on steroids.

Modi had threatened to leave Twitter, and the big 'debate' was about how Western media and tech companies were spreading 'fake news' about the recent deadly riots. Goswami, a host for whom objectivity was by no means a watchword, animatedly condemned Twitter as 'anti-India' before running a package that attacked 'Western media lies', 'fake news campaigns' and the West's 'twisted pogrom narrative'. One of the small talking heads then announced: 'There was a journalist in the UK called Anthony sent to prison for telling the truth about Pakistani grooming gangs!' I instantly knew he meant Tommy, not Anthony. The notorious British Islamophobe Tommy Robinson (aka Stephen Yaxley-Lennon, who we met in earlier chapters) had been jailed for thirteen months in May 2018 after breaking reporting restrictions by filming and broadcasting from outside the court of an ongoing trial. Robinson presented himself as a martyr throughout his legal woes and became a lightning rod for anti-Muslim and far-right pro-'free speech' activists in the UK – and, it turns out, in India too.

Each year the world seems to get a little bit smaller and more uniform, making it quite easy to visit a new country and feel at home there straight away. India isn't like that, and it's all the better for it. The fact that my mother is half-Indian made the country no less unsettling. No matter where you go in India you can always hear the faint rhythmic pulse of drumming in the distance. The country seems to march to a tabla beat just out of earshot. However, sitting on my bed watching that TV with its right-wing commentators shouting about fake news and attacking the 'mainstream media', with a prime minister obsessed by social media, open and unchallenged anti-Muslim rants and even the mention of a British far-right activist, it all felt sadly familiar. In a country so unimaginably complex and diverse I had, with one hour of TV, found a touchstone, something I recognised: the populist far-right.

In his magisterial *India: A Million Mutinies Now*, the Nobel laureate V.S. Naipaul wrote:

> To awaken to history was to cease to live instinctively. It was to begin to see oneself and one's group the way the outside world saw one; and it was to know a kind of rage. India was now full of this rage. There had been a general awakening. But everyone awakened first to his own group or community; every group thought itself unique in its awakening; and every group sought to separate its rage from the rage of other groups.[1]

Though he was writing about a Sikh insurgency in Punjab in the 1980s, Naipaul's words about ethnic and religious division, anger and rage still ring true in Narendra Modi's modern-day India. At the time I arrived in the country, Modi, the *chaiwala* boy from Gujarat turned prime minister, had recently won re-election; he had been in power since 2014. I missed the visit of Donald Trump by just a few days. His 'Namaste Trump' tour, a response to the 'Howdy Modi' event held in Texas in 2019, had recently ended with newspapers around the world talking of the two leaders' 'bromance' and mutual outlook. In some ways, however, they couldn't be more different. Trump, the son of a wealthy New York real-estate mogul; Modi, an 'ascetic Gujarati from a poor background' whose father ran a railway station canteen in Vadnagar.[2] Yet they had both risen to power using a platform of divisive and exclusionary rhetoric and now ruled over the two largest democracies in the world.

Modi's journey to world leader is a remarkable one. It's worth remembering that not long before his 2014 election he had been ostracised by the international community and diplomatically frozen out by Britain and the European Union.[3] In 2005 he was even refused entry into America under a little-known 1998 law that held him responsible for 'severe violations of religious freedom'. The refusal came as a result of his failure to stop anti-Muslim violence in his home state of Gujarat. In early 2002 India once again erupted into ethnic and religious violence. A train of Hindu pilgrims was stopped and set on fire, killing 59 people. Hindu gangs responded with anti-Muslim rioting across Gujarat that saw Muslim families dragged from their houses and hacked to death, and Muslim holy sites levelled while the police stood by. The result was 2,000 dead. When asked about the events Modi responded:

> After that [the train attack], riots took place, and Hindus and Muslims all died. Violence is bad, but your object-
> ives should be to prevent the train being surrounded.
> If Congress wants to take up the issue of Gujarat, they

should also take up what happened to the indigenous Hindus who were driven out of their houses in Kashmir. [...] Hindus do not have the chance to represent themselves. [...] It's part of the programme of trivializing our civilisation.[4]

In the words of the journalist and historian Patrick French, 'Modi made no expression of regret, and focused on the victims of the attack on the train, implying that the Muslims deserved what had come to them'.[5] Despite this, Atal Bihari Vajpayee's government failed to dismiss Modi as Chief Minister. What is so striking is how similar this rhetoric is to that I heard from the far right in America. The claim is of victimisation against the majority community, in the US white men, in this case Hindu Indians.

Modi ascended to power in 2014 as leader of the Bharatiya Janata Party (BJP), the biggest political party in the world, claiming to have 100 million members.[6] The party motto is 'Country first, party second, self last',[7] and their mission, according to Patrick French, is 'to redefine Indian identity by linking it to a mythologized Hindu past'.[8] As with the rise of many European far-right parties, the BJP grew into the force it is today over a series of decades. At the 1984 election, it won just two seats out of 542 in the lower house of Parliament (the Lok Sabha) but just a decade later, 'the BJP was becoming the most important force in Indian politics'.[9] French explains how its rise was the result of a 'perfect storm of events' that shot the BJP and the wider Hindutva movement 'to the centre of national life'. It included the Gandhi family, still the first family of Indian politics, having 'disappeared'; middle-class anger over 'the stifling web of controls and regulation' instituted by numerous Congress Party governments, and the willingness of the movement to 'manipulate communal politics for political gain'.[10] However, as Achin Vanaik explains, its 'electoral rise, both in the provinces and at the centre is part of a wider cultural-ideological advance, and a deeper implantation in the country's structures and institutions'.[11] This is a reference to the broader Hindutva movement of which the BJP is part.

Hindutva, essentially 'Hindu-ness', is a concept that fuses religion, culture and geography into a national identity. Cas Mudde calls Hindutva ideology 'perhaps the most perfect mix of nativism and religion',[12] while Vanaik has described Hindu nationalism as the 'communal phoenix' rising to cast its 'shadow over India's body politic'.[13] The growth of political Hindutva happened slowly at first, between 1947 and 1990, but has accelerated since then. Cas Mudde describes Modi and the BJP as the 'party representative of the well-established and organized Hindutva movement, which includes violent, extremist groups like the National Volunteer Organization (RSS)'.[14] According to Walter Andersen and Shridhar D. Damle, 'To understand India therefore requires an understanding of the RSS'.[15] The organisation was founded in 1925 by Dr Keshav Baliram Hedgewar, who believed that 'the deep social divisions among the Hindus of India were responsible for what he considered a thousand years of foreign domination on the subcontinent'.[16] Not long after independence in February 1948 the RSS was banned due to suspicion that it was involved in the assassination of Mahatma Gandhi, the killer, Nathuram Godse, being a former RSS member. The ban was lifted not long after in July 1949 but had severely damaged the organisation's reputation in the eyes of many Indians. It began to recover in the 1960s and then grew rapidly from the early 1990s onwards. Today the RSS has been described as 'Arguably, the most powerful violent far-right group in the world'.[17] Central to its worldview is a rejection of Western Enlightenment ideas and a belief that ethno-nationalism is more important than economic class struggle in shaping Indian society.[18] As of 2016 it had an estimated 1.5–2 million regular participants, 6,000 full-time workers and nearly 57,000 local daily meetings, 14,000 weekly and 7,000 monthly meetings (*shakhas*) in 36,293 different locations.[19]

Central to understanding the rise of the RSS and Hindu nationalism is the events surrounding the Ram Temple Movement, culminating in the destruction of the Babri Masjid mosque in December 1992. It was during these events 'that the transformative power of Hindu communal forces in India really became apparent'.[20] At the centre of a centuries-old dispute between Hindus and Muslims in the city of Ayodhya was a 16th-century mosque that many Hindus believe was constructed on top of the ruins of a Hindu temple marking the birthplace of one of their most admired deities, Lord Ram. In 1992 a crowd of 150,000 protesters, spurred on by a six-year campaign spearheaded by the BJP, broke through police lines and destroyed the mosque.[21] In the days that followed bloody riots broke out across the country, the worst of which tore through Mumbai, killing an estimated 900 people. These events did not lead to the nationwide destruction of mosques as many had feared, thanks to the 'structures of the Constitution and the broader Indian allegiance to secularism'.[22] However, for Indian secularists, 'the destruction of the Babri Masjid appeared to mark the end of India as a secular state, with no mosque or Muslim now safe from Hindu fundamentalism'.[23] At the general election four years later, the BJP displaced Congress as the largest party.

In August 2020, Prime Minister Narendra Modi travelled to Ayodhya with the eyes of India on him. On the site of the destroyed Babri Masjid he laid the foundation stone of the new Ram Temple, placing a symbolic silver brick in the sanctum sanctorum. The act was a powerful statement to the BJP's Hindu nationalist base. It was made possible following a report by the Archaeological Survey of India providing evidence that the remains of a non-Islamic building were beneath the now-demolished mosque. The struggle to create the Ram Temple has 'played the most significant part in the RSS's socio-political acceptance in India', and indeed it was well represented at the ground-breaking ceremony.[24] The chief Bhagwat of the RSS, in front of Modi, said: 'We had taken a resolution. The then RSS chief Balasaheb Deoras had told us that be prepared [*sic*] for a struggle of 20 to 30 years for realising this dream. We struggled and at the beginning of the 30th year, we have attained the joy of fulfilling our resolution.' It should come as no surprise that Modi was eager to be at the event. He has long been closely aligned with the RSS, having been a member since he was eight years old[25] and started working as a *pracharak* (campaigner) for them at the age of 21.[26] Modi's ties to the RSS go beyond symbolism and extend to policy, a point reiterated in September 2015, when the RSS held one of their 'coordination' meetings with dozens of their affiliates to consider public policy issues, after which Modi and several other senior government ministers turned up to discuss the issues raised in person.[27]

The destruction of a mosque and its replacement with a Hindu temple is a highly symbolic act and one that, for many, is archetypal of the supremacist attitude of extreme Hindu nationalism. For this reason, just as there was with Trump in America, there is a debate within the Indian left over whether Modi and the wider Hindu far right is, or is not, fascist. The dominant position among Indian Marxists is that it is.

However, Vanaik argues that it is 'not correct to characterize the forces of Hindutva as fascist, despite its undeniable fascist aspects',[28] though he admits that 'Theirs [RSS and BJP] is the most pernicious kind [of Hindu nationalism], posited as it is on hostility to the Muslim "other"'.[29] Patrick French describes some in the BJP as 'similar to men I had talked to in Pakistan who imagined a purer nation. Their vision of Hinduism was a direct match for political Islam' in part, due to their similar 'reductive way of viewing humans and the world', which is 'exclusivist, reductive, relentlessly male prejudice'.[30]

In many ways, the RSS and elements of the BJP would reach Roger Griffin's 'fascist minimum' and his definition of fascism as a 'palingenetic form of populist ultra-nationalism'.[31] Modi and the BJP certainly call for the rebirth of India, distinguish between a supposedly pure people and a corrupt elite, and push ultra-nationalist politics. The left-wing journalist Sumanta Banerjee even told BBC Radio 4 that 'members of the present Modi-led BJP government have imbibed Savitri Devi's ideology'.[32] A French fascist who moved to India in the early 1930s, Devi believed Hinduism to be 'the custodian of the Aryan and Vedic heritage down through the centuries, the very essence of India', and saw Hitler's Third Reich as the rebirth of Aryan paganism in the West.[33] Any flirtation with her views is a clear sign of fascist affiliation. However, Modi has been in power since 2014 and failed to create anything like a fascist dictatorship, which poses a difficult question for those who describe him as a fascist. What can be agreed on, though, is that Modi and the BJP fit comfortably in the category of far-right.

While Modi emerged out of the RSS, and the Hindu nationalist movement is central to his rise, this alone doesn't explain his remarkable victory in 2014. Central to this was his ability to successfully weaponise the power of populism. In many ways Modi is the perfect example of a populist. In April 2018, for example, he declared that the Congress Party is for the *namdaar* (elite), while he and the BJP are for the *kaamdaar* (people).[34] Like many populist leaders, Modi is lauded for his rhetorical style and ability to hold often vast audiences, though perhaps his most astute skill is his simultaneous embrace of 'India's future, through its young IT-savvy generation, and its past, embodied in the myths and legends of its cultural heritage'.[35] In one speech he can hit out at his political opponents for 'opposing technology' and declare that 'for a modern India, in every field of life we want to give importance to technology',[36] and in another tell the crowd that 'I strongly believe in the words of legends. I have great faith in the statements made by ascetics, sages and saints', even quoting Swami Vivekananda: 'I can see before my eyes Mother India awakening once more.'[37]

Using these tools, in 2014 the BJP secured 31% of the vote and was aligned with numerous other smaller parties in what is called the National Democratic Alliance (NDA), which together achieved 39%. Central to Modi's victory was the decline of the long-dominant Congress Party, which achieved just 19%. Despite falling well short of a majority, the electoral maths worked out and he became the absolute winner. Lance Price, formerly a special advisor to British Prime Minister Tony Blair, has described the victory as 'a masterclass in modern electoral politics',[38] a conclusion that is hard to disagree with, considering the BJP more than doubled its vote compared to the previous election in 2009.

Modi's victory was warmly welcomed by far-right figures around the world. Trump's close ally Steve Bannon declared it part of a 'global revolt' while the leading European alt-right figure Daniel Friberg described it as part of a 'historical paradigm shift'.[39] Interestingly, Friberg and his colleagues at the prominent alt-right publisher Arktos claim to have conducted over a hundred meetings with Indian politicians and religious leaders and at least two meetings with members of the BJP and RSS. In fact, in December 2013, a post on Arktos' Facebook page claimed that at one meeting with BJP officials:

> We discussed possibilities for cooperation between traditionalist and conservative movements in Europe and Asia, as well as potential strategies to counter liberal globalist hegemony, and, of course, future book projects. [...] Arktos intends to become the Indian Right's gateway to the Western world, which will be fruitful both for our friends in India as well as for those interested in contemporary India elsewhere, and the lessons it can offer us worldwide.[40]

Sections of the international far right watched India closely, and Modi's victory caused great excitement and inspired many. However, the question remained: how radical would his agenda be once in power?

By the time I arrived in Chennai the cricket had already been cancelled. The plan had been for a few quick days of work before I flew to Sri Lanka to meet up with a friend and watch the England cricket team play at the Galle International Stadium. With the Indian Ocean just beyond the boundary and the crumbling walls of Galle Fort towering imperiously over the ground, there is surely no better place to watch a game of cricket. Sadly, the tour was cancelled with a few days' notice due to the relentless spread of Covid-19.

For the past few weeks I had been languidly making my way up the west coast of India. I'd spent several wonderful days in the backwaters of Kerala before heading north to Panaji, the extremely unlikable capital of Goa. The guide-book promised me a city of terraced hills covered in fetching Portuguese-era buildings with red-tiled roofs, all overlooking the expanse of the Mandovi River estuary. I found a rather shabby city with a riverside ruined by gaudy casino boats and neon advertisements. It was only as I arrived at my hotel that I realised quite how bad things had become with Covid. I dropped my bag to the floor and rang the bell. 'How long have you been in India?', came a voice from behind the door.

'Two weeks', I replied.

'No rooms', came the response.

'I've already booked and paid for the room.'

'No rooms.'

'But I've already paid for it so there must be a room.'

'No rooms. Full.' And with that my conversation with the closed door was over.

I had booked through a website so I called customer services in the UK, who said they would contact the hotel to find out what the problem was. Rather comically, I heard the owner's phone ring from behind the door. 'No rooms', he said. With perfect timing my phone then rang and someone sitting in London proceeded to explain to me that the hotel owner, roughly two feet away from me, claimed to have no rooms. Just as I was about to eat my phone with frustration I heard a shuffle from behind the door. 'Sorry, Covid. No rooms.'

The answer was the same everywhere. No one wanted to take foreign visitors because of the spreading pandemic.

That evening I walked the streets of Panaji from hotel to hotel, getting increasingly tired and angry with each rejection, until finally I found a bed in Hotel Arcadia. The air conditioning didn't work and there was nowhere to wash except a hand basin but I gratefully accepted the room and quickly fell asleep.

I woke early and headed south on the bus to the staggeringly beautiful beach at Palolem; a crescent moon of butterscotch-coloured sand walled off from the world by a thicket of palm trees and wooden beach huts. The odd clip of news or glimpse at a newspaper reminded me of the still bubbling racial tensions in the north and the rapidly spreading pandemic. With the cricket cancelled and India revoking all tourist visas, I knew my time in the country was limited, so I had packed my bags and flown to Chennai.

My host in the city was Nithi Sevaguru, an unusually kind man whom I met via a family friend in the UK. Over the coming three days he was my guide, taking me for dinner, organising my travel and shouting at the hotel staff when I was bitten to within an inch of my life by bed bugs. Chennai, formerly Madras, is an infectiously bustling city that sprawls along the Coromandel Coast where the warm water of the Bay of Bengal laps against the longest natural urban beach in the whole of India. I squeezed in a visit to the Government Museum – the third-largest in the world – and filled up on imperial guilt at Fort St George, the first English fortress in India, dating to 1639. However, I was in Chennai for one reason, to visit a sit-in protest, then in its 31st day.

In addition to the violence seen in Delhi, protests against Modi's Citizenship Amendment Act (CAA), the National Register of Citizens and the National Population Register had exploded across India. These policies answered the question of how radical Modi's agenda would be once in power. Protests had taken place in Chennai since the passing of the CAA in December 2019, some of them huge. By the time I arrived there was just an echo of the fury that had passed in the previous months.

I exited the modern Mannadi metro station and walked towards the faint sound of chanting in the distance. A small side road was blocked off with metal barriers, the ground covered in bamboo matting and an orange tarpaulin stretched from building to building to provide shade from the baking heat. At the front were a dozen or so teenage boys sitting cross-legged and chanting. Behind them, with a thin line of rope as separation, was a larger group of women and young girls in colourful headscarves. Flapping above the demonstration site was a large Indian flag with the words 'Who the hell are you to say I am not Indian. I am proud to be Indian' written across it. In the centre of the group was a whiteboard with 'No-CAA-NRC-NPR, Mannady Shaheen Bagh, Day 31, 15/03/20' scrawled on it in marker pen.

The protest was watched without interest by a smattering of police officers, and locals passed by unfazed as they went about their evening shopping. Every few minutes the group burst into noisy chanting; call and response. Their passion and enthusiasm after 31 days was quite something to watch. I nervously leaned on the metal fence and took the odd photograph. Being white in a part of town with no tourists, it didn't take long before I attracted attention from both the police and the protesters. A boy in his late teens walked over and confidently shook my hand. 'How can I help you?' he said. 'I'm a journalist and thought I would come and have a look as I saw you in the newspaper', I offered, unsure about how he felt about my arrival. 'You must join us', he replied, ushering

me around the barrier and into the protest. I paused, thanked
him but explained I was merely there to observe. He looked
crestfallen, so I quickly asked if he would be happy to have
a chat about why he was protesting. He nodded enthusiastically, a broad, friendly smile returning to his face. 'We're here
24 hours to oppose CAA, NRC, NPR', he said, the three acro-
nyms rolling off his tongue from muscle memory built up by
a month of chanting. We talked for a while and I assured him
I would return tomorrow and spend the day at the protest.

The following afternoon he ran straight over to me as I
approached the metal gates cordoning off the demonstration.
'You came!' Before we had even spoken he had ushered me
into the demonstration, motioned for me to take off my shoes
and sat me down on the floor. He was so happy to see me
that I felt quite touched. His friend came over and handed me
a small samosa, a bottle of water and a badge reading 'NO
CAA'. 'My name is Ibrahim Mohammed', he said. I asked if
he would be happy to talk and he agreed, telling me: 'We will
stay here until we stop the bill. They want me to prove my
father and my father's father are citizens. My father was born
in a village so has no birth certificate.' I asked what would
happen to him if the bill passes. 'They will come to my house
and if I can't prove my papers I become a refugee.' I asked if
this was a Muslim demonstration. 'No, it's an Indian demonstration', came the response. I heard the same story numerous
times from different protesters, each genuinely scared that
Modi's laws would take their country away from them.

As we spoke, an elderly man with a long ginger beard
chanting through a microphone walked over and stood
next to me. 'A white person has joined us! We have a white
supporter!' he boomed over the PA. I looked around and
realised he was pointing at me. A phone on a tripod that

was livestreaming the demonstration was thrust in my face as the group cheered. 'Speak, explain why you support us, explain why people in England support us.' Of course, I did support them; I felt their anger, was touched by their passion and in agreement about Modi, but I didn't feel knowledgeable enough to stand up in front of a crowd on the streets of Chennai and give a speech. I merely wished them good luck and told them to stay safe. Thirty-one days was a long time but I feared it was going to take a lot more than protests like this to stop Modi's laws.

Watching the news that evening it became clear that my days in India were numbered. Covid-19 was still spreading and the Taj Mahal had just been closed to visitors. I had only just started my research and was desperate not to fly home just yet, so I walked across the road from my hotel to Chennai Egmore train station, an imposing red-brick building crowned by white domes, and booked the next train to Delhi. The trip was an eye-watering 33 hours but I boarded at 9.05 the following morning excited about the adventure. My enthusiasm soon waned when I found that my bunk was crammed against the ceiling of the carriage, with no window. My romanticised image of crossing India by rail with majestic scenery whizzing past my window was dashed, and I settled in for a day and a half of staring at the wall and desperately trying not to use the toilet. I arrived in a strangely subdued Delhi and checked into the YMCA hotel. As far as I could tell, except for the staff, I was the only person there. The dining room was deserted, the pool closed. They took my temperature, asked me to fill in my details and handed me my key.

The following morning it became clear just how bad things had become. I woke to a knock on the door and opened it to find a uniformed man with a camera. 'We need to take a picture for your embassy', he said. I knew it was probably time to go home. With what little time I had left I walked down to Rajpath, with India Gate at one end and the vast Presidential Palace at the other. Everything was closed. The monuments were fenced off. India was going into lockdown and I started to worry about being trapped. India is a glorious country but I'm a smoking asthmatic and wasn't keen on being stuck there during a global pandemic. I hurriedly booked a flight home for that evening, checked my watch and realised I had time for one last trip.

'I need to go to Jamia Millia Islamia', I said to the driver of a battered yellow auto rickshaw. 'Why?' said the paunchy driver. 'I want to go to the protest.' The university, some way out of the centre of the city in the eastern district of Okhla, had been host to another long-standing anti-CAA protest. 'I'm not taking you there', he replied in perfect English. 'Too far?' I asked. 'You'll get shot', he said. I laughed. He didn't.

It transpired that rumours were circulating that the government was making ready to clear the protest, using Covid as a pretence. I paused and considered my options. Getting shot was certainly not how I intended for my truncated India trip to end, but I made the snap decision to head to the protest anyway. The next rickshaw driver had no reservations. We sped through the traffic for a good 45 minutes before reaching the university. The protest occupied one half of the road, sheltered from above by a motorway bridge. 'I'll wait here', said the driver.

Every pillar of the motorway bridge was covered in graffiti or with posters reading 'If we do not oppose the ghastly CAA 2019, NRC & NPR our generation will be buried alive'. I was handed a leaflet featuring an Indian flag and the famous Mark Twain quote: 'Loyalty to country always. Loyalty to government when it deserves it.' Along the wall that bordered the university were lines of tents where protesters slept, and at one end was a large blue marquee. Women filled the tent while a small group of men stood just outside, all listening to a speech. I couldn't understand anything until the speaker broke into English and said 'No to fascism'. That, I understood. There was a thick tension in the air – the rumours that the site would imminently be cleared had reached here too. Most of the crowd seemed understandably wary of me, though some were friendly. One man came over, shook my hand and offered me a mask. Signs about Covid were everywhere. These people were not ignorant of the threat of the virus, they were just more scared of a different pandemic. More scared of the spread of intolerance and hatred. More scared of losing their citizenship. More scared of losing their country, their home.

10

BOLSONARO'S BRAZIL, THE GLOBAL PANDEMIC AND CLIMATE CHANGE

If Covid-19 truncated my trip to India, it demolished any hope of making it to Brazil. By the summer of 2020 the pandemic had spread to every corner of the world and international travel was becoming harder by the day. Making things worse was the situation in Brazil itself. The country's President, Jair Bolsonaro, was, like many of his fellow far-right leaders around the world, utterly failing to grasp the seriousness of the situation. He described it as the 'little flu', called on citizens to go back to work, mocked social distancing measures and said 'We'll all die one day'.[1] He even bizarrely claimed the virus was a media 'fantasy' and 'trick' and that he 'wouldn't feel anything' if personally infected.[2] This created the remarkable situation where, as with Trump in America, the president was actively disrupting attempts to contain the virus in his own country. As the death toll passed 162,000 in November, the second highest anywhere in the world, he declared: 'Everyone is going to die. There is no point in escaping from that, in escaping from reality. We have to stop being a country of sissies.'[3] The word he actually used was '*maricas*', a derogatory slang term for gay people.

The Covid-19 pandemic had dominated the news since the beginning of 2020 and for each heart-warming story of communities coming together and neighbours helping each other was another of division, calls for ever-stronger borders and rises in hate crimes against Asian communities across the globe. Since the pandemic started there had been increased accounts of anti-Asian assaults, harassment and hate crimes. This ranged from verbal aggression along the lines of 'Go back to China' and accusations of 'bringing in the virus' to physical assaults on victims assumed to be Chinese, or even just Asian. The European Union's Agency for Fundamental Rights noted a general spike in hate against people of Chinese or Asian descent across the EU. The hate has also impacted their access to health services.[4]

In the UK, which has a significant population of Asian origin, figures show that attacks against 'Orientals' recorded by the Metropolitan Police rose steeply as the pandemic spread, fell during the first lockdown and then, with the easing of restrictions in May, started to steadily rise again.[5] In February 2020 Dr Michael Ng of a Chinese association in the south of England told the *Guardian* that hostility against the Chinese community was at the worst level he had seen in 24 years.[6] This hostility translated into hate crimes, and in May it was announced that such crimes directed at South and East Asian communities had increased by 21% during the coronavirus crisis.[7] This pattern was seen across large parts of Europe. In France the hashtag #JeNeSuisPasUnVirus (I'm not a virus) was used by French Asian citizens facing stigma and attacks.[8] This followed the outrage caused when a local newspaper, *Le Courier Picard*, used the headline '*Alerte jaune*' ('Yellow alert') and '*Le péril jaune?*' ('Yellow peril?'), complete with an image of a Chinese woman wearing a protective mask.[9]

In Italy, the NGO Lunaria collected over 50 reports of assaults, discrimination and bullying of people perceived to be Chinese. The barrage of hateful rhetoric can also be traced to politicians and even parties in power. The governor of the Veneto region of Italy, an early epicentre of the pandemic, told journalists in February that the country would be better than China in handling the virus due to Italians' 'culturally strong attention to hygiene, washing hands, taking showers, whereas we have all seen the Chinese eating mice alive'.[10] Gianni Ruffin, director general of Amnesty International Italy, spoke out on the issue: 'Scientifically incorrect information, irresponsible affirmations by politicians and incomprehensible local measures [taken against the virus' spread] have led to a shameful wave of Sinophobia.'[11] Similar rises of anti-Asian racism were seen across Europe, notably in Sweden and Poland,[12] while in Hungary, Asians of non-Chinese heritage felt the need to make clear they were not Chinese, with at least two shops in Budapest displaying signs reading '*Vietnamiak vagyunk*', meaning 'We are Vietnamese'.[13]

The hate experienced by Asians due to Covid-19 does not exist in a political vacuum. It would be wrong to say that the upswing in anti-Asian racism during the pandemic was the result of the far right alone, not least because there is a broader societal racism at play. However, the far right has certainly sought to exploit this existing prejudice and in some cases exacerbate it. The emergence of Covid-19 coincided with a broader shift towards anti-Chinese politics by the international far right. Over the last few years, as we have seen the 'decoupling' of the US and Chinese economies and a shift towards what some are calling a 'cold war chill' between the West and China, nationalist and far-right figures have increasingly targeted Chinese people.

It is of course too soon to know the long-term effects of the pandemic. Unlike previous major trigger events such as the financial crisis or the migrant crisis, the international far right have not as yet enjoyed a major rise in popularity. In fact, the terrible handling of the pandemic by Donald Trump likely contributed to his election loss in 2020. Many European far-right parties failed to respond coherently and have been marginalised from national debates on the issue, and both Bolsonaro in Brazil and Modi in India have seen their popularity decline due to their handling of the pandemic. Whether the far right will be able to capitalise on the likely long-term economic difficulties arising from the pandemic is a worrying unanswered question.

However, the pandemic has certainly provided new opportunities for the far right, engendered by an explosion of conspiracy theories, including the idea that China designed the virus as a bioweapon, that Bill Gates is seeking to implant people with microchips via a vaccine, and that 5G internet is somehow to blame. While some of these conspiracies are new, many are extensions of long-standing theories being disseminated by existing far-right networks. The most significant development has been the growth and spread of QAnon, the conspiracy theory alleging that Trump is engaged in a secret war against a vast cabal of Satanic paedophiles who kidnap, torture and cannibalise children. While it started in America some years ago, the pandemic has given new impetus to this theory and caused its growth across Europe.

It is tempting to dismiss conspiracy theorists as harmless eccentrics, gathering in online forums to discuss peculiar, but ultimately ineffective, ideas. In truth, conspiracy theories are the lifeblood of far-right extremism, providing simple and monocausal explanations for the world's problems, all too often blaming secret cabals; usually Jews. With so many people engaging with conspiracy theory content online, there is a genuine danger that a new generation of people will be introduced to conspiratorial antisemitism and the far right more broadly.

Not making it to Brazil was a huge disappointment. Growing up in rainy Britain, Brazil was always a country of great excitement and fascination. Now as an adult whose job it is to research and monitor the international far right, my vision of Brazil has begun to change. Rio remains the vibrant metropolis I always dreamed of, but clouds have begun to gather above the statue of Christ the Redeemer.

I watched in horror in 2018 as Jair Bolsonaro became President with his slogan '*Brasil acima de tudo, Deus acima de todos*' ('Brazil above everything, God above everyone'). It reminded me of the British far right's traditional slogan 'Britain First', or the chants of 'America First' that I had heard at Trump rallies in Ohio in 2016. Sometimes it's comforting to realise you are not alone. Other times, realising that similar phenomena are happening elsewhere in the world only makes things scarier. The election of Bolsonaro was one of those moments, another data point indicating a terrifying direction of travel. His victory meant Brazil joined India, America and parts of central Europe in having fallen under the leadership of far-right xenophobes. Trump, Modi and Bolsonaro forged a far-right bloc at the very top of world politics, meaning hundreds of millions of people lived in countries run by the electoral far right, destabilising three of the largest democracies on earth. Today, Brazil has become a central player in the global story of the rising far right.

In July 2018 Jair Bolsonaro, a former army captain from

a humble background, was nominated as the presidential candidate of the conservative, some would say far-right, Social
Liberal Party. On 6 September, while campaigning in the city
of Juiz de Fora, he was stabbed. A later tweet by his son Flavio
confirmed that the knife had perforated parts of his liver, lung
and intestine.[14] Despite being unable to campaign for much of
the election, he swept to victory with a commanding 55.2%
of the vote against just 44.8% for Fernando Haddad of the
Workers' Party. For some of his supporters, surviving the
knife attack was 'evidence of divine grace' and 'remodelled the
populist politician into [an] indestructible messianic hero'.[15]
President Trump was quick to call and congratulate the figure
who had been dubbed the 'Trump of the Tropics'.[16] However,
while the media were right to draw parallels between the two
far-right leaders, and to place his victory in the context of a
wider trend of radical and far-right electoral success around
the world, in many ways Bolsonaro is an order of magnitude
more extreme than his American ally.

There are few minority communities that Bolsonaro
doesn't have a history of attacking, though some of his most
shocking outbursts have come against homosexuality. In
2002, in the *Folha de São Paulo* newspaper, he said: 'I'm not
going to fight or discriminate, but if I see two men kissing
on the street, I'll hit them';[17] then in 2011: 'I would be incap-
able of loving a homosexual child. I'm not going to act like a
hypocrite here: I'd rather have my son die in an accident than
show up with some moustachioed guy. For me, he would have
died.'[18] He even suggested that if your son 'starts acting a little gay, hit him with some leather'.[19] In 2011, in an interview
with *Playboy* magazine, he added: 'If a homosexual couple
comes to live next to me, it will devalue my home! If they
walk around holding hands and kissing, that devalues it.'[20]

To hear such extreme homophobia from a president is shocking but sadly not unique. The strongest parallel is with the dangerous anti-LGBT+ agenda being pushed by the governing far-right Law and Justice (PiS) party in Poland and their President Andrzej Duda. During the delayed 2020 presidential election campaign Duda pledged to 'defend children from LGBT ideology' and described gay marriage and adoption as part of 'a foreign ideology'.[21] In an outburst reminiscent of Bolsonaro, an MP from PiS, Przemysław Czarnek, said: 'Let's stop listening to these idiocies about human rights. These people are not equal with normal people.'[22] Despite, or perhaps because of, his homophobic campaign, Duda narrowly beat his socially liberal challenger Rafał Trzaskowski in the July election, retaining the office of President.

There was a time when vitriolic homophobia was the absolute norm across the international far right. Homosexuality was decried as 'degenerate' and 'dangerous'; attitudes that remain unchanged within the far right. However, the picture has recently become more mixed when it comes to the wider radical and far-right spectrum, making Bolsonaro's outbursts sound even more anachronistic. The issue of attitudes to LGBT+ rights in the modern far right is a complex one, but many now engage in a limited discourse with gay men, largely for strategic purposes. As my colleagues David Lawrence and Simon Murdoch have shown in numerous articles, positioning the right to be gay as a core Western value has enabled the contemporary far right to attack Islamic and non-Western cultures for their perceived intolerance, bolstering the argument that such cultures are incompatible with the West. Sometimes cynically, sometimes completely genuinely, elements of the modern far right use gay rights as a 'wedge issue' between LGBT+ individuals, liberal left-wingers and

Muslims. Whether tokenistic or real, this development has served to make the modern far right appear more palatable during a period of improving societal attitudes towards the gay community.[23] This is part of a broader attempt by many on the far right to co-opt the language of human rights and oppression, with some even publicly identifying with figures such as Martin Luther King, Gandhi or Mandela. Increasingly we see a rhetorical gymnastics that frames far-right activism as a struggle for human rights and equality, shorn of overtly crude epithets. However, as Bolsonaro and Duda have shown, this is certainly not the case everywhere.

Bolsonaro's ugly track record of homophobia goes hand in hand with a deep-seated misogyny. In February 2016 he said: 'I would not employ [a woman] with the same salary [of a man]. But there are many women who are competent.'[24] His prejudice even extends to his own family. While giving a speech at the Hebraica Club in Rio, he said of his children: 'I had four men and on the fifth, I had a moment of weakness and a woman came out.'[25] Most shockingly, while on a TV debate with Congresswoman Maria do Rosário he said: 'I would never rape you, because you do not deserve it [...] slut!'[26] He also admitted to hitting a woman when a boy in Eldorado because 'a girl was getting in my face'.[27]

Adding to his homophobia and misogyny is his history of racist outbursts. As historian Federico Finchelstein argues, he denigrates Afro-Brazilians.[28] For example, during a speech in Rio in 2017 he talked of visiting a settlement in El Dourado Paulista founded by people of African origin: 'Look, the lightest African descendant there weighed 100 kg. They don't do anything. They don't even serve to reproduce.'[29] He has also lashed out at other South Americans, describing Venezuelan immigrants as 'scum of the earth'.[30]

However, Brazil was an unequal society long before the election of Bolsonaro. While 51% of the population identifies as black, they experience the highest levels of unemployment and illiteracy, the lowest salaries, and are most likely to be homicide victims, victims of police violence, and to be incarcerated.[31] On average, black and brown Brazilians have an income that is slightly less than half that of whites. More than half of the people living in the favelas of Rio de Janeiro are black, as opposed to just 7% in the city's more prosperous districts.[32] The black activist Ivanir dos Santos described the situation: 'In Brazil you have an invisible enemy. Nobody's racist. But when your daughter goes out with a black, things change.'[33] The idea that 'nobody's racist' refers to many Brazilians' pride in the ethnic diversity of the country. Michael Reid, for example, argues that: 'Until the invasion of American academic ideas, most Brazilians thought that their country's racial rainbow was among its main assets. They were not wholly wrong.' Reid points out that the country has anti-discrimination legislation dating back to the 1950s, and since the 1988 constitution, racial abuse and racist crimes have been illegal.[34] Despite this, 'Many Brazilians simply assumed that blacks belonged at the bottom of the pile. Supporters of affirmative action were right to say that the country turned its back on the problem.'[35]

The election of Bolsonaro has done nothing to help racial inequality in the country, least of all for the indigenous people of Brazil, whom he has regularly attacked using extreme racist language. In 2020 he said: 'The Indians are evolving, more and more they are human being like us'; and back in 1998 he went as far as to laud the genocide of native communities in the USA: 'It's a shame that the Brazilian cavalry hasn't been as efficient as the Americans, who exterminated the Indians.'[36]

Since taking office, his racist politics have been turned into racist policies. Human Rights Watch warns of 'Bolsonaro's plan to legalize crimes against indigenous peoples'.[37]

Bolsonaro's extreme and explicit homophobia, misogyny and racism pose a genuine threat to the people of Brazil – but also to the very survival of democracy in the country. His presidency has to be viewed in the context of his own long history of anti-democratic and pro-dictatorial beliefs, coupled with the fragility of Brazil's democratic institutions. Central here is Bolsonaro's positive view of the bloody military dictatorship that ruled the country between 1964 and 1985. According to the Brazilian Truth Commission, the dictatorship was responsible for 434 deaths and disappearances of opponents and the massacre of 8,000 native people.[38] Despite this, Bolsonaro has denied it was truly a dictatorship and even told Viktor Orbán, the far-right leader of Hungary, that the military junta could not be described as such.[39] In part this was because, unlike many other Latin American dictatorships of the period, 'it maintained a façade of constitutional rule' and 'manipulated elections but did not abolish them'.[40] Bolsonaro has also lavished praise on other dictators such as Paraguayan president Alfredo Stroessner and Chilean president Augusto Pinochet,[41] leading Federico Finchelstein to accuse him of unabashedly using 'history as a mere propaganda tool', and claiming that he 'invented and then sought to personify a mythical age of Latin American dictatorships'.[42]

Bolsonaro has not confined his pro-dictatorship views to history – he has himself advocated for violent and bloody change. In 1999 he said:

> Through the vote, you will not change anything in this
> country, nothing, absolutely nothing! It will only change,

unfortunately, when, one day, we start a civil war here and do the work that the military regime did not do. Killing some 30,000, starting with FHC [then-President Fernando Henrique Cardoso], not kicking them out, killing! If some innocent people are going to die, fine, in any war, innocents die.[43]

When asked by the interviewer, 'If you were the president of the Republic today, would you close the National Congress?', he responded:

There's no doubt about it. I'd do a coup on the same day! It [the Congress] doesn't work! And I'm sure at least 90 percent of the population would throw a party, would applaud, because it does not work. Congress today is good for nothing, brother, it just votes for what the president wants. If he is the person who decides, who rules, who trumps the Congress, then let's have a coup quickly, go straight to a dictatorship.[44]

He also said: 'I'm in favour of torture, you know that. And the people are in favour as well.'[45]

When campaigning to be president he didn't hide such views. In fact, asked about rampant police violence, he replied: 'If a police officer kills ten, fifteen, or twenty alleged criminals with ten or thirty bullets each, he needs to get a medal and not be prosecuted.'[46] In the words of Damian Platt, this amounted to Bolsonaro promising 'to make it easier for more police to kill more people'.[47] It is unsurprising, then, that gun ownership rose by 98% during his first year as president, and in April 2020 he revoked decrees designed to enable the tracing of weapons and tripled the quantity of ammunition available to civilians.[48] The journalist Fernando de Barros e Silva described this as 'the victory of the militia model of management of Brazilian violence'.[49] In his first two years in power Bolsonaro had already 'ratcheted up his campaign to undermine democratic institutions with constant attacks on the judiciary, congress, state governments and the traditional media',[50] representing 'the greatest setback for social progress in Brazil since the military coup of 1964', according to Platt.[51] Finchelstein has stated that 'Bolsonaro's style and substance, steeped in political violence, national chauvinism, and personal glorification, have essential fascist hallmarks'.[52] The pillars of Brazilian democracy and rule of law are trembling.

When measuring the danger of a far-right politician or government, most would understandably and correctly think about the terrible effect that their election will have on minority communities, the rule of law and liberal democratic norms. However, in a globalised world, the election of a far-right figure in one country can have reverberations around the globe. Victory in one place can spur on victory in another and create a sense of epochal change that becomes self-realising. Policies enacted by far-right governments can also have dramatic effects outside their own country. This was most obvious with the election of Trump in the US, but it can also be the case in smaller countries such as Poland and Hungary, as every election of a far-right government contributes to the normalisation of far-right politics in the eyes of the global community. One issue more than any other shows the dramatic global effects that can result from the election of a far-right government: climate change.

With the victory of Bolsonaro the earth's lungs have been thrown into even worse peril. In August 2020, with fires ripping through the Amazon, he went on TV to declare that his government would take a 'zero tolerance' approach to environmental crimes. Yet in truth, it is Bolsonaro himself who is the environmental criminal. Since taking office he has, as pointed out by the *New York Times*, 'worked relentlessly and unapologetically to roll back enforcement of Brazil's once-strict environmental protections'.[53] In his first few years in power he has 'championed industries that want greater access to protected areas of the Amazon, sought to weaken the land rights of Indigenous people and scaled back efforts to combat illegal logging, ranching and mining'.[54] He has even called for the abolition of what he calls the 'industry' which issues fines for environmental crimes. 'With Bolsonaro's speeches since 2018, what they understand on the ground is that environmental crime is now free of charge', said Suely Araújo, a political scientist at the University of Brasília.[55]

It is perhaps no surprise, then, that data for the first four months of 2020 indicated that deforestation in Brazil's section of the Amazon was up 55% from the previous year.[56] In part this is the result of a substantial drop in government spending on forest inspection activities by the Brazilian Institute of Environment and Renewable Natural Resources (IBAMA). The government also significantly reduced funding for the country's national climate change plan, falling from R$436 million in 2019 to just R$247 in 2020.[57] This cut in funding was the direct result of Bolsonaro's personal scepticism over climate change and his vocal opposition to the environmental movement. When asked by a journalist how to combine agricultural development with environmental protection, he replied: 'It's enough to eat a little less. You talk about environmental pollution. It's enough to poop every other day. That will be better for the whole world.'[58] In September 2019 his Foreign Minister, Ernesto Araújo, claimed that 'There is no climate change catastrophe', and continued: 'From the debate that is going on it would seem that the world is ending.'[59] He even argued that climate change is part of a plot by 'cultural Marxists' to compromise Western powers and increase Chinese and non-Western global influence.[60] For these reasons, the Brazilian politician and environment activist Marina Silva, together with numerous other former environmental ministers, stated that the Bolsonaro administration is turning Brazil into an 'exterminator of the future'.[61] It's perhaps no great surprise that Bolsonaro failed to attend the COP26 climate change conference in Glasgow in November 2021.

The damaging rhetoric and policies of the Bolsonaro administration, and their already measurable effects on the Amazon, could have long-lasting effects on the battle against climate change, an issue severely compounded by Donald Trump's similarly overt climate denial while in office. In 2012 Trump tweeted: 'The concept of global warming was created by and for the Chinese to make U.S. manufacturing non-competitive.' Then in 2013 he claimed: 'Global warming is a total, and very expensive, hoax!'[62] As with Bolsonaro and the Amazon, Trump's climate denial has had disastrous effects, promoting the use of fossil fuels in America, and in June 2017 he announced US withdrawal from the 2015 Paris Agreement on climate change mitigation, a decision quickly reversed by his successor Joe Biden upon becoming president.

However, climate change denial is by no means confined to the far right in the Americas. Much of the European far right has followed suit. Following the 2019 European Parliament elections the radical and far right held almost a quarter of the seats, as well as being represented in eight national governments, meaning they had a very real ability to affect climate policy in Europe. A 2019 report by Stella Schaller and Alexander Carius explored the European radical right's attitudes towards climate change and found that:

> Two out of three right-wing populist Members of the European Parliament (MEPs) regularly vote against climate and energy policy measures. In Europe's only directly elected body, the European Parliament, half of all votes against resolutions on climate and energy come from the right-wing populist party spectrum. Seven of the 21 right-wing populist parties analised [*sic*] deny climate change, its anthropogenic causes, and negative consequences.[63]

One of the worst climate denial offenders in Europe is the AfD in Germany, which ran a pro-diesel campaign and claimed that 'CO_2 is not a pollutant but an indispensable component of all life' in its 2017 federal election programme.[64]

The far right's interest in climate politics can, in part, be explained by their brazen rejection of accepted mores of mainstream, liberal-left political discussion and their railing against 'globalist elites' who are supposedly suppressing and controlling the common-sense views and freedoms of the people.

That said, climate denial is not ubiquitous across the far right. In coming years we are likely to see far-right individuals and parties attempt to co-opt environmentalism for their own aims. There has always been a strand of the far right that has placed environmentalism at the core of its politics, often expanding the definition to include the preservation of traditional societies as well as ecology, a nationalism rooted in '*Blut und Boden*' (blood and soil), a Nazi-era slogan that was chanted at the alt-right Charlottesville rally in 2017.[65] As pointed out by my colleague David Lawrence: 'Murky nazi forums are now often flooded with propaganda produced by the so-called "Eco Gang", referencing a mystical connection to the land, the violent enforcement of animal rights, the dangers of overpopulation, and a looming ecological collapse.'[66] This 'eco-fascism' has shown itself to be deadly in recent years: both of the far-right terrorist attacks in Christchurch and El Paso were carried out by people who sought to frame their murderous hate crimes as solutions to environmental decline and supposed overpopulation.[67]

To be honest, at HOPE not hate we were slow to realise the importance of climate change to our work on the far right. The impending climate crisis and the rise of the far right were understood by us to be vitally important but essentially separate phenomena. This began to change in 2018 following a chance conversation in a crowded pub in Westminster. A group of HNH researchers, including myself, was huddled around a small table with Craig Fowlie, the Global Editorial Director of Routledge publishing. Someone asked what the biggest threat to anti-fascism would be in the next few decades and we all came up with the usual replies: 'terrorism', 'online radicalisation', 'normalisation'. Then, as if it was the most obvious answer in the world, Craig said: 'It's climate change.' Furrowed brows and bemused glances shot around the table. Yet, by the end of that evening we were all convinced he was right, and the following day I sat down with Nick Lowles and began to plan for a whole new research area for us, one that continues to this day: climate change and the far right. That culminated in a major report, *Extreme Weather. Extreme Denial. Extreme Politics*, alongside a series of talks and conferences I organised in New York in 2019.

During the research for the project it became terrifyingly clear that the far right wouldn't just block effective action against climate change, it would also be in the best position to exploit its negative effects in the medium to long term. So in 2019, I headed to Africa to find out more about how climate change could affect migration to Europe – and what the possible far-right backlash might look like.

━━━

If you stand on the beaches of Tangier in Morocco and look out towards the horizon, you can see southern Spain. At its narrowest point the crossing is just over 14 kilometres, a mere one hour on the ferry, or a tantalising two or three hours if you're paddling in a dinghy. For Stephen (not his real name) it's taken five years to reach these beaches. He left Liberia on the southern coast of West Africa in 2014 and started his journey north, eventually hoping to make his way to Europe and a new life. He'd worked in the diamond trade, and after a deal went bad in Mali – he kept the details purposely vague – was forced to flee for his safety, leaving behind his daughter. 'I've stopped calling her', he said. 'I couldn't keep lying to her, being optimistic. It's better to just be silent.' He'd arrived in Tangier two weeks previously after taking a packed bus across the Sahara. Most migrants took buses, but the train from Marrakesh to Casablanca and the capital Rabat also had small groups of young West African men heading north, most in flip-flops and carrying no luggage save the odd plastic carrier bag.

Stephen was sleeping rough, along with 30 or so other migrants from across West Africa, in the grounds of the Our Lady of the Assumption Cathedral, a Roman Catholic church replete with beautiful blue stained glass. Most slept on the concrete floor with no covers, or at best a thin sheet or towel. A pungent smell of meat and burnt hair hung in the air around the camp, as the adjacent road was used to barbecue sheep's heads and shins. Locals hacked off the horns on the kerb of the street and plunged the skulls into charcoal pits, producing an acrid smoke. Despite not speaking Spanish, Stephen attends Mass each evening at seven o'clock. 'They are good to us', he explained, but food was hard to come by and whole days could pass without a meal. The dream was to secure the 150–200 euros necessary to get a place on a small inflatable boat. 'It's dangerous', he admitted, while tucking into a fried egg topped by a solitary triangle of Dairy Lea cheese, 'but it's worth it.' The small rubber dinghies are designed for nine people but can often be filled with up to twenty, and at 47 years old Stephen was much older than most making the perilous journey.

Tangier itself felt like a city experiencing a second wind. In the mid-20th century it played host to Tennessee Williams, Allen Ginsberg, Jack Kerouac, Brion Gysin and the Rolling Stones. With its tangled old streets and panoramic views of the Mediterranean it drew artists from around the world. Now the city boasted top-end glass-clad hotels overlooking a marina scattered with yachts and a smart promenade packed with evening walkers taking in the view of the wide sandy beach and the tranquil sea.

The migrant and refugee community in the city was largely invisible, with only a few black faces to be seen. Most of the migrants were living rough outside Tangier in so-called 'jungles' (makeshift camps), trying to avoid detection or arrest and the threat of being driven back to the Sahara and dropped off, only to start the journey all over again. The situation in Morocco regarding migrants and refugees was unsurprisingly complex. Most people enter by crossing the Algerian border, and the refugee population at the time was spread across 51 different cities and towns around the country. According to the UNHCR there were just 6,272 official refugees in Morocco, and a further 2,889 asylum seekers awaiting a decision, when I was in the country. If these numbers sound small it's because only a fraction of those who enter Morocco intend to stay. It's hard to estimate, but the true number of refugees and migrants in the country is likely much closer to 80,000 or 90,000, the vast majority of whom are aiming for Europe. 'We try to convince them [the refugees] not to make the risky journey across the sea and to make their life here in Morocco', explained Masaki Miyoshi, the Protection Officer at the UNHCR whom I met in Rabat. However, it's a hard argument to win and even the majority of those who do claim asylum will still try to make the journey to Europe at some point.

That journey is not easy, especially since the Moroccan and Spanish governments struck a deal to limit irregular migration in February 2019, and some, tired of being 'on standby', resign themselves to staying put and starting a new life in North Africa. This is why there has been a rise in asylum claims in the northern city of Nador, where people have realised it's now too hard to make it across. However, contrary to common belief, especially if you listen to the far right in Europe, the vast majority of migration in West and Central Africa is not heading towards Europe but is actually inter-regional. As Damien Jusselme, from the West and Central Africa Office of the UN's International Organization for Migration (IOM) explained to me: 'We estimate that around 95% of the flows in the region are inter-regional. People are migrating a lot within western and Central Africa and for a whole variety of reasons.' In fact, he added, 'arrivals in Europe are significantly down this year'.

According to the UNHCR's Operational Portal, as of 19 August 2019, just 53,761 refugees and migrants had arrived in Europe that year, 43,105 of whom arrived by sea to Italy, Greece, Spain, Cyprus and Malta. Greece had taken in over 29,000, followed by Spain with 18,458 and Italy with 4,393 people. The countries of origin vary, but as of June that year 14.4% came from Afghanistan, then Morocco with 12.9% and the Syrian Arab Republic with 9.9%. In the top ten countries of origin, West and Central Africa are well represented, with Mali, Guinea, Côte d'Ivoire and the Democratic Republic of the Congo making the list. These numbers, while significant, are much smaller than in previous years. 2015 saw the peak with 1,032,408 people making the trip to Europe, while 2020 saw 95,031 arrivals.[68] The journey to Europe remains extremely dangerous nonetheless, and the UN estimate that there were already 839 dead or missing people in 2019 by the time I stood on those beaches.

The reasons that people make the journey are extremely complex. Overwhelmingly, though, the primary 'push factors' are conflict and economic migration. The latter is often greeted with scepticism in Europe, framing these migrant stories as a simple economic 'choice', yet the truth is usually more complicated, as Jusselme from the IOM explains: 'It is indeed a choice, but within your economic migration, what part is a choice and what part is you being forced to actually move?' At present, climate change comes well down the list of push factors that are causing people to leave their homes and head north towards Europe. Daniel Trilling, author of *Lights in the Distance*, a book about migration and refugees in Europe, explains: 'Climate change may well result in displacement but by far the biggest causes of people moving along the refugee routes to Europe are war and inequality.' However, climate is likely to become a factor for migration in the future, and while the majority of those affected at present become IDPs (internally displaced people), this won't last for ever. We are likely to see increasing levels of trans-boundary migration caused by the effects of global heating.

At present there is an understandable tentativeness when discussing the issue of climate refugees. The fear is that talk of climate change causing mass migration to Europe will cause a backlash. In fact, for some NGO workers I spoke with, such as Hannes Stegemann, Director of Caritas Rabat in Morocco, climate change is supposedly 'not a worry'. Rather the real concern is that 'false links are often used for political manipulation. You induce fear – millions on the run because of climate change – and you get a xenophobic response out of fear.' Stegemann is right that we should not exaggerate and stoke a xenophobic backlash, but the evidence of the effect of a changing climate is so clear that you can't help feeling there is something of a 'duck and cover' reaction going on in parts of the NGO world when it comes to this issue.

One person for whom that can't be said is Steve Trent, co-founder and Director of the Environmental Justice Foundation. He argues that it is 'absolutely clear that the numbers involved, even if we went to net zero [emissions] tomorrow, are going to be in the order of many tens of millions, and possibly hundreds of millions'. When asked where these affected populations will head for, he didn't hesitate: 'If you look for example at the Sahel, large swathes of sub-Saharan Africa, countries like Mali where it's already effectively in permanent drought, those people are not going to head south, they are going to head north.' In fact Trent lamented the lack of legislative and humanitarian preparation, without which he believes we will see Europe 'stress-tested to the point at which it breaks [...] and it's climate that's going to do it'. However, while it seems extremely likely that a changing climate will indeed force millions from their homes, and many will no doubt look to Europe for sanctuary, we must proceed with caution when making predictions. As Trilling succinctly puts it: 'It's important to recognise the threat climate change poses without being alarmist about migration.'

The attendance at the church that evening was pretty sparse. A few local Spanish Catholics were joined by a handful of migrants, some using the time to rest in the shade, others grabbing an hour to charge their phone at one of the plugs by the side of the pews. Stephen grinned and refused a prayer book when offered: 'I don't speak Spanish.' As the service finished he offered me his phone number and promised to get in contact when he reached Europe. When asked how long he thought it would take, he made a paddling motion and laughed: 'It depends how much energy I have!' In reality, it all depended on when he could scrimp and save the money to pay a people-smuggler, and whether he would then be one of the lucky ones who makes it across the Straits of Gibraltar unscathed. It had taken him five years to finally reach the Mediterranean and now he could see Europe on the horizon. He seemed optimistic and eager to start his new life, raise some money and be able to call his daughter again, this time with genuine good news. I didn't have the heart to tell him that I feared the welcome he might receive, having seen the far-right backlash during the so-called migrant crisis.

If even some of the predictions about the tragic effects of climate change on developing countries come true, we can expect increased migration to Europe and the West more generally. The far right are poised and ready to exploit the situation.

CONCLUSION

On 3 November 2020 Donald Trump lost the US Presidential election. However, on 6 January 2021, just days before the planned inauguration of Joe Biden, Trump supporters descended on Washington, DC in a shocking but ultimately unsuccessful attempt to overturn his electoral defeat. For months Trump had failed to concede the election, instead taking to social media to push unsubstantiated claims and outright misinformation about voter fraud. For many Trump supporters, especially those who believe in the bizarre QAnon conspiracy theory, the election had been stolen from them and they headed to the Capitol to take it back. With Trump's direct encouragement, thousands of his supporters marched on the Capitol Building while Congress was in session and beginning the Electoral College vote count that would confirm Biden's victory.

What followed shocked the world. Far-right protesters stormed past police lines, climbed the walls and broke through doors into the building itself. Live pictures showed Trump supporters entering the hallowed halls of American democracy, many dressed in military fatigues, some carrying weapons, others zip ties for the taking of hostages. For the first time in US history the Confederate battle flag flew inside the Capitol. Analysis of the footage in the days that followed proved the rioters to be from an array of far-right and neo-nazi organisations, though in a testament to the radical transformation of the GOP, many were just supporters of the Republican Party. Within a few blocks of the building two pipe bombs were found, one next to the Republican National Committee building, the other at the headquarters of the Democratic National Committee. This was not a protest, it was an attempted coup – and while it proved unsuccessful, it has left scars on American democracy that will take some time to fade.

The events surrounding the 2020 US election and the behaviour of many Trump supporters since are another reminder that the far right don't believe in democracy. They may stand in elections. They may ask for your vote. They may claim they believe in the rule of law and equal rights, but they don't believe in democracy. The far right believe in power. They believe in their rights but not your rights. They believe in their right to free speech but not your right to free speech. They condemn violence until they use it. Donald Trump has reminded us of this.

There is no doubt that Trump's defeat is good news, but any talk of it being the beginning of the end for the global far right is wildly misplaced. Over 74 million Americans voted for him in 2020. They voted for him after he called the neo-nazis and fascists at Charlottesville 'very fine people'; after he imposed a Muslim travel ban; after he withdrew from the Paris Agreement on climate change; after he retweeted anti-Muslim videos from the deputy leader of Britain First and after he separated migrant children from their parents at the Mexican border. Trump may have lost but there are millions and millions of people in America and around the world who still agree with him. His defeat is a welcome setback and further proof that the rise of the right is not inevitable; but across large parts of the globe, societies are moving away from liberal, progressive and democratic norms and towards fragmented, divided and anti-egalitarian societies. At the time of writing in late 2021, polls for the 2022 French presidential election show Marine Le Pen, who has proposed a hijab ban, still on course to reach the run-off round. There has also been the rise of the far-right, racist and antisemitic media commentator Eric Zemmour who has thrown his hat into the ring, dragging the debate in France even further to the right. Now is not the time for complacency. The pillars of liberal democracy continue to wobble.

The reasons for this are complex, and any book that gives you a simple explanation is lying to you. As we have seen, in part it is the negative effects of globalisation and neoliberal economics which have stratified communities and created ever more unequal societies. It is also the fault of political elites around the world who have failed to address the needs of whole sections of society for too long, leading them to think they had nowhere else to go until they eventually turned to the radical and far right. The battle between cultural and economic arguments will continue for years, but the historians of the future will likely settle on a combination of the two. We must also look at the role of the internet and the online world. It has offered us many wonderful opportunities to find knowledge, friends and lovers, but it has also provided tools that have been successfully exploited by those who seek to divide societies and destroy democracy. While globalisation and the internet have made the world smaller than ever before, they also seem to be dividing it. However, central to understanding our current situation is remembering the enduring nature of hatred, of prejudice and discrimination. Not everyone who voted for Trump, Bolsonaro or Modi is a racist or misogynist – but none of them minded enough about racism or misogyny not to. This is how we will lose. It won't be that everyone will become far-right, it will be not enough people caring about those who are.

Finally, there is a self-importance to this book that I have failed to avoid. I am of course an irrelevance in the vast world events which this book covers, a footnote I have arrogantly added myself. The personal stories I tell here are merely to add colour to a much larger and more important story. A story about the slow but steady rise of a form of ugly politics that has made millions of people's lives worse and will continue to do so.

My overriding feeling while writing this book has been one of fear but hope. The closer I have looked at what is happening in different parts of the world the more concerned I have become. It feels less like a series of unfortunate simultaneous events and more like a broad direction of travel. Writing it has convinced me more than ever that history isn't an inevitable linear journey towards ever more progress but rather a continuing fight that has to be won again and again. The other key reflection is that bad things are believed and done by normal people. If I think back on all the far-right activists I met, many of them I personally liked, even while despising their beliefs and wanting to stop them. It's so easy – and comforting – to dehumanise these people. To make them an abstract evil, a monster. In reality they are people, often not too different from you and me. That makes it all the more scary.

I hope this book does not overly romanticise my own story. There have been many times when I thought the cost of this work was too high, when the effect it had on my life seemed to outweigh the personal rewards or political successes. Taking on bad people comes with a cost. I have been physically threatened, chased, abused, thrown down stairs – and most painfully of all, I have been lied about and smeared in ways that nearly destroyed me. There have been moments when I thought it had taken everything from me and left me broken. It has hardened parts of me I wish it hadn't and softened others in a way that has left me vulnerable. It has created periods of pain, fear and loneliness from which I hid, all too often in the arms of hedonism.

Worst of all, there were times when I behaved in ways that made me worry I might be becoming a bad person, or at the very least doing things that bad people do. To be good at this job I had to become good at lying and ready to betray; and with time I have become better at both than I ever wanted to be. I told myself that the ends justify the means, that the danger of fascism excuses such behaviour. Maybe it does; possibly it doesn't. Yet I signed up for this, but my family did not, and seeing their names and addresses published by the far right was one of the lowest moments I've ever experienced doing this job.

While I have tried to be as honest as possible, there are of course stories missing, some because the people involved didn't want to be mentioned, others because it's simply not safe to do so yet. There are others missing because I don't feel ready to tell them. At times this job has taken over my whole life, consumed me. Times when the mission came above all else, when nothing and nobody mattered more. Moments when I put myself at unnecessary risk or, more shamefully, when I chose to put others in danger. I had no right. Some of these moments are in this book but others are not, because I am too cowardly to tell them. Too scared to take the time to think about them, reflect on my behaviour and how it affected me, but also how it affected the people around me. There are things I have done that are still too raw to explore, barely healed scabs I'm not ready to pick off just yet.

I also don't want to give the impression that everything I did, I did for the right motives; 'to fight the good fight'.

Sometimes I did it because it was fun or exciting. Fear and adrenalin are intoxicating, more addictive than any drug I've ever taken. I have rationalised that things were 'necessary' when actually I just wanted to do them, for the thrill, for the *glory*. Anyone in this game who tells you any different is lying.

Yet, I am still here doing it. That's because on balance the positives have far outweighed the negatives. This book is full of moments about which I am incredibly proud, fleeting minutes when I felt I made a difference. I have seen the world, made stories, had fun, fallen in love, fallen out of love, and most importantly made friends without whom none of it would have been possible and certainly not worthwhile.

The moments of victory in this tale are fleeting; the wider struggle continues and always will. But each win, however small, creates hope, and if anything will ever lead to a final victory over the far right it will indeed be HOPE.

NOTES

Introduction

1. Jean-Yves Camus and Nicolas Lebourg, *Far-Right Politics in Europe* (London: Belknap Press, 2017), 22.
2. Cas Mudde, *The Far Right Today* (Cambridge: Polity Press, 2019), 7.
3. Mudde, *The Far Right Today*, 7.
4. George Orwell, 'What is Fascism?', available here: https://www.orwell.ru/library/articles/As_I_Please/english/efasc
5. Roger Griffin, quoted in Dylan Matthews, 'Is Trump a fascist? 8 experts weigh in', *Vox*, 23 October 2020. Available here: https://www.vox.com/policy-and-politics/21521958/what-is-fascism-signs-donald-trump
6. Orwell, 'What is Fascism?'
7. Robert O. Paxton, *The Anatomy of Fascism* (London: Allen Lane, 2004), 21.
8. Gilbert Allardyce, 'What Fascism is Not: Thoughts on the Deflation of a Concept', *American Historical Review*, 84:2 (1979), 367–88.
9. Graham Macklin, *Failed Führers: A History of Britain's Extreme Right* (Abingdon: Routledge, 2020), 8.
10. Roger Griffin, *The Nature of Fascism* (London: Routledge, 1991), 26.

Chapter 1: From the British National Party to Brexit

1. Joe Mulhall, *British Fascism After the Holocaust: From the Birth of Denial to the Notting Hill Riots, 1939–1958* (Abingdon: Routledge, 2021), 54–6.
2. Matthew J. Goodwin, *New British Fascism: Rise of the British National Party* (Abingdon: Routledge, 2011), 37.
3. Daniel Trilling, *Bloody Nasty People: The Rise of Britain's Far Right* (London: Verso, 2013), 61.
4. Trilling, *Bloody Nasty People*, 11–19.
5. Quoted in Alan Sykes, *The Radical Right in Britain* (Basingstoke: Palgrave Macmillan, 2005), 136.
6. Graham Macklin, *Failed Führers: A History of Britain's Extreme Right* (Abingdon: Routledge, 2020), 481–5.
7. *Freedom* (Cumbria: British National Party, 2001).

8. Richard Thurlow, *Fascism in Britain: From Oswald Mosley's Blackshirts to the National Front* (London: I.B. Tauris, 2009), 212. See also Joe Mulhall, 'The Unbroken Thread: British Fascism, Its Ideologues and Ideologies, 1939–1960' (PhD dissertation, Royal Holloway, University of London, 2016).

9. Martin Walker, *The National Front* (Glasgow: Fontana/Collins, 1977), 134–8.

10. Matthew Collins, quoted in 'It's Not Easy to Burn A Book' (BBC Radio 4 podcast audio, 2019), https://www.bbc.co.uk/programmes/m0002cxn, accessed 29 July 2020.

11. *Freedom* (2001).

12. Nick Griffin, 'Our Fight in the Culture Clash', *Identity* 64, 2006, quoted in Matthew Feldman, Paul Jackson (eds.), *Doublespeak: The Rhetoric of the Far Right Since 1945* (New York: Columbia University Press, 2014), 129–30.

13. Goodwin, *New British Fascism*, 56–61.

14. Trilling, *Bloody Nasty People*, 139.

15. https://www.youtube.com/watch?v=R7CUHhJzDc8

16. https://www.youtube.com/watch?v=R7CUHhJzDc8

17. https://www.youtube.com/watch?v=R7CUHhJzDc8

18. https://www.youtube.com/watch?v=R7CUHhJzDc8

19. Trilling, *Bloody Nasty People*, 181.

20. Tim Wigmore, 'What Killed the BNP?', *New Statesman*, 12 January 2016, https://www.newstatesman.com/politics/staggers/2016/01/what-killed-bnp

21. Robert Ford and Matthew Goodwin, *Revolt on the Right: Explaining Support for the Radical Right in Britain* (Abingdon: Routledge, 2014), xiiv.

22. Ford and Goodwin, *Revolt on the Right*, 97.

23. Nick Lowles, 'Straight out of the Far Right Playbook', HOPE not hate e-newsletter, 15 February 2016.

24. Nigel Copsey, *Anti-Fascism in Britain* (Abingdon: Routledge, 2017), 218.

25. 'Hatred not hope', *Jewish Chronicle*, 17 December 2015.

26. Dave Renton, *The New Authoritarians: Convergence on the Right* (London: Pluto Press, 2019), 69.

27. Maria Sobolewska and Robert Ford, *Brexitland: Identity, Diversity and the Reshaping of British Politics* (Cambridge: Cambridge University Press, 2020), 10.

28. Renton, *The New Authoritarians*, 73.

29. Sobolewska and Ford, *Brexitland*, 3.

30. Paul Stocker, *English Uprising: Brexit and the Mainstreaming of the Far Right* (London: Melville House UK, 2017), 11.
31. Stocker, *English Uprising*, 11.
32. Stocker, *English Uprising*, 12.
33. Stocker, *English Uprising*, 11.
34. Stocker, *English Uprising*, 11.
35. Simon Winlow, Steve Hall and James Treadwell, *The Rise of the Right: English Nationalism and the Transformation of Working-class Politics* (Bristol: Policy Press, 2017), 201.
36. Winlow, Hall and Treadwell, *The Rise of the Right*, 204.
37. Winlow, Hall and Treadwell, *The Rise of the Right*, 205.

Chapter 2: The 'Counter-Jihad' Movement and Anti-Muslim Street Protest

1. http://www.britishfuture.org/articles/news/million-british-muslims-reject-extremists-on-poppy-wearing/
2. Joel Busher, *The Making of Anti-Muslim Protest: Grassroots Activism in the English Defence League* (Abingdon: Routledge, 2016), 5.
3. Busher, *The Making of Anti-Muslim Protest*, 5.
4. George Kassimeris and Leonie Jackson, 'The Ideology and Discourse of the English Defence League: "Not Racist, Not Violent, Just No Longer Silent"', *The British Journal of Politics and International Relations* 17, 2015, 174.
5. Kassimeris and Jackson, 'The Ideology and Discourse of the English Defence League', 175.
6. Hilary Pilkington, *Loud and Proud: Passion and Politics in the English Defence League* (Manchester: Manchester University Press, 2016), 37.
7. Kassimeris and Jackson, 'The Ideology and Discourse of the English Defence League', 185.
8. 'EDL Mission Statement', Gates of Vienna, 15 January 2011, http://gatesofvienna.blogspot.com/2011/01/edl-mission-statement.html
9. Kassimeris and Jackson, 'The Ideology and Discourse of the English Defence League', 172–3.
10. Nigel Copsey, *The English Defence League: Challenging Our Country and Our Values of Social Inclusion, Fairness and Equality* (London: Faith Matters, 2010), 5.
11. Busher, *The Making of Anti-Muslim Protest*, 135.
12. 'EDL leader Tommy Robinson quits group', BBC News, 8 October 2013, https://www.bbc.co.uk/news/uk-politics-24442953

13. Paul Golding, quoted in 'Feeble fascist criminals Britain First finally banned from Facebook', *GQ*, 14 March 2018, available here: https://www.gq-magazine.co.uk/article/britain-first

14. Bennett Clifford and Helen Christy Powell, 'De-Platforming and the Online Extremist's Dilemma', *Lawfare*, 6 June 2019, available here: https://www.lawfareblog.com/de-platforming-and-online-extremists-dilemma

15. Clifford and Powell, 'De-Platforming and the Online Extremist's Dilemma', 6 June 2019.

16. Lella Nouri, Nuria Lorenzo-Dus and Amy-Louise Watkin, 'Following the Whack-a-Mole: Britain First's Visual Strategy from Facebook to Gab', Global Research Network on Terrorism and Technology, Paper No. 4, Royal United Services Institute, available here: https://rusi.org/sites/default/files/20190704_grntt_paper_4.pdf

17. Nouri, Lorenzo-Dus and Watkin, 'Following the Whack-a-Mole: Britain First's Visual Strategy from Facebook to Gab', Global Research Network on Terrorism and Technology: Paper No. 4. *Royal United Services Institute*. Available here: https://rusi.org/sites/default/files/20190704_grntt_paper_4.pdf

Chapter 3: The Effect of Islamist Extremism and the Islamic State

1. Roger Eatwell, quoted in Chris Holmsted Larsen, 'Partners in crime? A Historical Perspective on Cumulative Extremism in Denmark', *CREX*, 14 April 2020, available here: https://www.sv.uio.no/c-rex/english/news-and-events/right-now/2020/partners-in-crime.html

2. Omar Bakri later claimed that he was born in Lebanon; see Kylie Baxter, *British Muslims and the Call to Global Jihad* (Clayton: Monash University Press, 2007), 53.

3. 'The Khalifah will return ...', www.muhajiroun.com, 14 August 2003.

4. 'Al-Muhajiroun – Islamists in the US: Part 2', *Spero News*, 2007 (accessed 18 July 2013), available from: http://www.speroforum.com/a/7541/AlMuhajiroun--Islamists-in-the-US-Part-2#.UlU0_WDgGWh

5. 'Luton parade protesters "were members of extremist group"', *The Telegraph*, 2009 (accessed 18 June 2014), available from: http://www.telegraph.co.uk/news/uknews/4976105/Luton-parade-protesters-were-members-of-extremist-group.html

6. Dominic Casciani, (2010), 'Profile: Islam4UK', BBC News, 2010 (accessed 18 June 2014), available from: http://news.bbc.co.uk/1/hi/uk/8441499.stm

7. 'Proposed Wootton Bassett Protest: A publicity Stunt that Deserves Disdain', Muslim Council of Britain, 2010 (accessed 12 October 2013), previously available from: http://www.mcb.org.uk/article_detail.php?article=announcement-853
8. 'Islam4UK Islamist group banned under terror laws', BBC News, 2010 (accessed 23 June 2014), available at: http://news.bbc.co.uk/1/hi/uk/8453560.stm
9. Jamie Doward and Andrew Wander, 'The Network', *The Observer*, 6 May 2007, available at: https://www.theguardian.com/world/2007/may/06/terrorism.jamiedoward
10. Anonymous interview, 2013.

Chapter 4: The European Far Right and the Migrant Crisis

1. https://dangerousspeech.org/wp-content/uploads/2019/11/Konvicka-Czech-Republic-case-study_Final.pdf
2. Waldemar Gurian, quoted in Dan Stone, *Goodbye To All That?: The Story of Europe Since 1945* (Oxford: Oxford University Press, 2014), 1.
3. Stone, *Goodbye To All That?*, viii.
4. Stone, *Goodbye To All That?*, 9.
5. Stone, *Goodbye To All That?*, ix.
6. Francis Fukuyama, 'The End of History?', *The National Interest*, Summer 1989, 1.
7. Paul Preston, quoted in 'Francisco Franco: Is it accurate to call the Spanish dictator a fascist?', *History Extra*, 21 August 2020, available at: https://www.historyextra.com/period/20th-century/was-spanish-dictator-francisco-franco-fascist/
8. Cas Mudde, *The Far Right Today* (Cambridge: Polity Press, 2019), 13.
9. Cas Mudde, *The Far Right Today*, 14.
10. Cas Mudde, *The Far Right Today*, 15.
11. Cas Mudde, *The Far Right Today*, 20.
12. Jamie Bartlett, Jonathan Birdwell, Mark Littler, *The New Face of Digital Populism* (London: Demos, 2011), 15.
13. Dave Renton, *The New Authoritarians: Convergence on the Right* (London: Pluto Press, 2019), 190.
14. Liz Fekete, *Europe's Fault Lines: Racism and the Rise of the Right* (London: Verso, 2019), 5–6.
15. Roger Eatwell and Matthew Goodwin, *National Populism: The Revolt Against Liberal Democracy* (London: Penguin Books. 2018), 5–6.
16. Cas Mudde, *The Far Right Today*, 87–8.

Chapter 5: American Militias and the Ku Klux Klan

1. https://www.thetimes.co.uk/article/we-faced-arrest-after-revealing-plot-to-kill-mp-rosie-cooper-say-anti-fascists-95dxjchpp

2. 'The Militia Movement', ADL, available here: https://www.adl.org/education/resources/backgrounders/militia-movement

3. David Neiwert, *Alt-America: The Rise of the Radical Right in The Age of Trump* (London: Verso, 2017), 80.

4. Cas Mudde, *The American Far Right* (Abingdon: Routledge, 2018), 5.

5. Leonard Zeskind, *Blood and Politics: The History of the White Nationalist Movement From the Margins to the Mainstream* (New York: Farrar, Straus and Giroux, 2009), xvii.

6. Terence McArdle, 'The Day 30,000 White Supremacists in KKK Robes Marched in the Nation's Capital', *The Washington Post*, 11 August 2018, available at: https://www.washingtonpost.com/news/retropolis/wp/2017/08/17/the-day-30000-white-supremacists-in-kkk-robes-marched-in-the-nations-capital/

7. The *Tampa Times*, quoted in: Sarah Churchwell, *Behold America: A History of America First and the American Dream* (London: Bloomsbury Publishing, 2019), 127.

8. Churchwell, *Behold America*, 130.

9. Churchwell, *Behold America*, 137.

10. Churchwell, *Behold America*, 196.

11. 'Ku Klux Klan', Southern Poverty Law Center, 2019, available at: https://www.splcenter.org/fighting-hate/extremist-files/ideology/ku-klux-klan

12. Zeskind, *Blood and Politics*, xvi.

13. Zeskind, *Blood and Politics*, xvii.

14. Quote taken from a report that is no longer available. Write-up of the report available here: Renee Lewis, 'Report: Anti-immigrant groups collude with homeland security employees', 30 June 2015: http://america.aljazeera.com/articles/2015/6/30/dhs-colluding-with-anti-immigrant-groups.html

15. 'Loyal White Knights – The Infamous Klan Group Falling Apart At the Seams', Southern Poverty Law Center, 7 December 2016, available at: https://www.splcenter.org/hatewatch/2016/12/07/loyal-white-knights-%E2%80%93%E2%80%93-infamous-klan-group-falling-apart-seams

Chapter 6: The Rise of President Trump

1. Brigitte Gabriel, quoted in Peter Beinart, 'America's Most Prominent Anti-Muslim Activist is Welcome in the White House', *The Atlantic*, 21 March 2017, available here: https://www.theatlantic.com/politics/archive/2017/03/americas-most-anti-muslim-activist-is-welcome-at-the-white-house/520323/

2. 'Robert Spencer Profile', Southern Poverty Law Center, available here: https://www.splcenter.org/fighting-hate/extremist-files/individual/robert-spencer

3. 'John Guandolo: America's Leading Anti-Muslim Conspiracist', Muslim Advocates, available here: https://muslimadvocates.org/advocacy/john-guandolo-americas-leading-anti-muslim-conspiracist/

4. David Lawrence and Gregory Davis, 'What is QAnon?', HOPE not hate, 22 October 2020, available here: https://www.hopenothate.org.uk/2020/10/22/what-is-qanon/

5. Gabriel, quoted in Beinart, 'America's Most Prominent Anti-Muslim Activist is Welcome in the White House'.

6. Michael Snyder, '19 Facts About the Deindustrialization of America That Will Make You Weep', *Business Insider*, 27 September 2010, available here: https://www.businessinsider.com/deindustrialization-factory-closing-2010-9?r=US&IR=T

7. William B. Bonvillian, 'US Manufacturing Decline and the Rise of the New Production Innovation Paradigms', OECD, 2017, available from: https://www.oecd.org/unitedstates/us-manufacturing-decline-and-the-rise-of-new-production-innovation-paradigms.htm

8. John Russo and Sherry Lee Linkon, 'The Social Cost of Deindustrialization' (first appeared in *Manufacturing a Better Future for America*, edited by Richard McCormack), available here: http://cwcs.ysu.edu/wp-content/uploads/2015/11/The-Social-Costs-Of-Deindustrialization.pdf

9. Annalyn Kurtz, '1 in 6 unemployed are substance abusers', *CNN*, 26 November 2013, available here: https://money.cnn.com/2013/11/26/news/economy/drugs-unemployed/index.html

10. 'Analysis of Drug-Related Overdose Deaths in Pennsylvania, 2015', DEA Intelligence Report, July 2016, available here: https://www.dea.gov/sites/default/files/2018-07/phi071216_attach.pdf

11. 'The Opioid Epidemic in the United States', State Health Access Data Assistance Center, available here: https://www.shadac.org/opioid-epidemic-united-states

12. Donald Trump's jobs plan speech, full transcript available here: https://www.politico.com/story/2016/06/full-transcript-trump-job-plan-speech-224891

13. Michelle Ye Hee Lee, 'How Many Trump Products Were Made Overseas? Here's the Complete List', *Washington Post*, 26 August 2016, available here: https://www.washingtonpost.com/news/fact-checker/wp/2016/08/26/how-many-trump-products-were-made-overseas-heres-the-complete-list/

14. Andrew Kaczynski, 'Trump on his Trump U Blog: "Outsourcing Jobs … Not Always A terrible Thing"', *Buzzfeed*, 2 March 2016, available here: https://www.buzzfeednews.com/article/andrewkaczynski/trump-on-his-trump-u-blog-outsourcing-jobs-not-always-a-terr

15. Cas Mudde, *The Far Right in America* (Abingdon: Routledge, 2018), 56.

16. Gino Spocchia, '45% of Republicans approve of the Capitol riots, poll claims', *The Independent*, 7 January 2021, available here: https://www.independent.co.uk/news/world/americas/us-election-2020/republicans-congress-capitol-support-trump-b1783807.html

17. 'Tea Party Supporters Overlap Republican Base', *Gallup*, 2 July 2010, available here: https://news.gallup.com/poll/141098/Tea-Party-Supporters-Overlap-Republican-Base.aspx?version=print

18. Ronald P. Formisano, *The Tea Party: A Brief History* (Baltimore: The John Hopkins University Press, 2012), 8.

19. Theda Skocpol and Vanessa Williamson, *The Tea Party and the Remaking of Republican Conservatism* (Oxford: Oxford University Press, 2012), 5.

20. Katie Connolly, 'What Exactly is the Tea Party?', BBC, 16 September 2010, available here: https://www.bbc.co.uk/news/world-us-canada-11317202

21. Jeremy W. Peters, 'The Tea Party Didn't Get What It Wanted, but It Did Unleash the Politics of Anger', *New York Times*, 28 August 2019, available here: https://www.nytimes.com/2019/08/28/us/politics/tea-party-trump.html

22. David Neiwert, *Alt-America: The Rise of the Radical Right in The Age of Trump* (London: Verso, 2017), 139.

23. Peters, 'The Tea Party Didn't Get What It Wanted, but It Did Unleash the Politics of Anger'.

24. Mudde, *The Far Right in America*, 68.

25. Gregory Krieg, 'How did Trump win? Here are 24 theories', CNN, 10 November 2016, available here: https://edition.cnn.com/2016/11/10/politics/why-donald-trump-won/index.html

26. Matt Grossman's research, discussed in Roger Eatwell and Matthew Goodwin, *National Populism: The Revolt Against Liberal Democracy* (London: Pelican Books, 2018), 4.
27. Dave Renton, *The New Authoritarians: Convergence on the Right* (London: Pluto Press, 2019), 121.
28. Diana Mutz's research, discussed in Eatwell and Goodwin, *National Populism*, 4–5.
29. Diana Mutz, quoted in Eatwell and Goodwin, *National Populism*, 5.

Chapter 7: Inside the International Alt-Right

1. Jack Donovan, *Androphilia: Rejecting the Gay Identity, Reclaiming Masculinity* (third edition; electronic) (Milwaukee: Dissonant Hum, 2012), 206.
2. https://www.altcensored.com/watch?v=Lvp8NZOauYw
3. Jason Jorjani, quoted in: Patrik Hermansson, David Lawrence, Joe Mulhall and Simon Murdoch, *The International Alt-Right: Fascism for the 21st Century?* (Abingdon: Routledge, 2020), 11.
4. I created this definition of the alt-right for the co-authored book as above: Hermansson, Lawrence, Mulhall and Murdoch, *The International Alt-Right*.
5. Richard Spencer, in 'Transcript: Richard Spencer Interview with James Allsup: "The Alt-Right's Future in Trump's America"', *Sons of Europa*, 19 April 2017, previously available at: http://sonsofeuropa.com/2017/04/19/transcript-richard-spencer-interview-with-james-allsup-the-alt-rights-future-in-trumps-america/
6. Rebel Media, *Gavin McInnes: What is the Alt-Right?* (online video), available at: https://www.youtube.com/watch?v=UQCZ9izaCa4 (accessed 8 November 2018).
7. Daniel Friberg, quoted in 'In Europe, Some Ultra-Conservatives Say Their National Identity is At Risk', ABC News (online video), available at: https://www.youtube.com/watch?v=xMxHrFabvt0 (accessed 23 November 2019).
8. Tamir Bar-On, *Where Have All the Fascists Gone?* (Abingdon: Routledge, 2007).
9. Simon Murdoch, 'The Manosphere', HOPE not hate, 18 February 2019, available at: https://www.hopenothate.org.uk/2019/02/18/state-of-hate-2019-manosphere-explained/
10. Patrik Hermansson, 'Libertarianism and the Alternative Right', HOPE not hate, 5 March 2018, available at: https://www.hopenothate.org.uk/2018/03/05/libertarianism-alternative-right/

11. For details on these movements, see: Joe Mulhall, Simon Murdoch, David Lawrence, Patrik Hermansson, *The International Alt-Right: From Charlottesville to the White House* (London: HOPE not hate, 2017), 12–13.

12. Attended by author; Truth Against The World, *The Alt-Right Press Conference | Richard Spencer, Peter Brimelow & Jared Taylor*, 2016 (online video), available at: https://www.youtube.com/watch?v=aJWLjRK2SRo (accessed 21 October 2019).

13. Paul Joseph Watson video; republished as: 3ilm MI, *the west is the best*, 2016 (online video), available at: https://www.youtube.com/watch?v=AeVyL5pLfZY (accessed 4 November 2019).

14. For more details on Colin Jordan's World Union of National Socialists, see: Paul Jackson, *Colin Jordan and Britain's Neo-Nazi Movement* (London: Bloomsbury Academic, 2016). For more information on the counter-jihad movement, see: Joe Mulhall and Nick Lowles, *The Counter-Jihad Movement: Anti-Muslim Hatred From the Margins to the Mainstream* (London: HOPE not hate, 2015).

15. Caitlin Dewey, 'The Only Guide to Gamergate You Will Ever Need to Read', *Washington Post*, 14 October 2019, available at: https://www.washingtonpost.com/news/the-intersect/wp/2014/10/14/the-only-guide-to-gamergate-you-will-ever-need-to-read/

16. Nick Lowles, Joe Mulhall, David Lawrence, Simon Murdoch, *Breitbart: A Rightwing Plot to Shape Europe's Future* (London: HOPE not hate, 2016).

17. Allum Bokhari and Milo Yiannopoulos, 'An Establishment Conservative's Guide to the Alt-Right', *Breitbart*, 29 March 2016, available at: https://www.breitbart.com/tech/2016/03/29/an-establishment-conservatives-guide-to-the-alt-right/

18. Sarah Posner, 'How Donald Trump's New Campaign Chief Created an Online Haven for White Nationalists', *Mother Jones*, 22 August 2016, available at: https://www.motherjones.com/politics/2016/08/stephen-bannon-donald-trump-alt-right-breitbart-news/

19. Betsy Swan and Gideon Resnick, 'Alt-Right Rejoices at Donald Trump's Steve Bannon Hire', *The Daily Beast*, 17 August 2016, available at: https://www.thedailybeast.com/alt-right-rejoices-at-donald-trumps-steve-bannon-hire

20. 'Jared Taylor Profile', Southern Poverty Law Center: https://www.splcenter.org/fighting-hate/extremist-files/individual/jared-taylor

21. 'Kevin MacDonald Profile', Southern Poverty Law Center: https://www.splcenter.org/fighting-hate/extremist-files/individual/kevin-macdonald

22. 'Peter Brimelow Profile', Southern Poverty Law Center: https://www.splcenter.org/fighting-hate/extremist-files/individual/peter-brimelow

23. Daniel Lombroso and Yoni Appelbaum, '"Hail Trump!": White Nationalists Salute the President-Elect', *The Atlantic*, 21 November 2016, available at: https://www.theatlantic.com/politics/archive/2016/11/richard-spencer-speech-npi/508379/

24. Mitch Smith, 'James Fields Sentenced to Life in Prison for Death of Heather Heyer in Charlottesville', *New York Times*, 28 June 2019, available at: https://www.nytimes.com/2019/06/28/us/james-fields-sentencing.html

25. Donald Trump, quoted in Glenn Kessler, 'The "very fine people" at Charlottesville: Who Were they?', *Washington Post*, 8 May 2020, available here: https://www.washingtonpost.com/politics/2020/05/08/very-fine-people-charlottesville-who-were-they-2/

Chapter 8: Identitarians At Sea and On Land

1. Lizzie Dearden, 'Christchurch Shooter Donated Thousands to Far-Right Groups and Websites Before Attack, Report Shows', *The Independent*, 8 December 2020, available here: https://www.independent.co.uk/news/world/australasia/brenton-tarrant-christchurch-donations-generation-identity-b1768056.html

2. Simon Murdoch, 'Man Accused of Halle Terror Attack Partly Inspired by Generation Identity', HOPE not hate, 22 July 2020, available here: https://www.hopenothate.org.uk/2020/07/22/man-accused-of-halle-terror-attack-partly-inspired-by-generation-identity/

3. Simon Murdoch and Joe Mulhall, *From Banners to Bullets: The International Identitarian Movement* (London: HOPE not hate, 2019).

4. Roger Eatwell, *Fascism: A History* (London: Pimlico, 2003), 313.

5. Andrea Mammone, Emmanuel Godin, Brian Jenkins (eds), *Varieties of Right-Wing Extremism in Europe* (Abingdon: Routledge, 2013), 55.

6. Alain de Benoist and Charles Champetier, *Manifesto for a European Renaissance* (UK: Arktos Media, 2012), 15.

7. de Benoist and Champetier, *Manifesto for a European Renaissance*, 32.

8. de Benoist and Champetier, *Manifesto for a European Renaissance*, 34.

9. Guillaume Faye, *Why We Fight: Manifesto of the European Resistance* (Budapest: Arktos Media, 2011), 334.

10. George Ritzer, *Globalization: A Basic Text* (Wiley-Blackwell, 2011), 207. This also assumes cultures are clearly demarcated entities linked to specific geographic locations. As Akhil Gupta and James Ferguson describe, this is an 'assumed isomorphism of space, place, and culture'. Akhil Gupta and James Ferguson, 'Beyond "Culture": Space, Identity, and the Politics of Difference', *Cultural Anthropology*, 7:1 (1992), 7.

11. De Benoist, quoted in José Pedro Zúquete, *The Identitarians: The Movement Against Globalism and Islam in Europe* (Notre Dame, IN: University of Notre Dame Press, 2018), 11, 14.

12. Guilliame Faye, quoted in Zúquete, *The Identitarians*, 14.

13. Philippe Vardon, foreword to Markus Willinger, *Generation Identity: A Declaration of War Against the '68ers* (UK: Arktos Media, 2013), 9.

14. Julius Evola, quoted in Daniel Friberg, *The Real Right Returns: A Handbook for the True Opposition* (United Kingdom, Arktos Media Ltd, 2015), 15.

15. Vardon, foreword to Willinger, *Generation Identity*, 9.

16. Willinger, *Generation Identity*, 14–15.

17. Willinger, *Generation Identity*, 24–7.

18. Willinger, *Generation Identity*, 71.

19. Stéphanie Trouillard, 'France to ban far-right group Generation Identity', France 24, 17 February 2021, available here: https://www.france24.com/en/france/20210217-france-to-ban-far-right-group-generation-identity

Chapter 9: Modi's India and Hindu Nationalism

1. V.S. Naipaul, *India: A Million Mutinies Now* (London: Picador, 2010), 490.

2. Patrick French, *India: A Portrait* (London: Penguin, 2012), 81.

3. Lance Price, *The Modi Effect: Inside Narendra Modi's Campaign to Transform India* (London: Hodder and Stoughton, 2016), 1.

4. French, *India*, 85.

5. French, *India*, 82.

6. Cas Mudde, *The Far Right Today* (Cambridge: Polity Press, 2019), 51.

7. Price, *The Modi Effect*, 19.

8. French, *India*, 62.

9. French, *India*, 61.

10. French, *India*, 61.

11. Achin Vanaik, *The Rise of Hindu Authoritarianism: Secular Claims, Communal Realities* (London: Verso, 2017), 2.

12. Mudde, *The Far Right Today*, 44.

13. Vanaik, *The Rise of Hindu Authoritarianism*, 1.

14. Mudde, *The Far Right Today*, 23.

15. Walter Andersen and Shridhar D. Damle, *Messengers of Hindu Nationalism: How the RSS Reshaped India* (London: Hurst and Company, 2019), xi.

16. Andersen and Damle, *Messengers of Hindu Nationalism*, xii.

17. Mudde, *The Far Right Today*, 93.

18. Andersen and Damle, *Messengers of Hindu Nationalism*, xviii.

19. Andersen and Damle, *Messengers of Hindu Nationalism*, xi.

20. Vanaik, *The Rise of Hindu Authoritarianism*, 1.

21. Mark Tully, 'How the Babri Mosque Destruction Shaped India', BBC, 6 December 2017, available here: https://www.bbc.co.uk/news/world-asia-india-42219773

22. French, *India*, 64.

23. French, *India*, 63.

24. Prabhash K. Dutta, 'How RSS and Ram Mandir Campaign Mainstreamed One Other', *India Today*, 6 August 2020, available here: https://www.indiatoday.in/news-analysis/story/rss-ram-mandir-campaign-1708330-2020-08-06

25. Mudde, *The Far Right Today*, 23.

26. Mudde, *The Far Right Today*, 74.

27. Andersen and Damle, *Messengers of Hindu Nationalism*, ix.

28. Vanaik, *The Rise of Hindu Authoritarianism*, 18.

29. Vanaik, *The Rise of Hindu Authoritarianism*, 17.

30. French, *India*, 89.

31. Roger Griffin, *The Nature of Fascism* (London: Routledge, 1991), 26.

32. Sumanta Banerjee, quoted in Patrik Hermansson, David Lawrence, Joe Mulhall, Simon Murdoch, *The International Alt-Right: Fascism for the 21st Century?* (London: Routledge, 2020), 244.

33. Hermansson, Lawrence, Mulhall, Murdoch, *The International Alt-Right*, 242.

34. Mudde, *The Far Right Today*, 30.

35. Price, *The Modi Effect*, 16.

36. 'Opposition is Against Technology but BJP Wants to Promote a Modern India, says Modi', *The Hindu*, 7 May 2018, available here: https://www.thehindu.com/news/national/bjp-wants-to-promote-modern-india-says-narendra-modi/article23799929.ece

37. Narendra Modi, quoted in Price, *The Modi Effect*, 17.
38. Price, *The Modi Effect*, 14.
39. Quotes in Hermansson, Lawrence, Mulhall, Murdoch, *The International Alt-Right*, 245
40. Quote in Hermansson, Lawrence, Mulhall, Murdoch, *The International Alt-Right*, 245.

Chapter 10: Bolsonaro's Brazil, the Global Pandemic and Climate Change

1. Alex Ward, 'Brazilian President Jair Bolsonaro's Failed Coronavirus Response, in One Video', *Vox*, 2 May 2020, available here: https://www.vox.com/2020/5/2/21245243/coronavirus-brazil-bolsonaro-response-video
2. Tom Phillips, 'Bolsonaro Says He "Wouldn't Feel Anything" if Infected With Covid-19 and Attacks State Lockdowns', *The Guardian*, 25 March 2020, available here: https://www.theguardian.com/world/2020/mar/25/bolsonaro-brazil-wouldnt-feel-anything-covid-19-attack-state-lockdowns
3. Antonia Noori Farzan and Miriam Berger, 'Bolsonaro Says Brazilians Must Not be "Sissies" About Coronavirus, as "All of Us Are Going to Die One Day"', *Washington Post*, 11 November 2020, available here: https://www.washingtonpost.com/world/2020/11/11/bolsonaro-coronavirus-brazil-quotes/
4. Samuel Stolton, 'Covid-19 Crisis Triggers EU Racism Against Asians, Rights Agency Says', *Euractiv*, 8 April 2020, available here: https://www.euractiv.com/section/global-europe/news/covid-19-crisis-triggers-eu-racism-against-asians-rights-agency-says/
5. Mark Townsend and Nosheen Iqbal, 'Far Right Using Coronavirus as Excuse to Attack Asians, Say Police', *The Observer*, 29 August 2020, available here: https://www.theguardian.com/society/2020/aug/29/far-right-using-coronavirus-as-excuse-to-attack-chinese-and-south-east-asians
6. Simon Murphy, 'Chinese people in UK targeted with abuse over coronavirus', *The Guardian*, 18 February 2020. Available here: https://www.theguardian.com/world/2020/feb/18/chinese-people-uk-targeted-racist-abuse-over-coronavirus-southampton
7. Jamie Grierson, 'Anti-Asian Hate Crimes Up 21% in UK During Coronavirus Crisis', *The Guardian*, 13 May 2020, available here: https://www.theguardian.com/world/2020/may/13/anti-asian-hate-crimes-up-21-in-uk-during-coronavirus-crisis

8. Vincent Coste, 'Coronavirus: France Faces "Epidemic" of Anti-Asian Racism', Euronews, 3 February 2020, available here: https://www.euronews.com/2020/02/03/coronavirus-france-faces-epidemic-of-anti-asian-racism

9. 'Coronavirus: French Asians Hit Back at Racism With "I'm Not a Virus"', BBC News, 29 January 2020, available here: https://www.bbc.co.uk/news/world-europe-51294305

10. 'Covid-19 Fueling Anti-Asian Racism and Xenophobia Worldwide', Human Rights Watch, 12 May 2020, available here: https://www.hrw.org/news/2020/05/12/covid-19-fueling-anti-asian-racism-and-xenophobia-worldwide

11. Yuebai Liu, 'Coronavirus Prompts "Hysterical, Shameful" Sinophobia in Italy', Al Jazeera, 18 February 2020, available here: https://www.aljazeera.com/news/2020/02/18/coronavirus-prompts-hysterical-shameful-sinophobia-in-italy/

12. 'Coronavirus-related Incidents of Xenophobia in Poland', All in for Integration, available here: http://www.forintegration.eu/pl/coronavirus-related-incidents-of-xenophobia-in-poland, and also: https://www.hrw.org/news/2020/04/06/abused-and-shunned-being-asian-descent-sweden-during-covid-19

13. https://www.ft.com/content/eeda65ea-4424-11ea-a43a-c4b328d9061c

14. Tweet by Flavio Bolsonaro, 6 September 2018, available here: https://twitter.com/FlavioBolsonaro/status/1037808900660256773

15. Damian Platt, Nothing By Accident: Brazil on the Edge (Damian Platt, 2020), 233.

16. 'Jair Bolsonaro: Brazil's Firebrand Leader Dubbed the Trump of the Tropics', BBC News, 31 December 2018, available here: https://www.bbc.co.uk/news/world-latin-america-45746013

17. Jair Bolsonaro, quoted in Andrew Fishman, 'Jair Bolsonaro is Elected President of Brazil. Read His Extremist, Far-Right Positions in his Own Words', The Intercept, 28 October 2018, available here: https://theintercept.com/2018/10/28/jair-bolsonaro-elected-president-brazil/

18. Bolsonaro, quoted in Fishman, 'Jair Bolsonaro is Elected President of Brazil'.

19. Bolsonaro, quoted in Fishman, 'Jair Bolsonaro is Elected President of Brazil'.

20. Bolsonaro, quoted in Fishman, 'Jair Bolsonaro is Elected President of Brazil'.

21. Shaun Walker, 'Polish President Issues Campaign Pledge to fight "LGBT ideology"', The Guardian, 12 June 2020, available

here: https://www.theguardian.com/world/2020/jun/12/polish-president-issues-campaign-pledge-to-fight-lgbt-ideology

22. Shaun Walker, 'Polish President Scales Down Homophobic Rhetoric as Election Nears', *The Guardian*, 19 June 2020, available here: https://www.theguardian.com/world/2020/jun/19/polish-president-scales-down-homophobic-rhetoric-poland-election-nears-andrzej-duda

23. See Simon Murdoch, 'From Attack to "Defence": The Changing Nature of Far Right and LGBT+ Politics', HOPE not hate, 28 June 2019, available here: https://www.hopenothate.org.uk/2019/06/28/attack-defence-changing-nature-far-right-lgbt-politics/; and Patrik Hermansson, David Lawrence, Joe Mulhall and Simon Murdoch, *The International Alt-Right: Fascism for the 21st Century?* (London: Routledge, 2020), 194–203.

24. Bolsonaro, quoted in Fishman, 'Jair Bolsonaro is Elected President of Brazil'.

25. Bolsonaro, quoted in Fishman, 'Jair Bolsonaro is Elected President of Brazil'.

26. Bolsonaro, quoted in Fishman, 'Jair Bolsonaro is Elected President of Brazil'.

27. Bolsonaro, quoted in Fishman, 'Jair Bolsonaro is Elected President of Brazil'.

28. Federico Finchelstein, *A Brief History of Fascist Lies* (Oakland: University of California Press, 2020), 4.

29. Jair Bolsonaro, quoted in Lucia Binding, '"Trump of the Tropics" – Controversial Quotes by Brazil's New President Jair Bolsonaro', Sky News, 1 January 2019, available here: https://news.sky.com/story/trump-of-the-tropics-controversial-quotes-by-brazils-new-president-jair-bolsonaro-11539063

30. Jair Bolsonaro, quoted in Cas Mudde, *The Far Right Today* (Cambridge: Polity Press, 2019), 33.

31. Platt, *Nothing By Accident*, 24.

32. Michael Reid, *Brazil: The Troubled Rise of A Global Power* (New Haven, CT: Yale University Press, 2015), 181.

33. Ivanir dos Santos, quoted in Reid, *Brazil*, 182.

34. Reid, *Brazil*, 184.

35. Reid, *Brazil*, 184.

36. Jair Bolsonaro, quoted in 'What Brazil's President, Jair Bolsonaro, Has Said About Brazil's Indigenous Peoples', Survival, available here: https://www.survivalinternational.org/articles/3540-Bolsonaro

37. Maria Laura Canineu and Andrea Carvalho, 'Bolsonaro's plan to legalize crimes against indigenous peoples', *Human Rights Watch*, 1 March 2020. Available here: https://www.hrw.org/news/2020/03/01/bolsonaros-plan-legalize-crimes-against-indigenous-peoples

38. Finchelstein, *A Brief History of Fascist Lies*, 99.

39. Finchelstein, *A Brief History of Fascist Lies*, 98–9.

40. Reid, *Brazil*, 100.

41. Finchelstein, *A Brief History of Fascist Lies*, 99.

42. Finchelstein, *A Brief History of Fascist Lies*, 100.

43. Bolsonaro, quoted in Fishman, 'Jair Bolsonaro is Elected President of Brazil'.

44. Bolsonaro, quoted in Fishman, 'Jair Bolsonaro is Elected President of Brazil'.

45. Bolsonaro, quoted in Fishman, 'Jair Bolsonaro is Elected President of Brazil'.

46. Bolsonaro, quoted in Mudde, *The Far Right Today*, 35.

47. Platt, *Nothing By Accident*, 18.

48. Platt, *Nothing By Accident*, 22.

49. Fernando de Barros e Silva, quoted in Platt, *Nothing By Accident*, 22.

50. Platt, *Nothing By Accident*, 21.

51. Platt, *Nothing By Accident*, 22.

52. Finchelstein, *A Brief History of Fascist Lies*, 100.

53. Mariana Simões, 'Brazil's Bolsonaro on the Environment, in His Own Words', *New York Times*, 28 August 2019, available here: https://www.nytimes.com/2019/08/27/world/americas/bolsonaro-brazil-environment.html

54. Simões, 'Brazil's Bolsonaro on the Environment'.

55. Mauricio Angelo, 'Brazil Slashes Budget to Fight Climate Change as Deforestation Spikes', Reuters, 2 June 2020, available here: https://uk.reuters.com/article/us-brazil-deforestation-climate-change-a/brazil-slashes-budget-to-fight-climate-change-as-deforestation-spikes-idUSKBN2392LC

56. Angelo, 'Brazil slashes budget to fight climate change as deforestation spikes'.

57. Angelo, 'Brazil slashes budget to fight climate change as deforestation spikes'.

58. 'Jair Bolsonaro: "Poop Every Other Day" to Protect the Environment', BBC News, 10 August 2019, available here: https://www.bbc.co.uk/news/world-latin-america-49304358

59. 'Brazil Foreign Minister Says 'There is no Climate Change Catastrophe'', *Reuters*, 11 September 2019, available here: https://uk.reuters.

com/article/us-brazil-environment-araujo/brazil-foreign-minister-says-there-is-no-climate-change-catastrophe-idUKKCN1VW2S2

60. Marina Silva, quoted in Flavia Bellieni Zimmermann, 'Bolsonaro's War on the Environment and Climate Change', Australian Institute of International Affairs, 6 August 2019, available here: https://www.internationalaffairs.org.au/australianoutlook/bolsonaros-war-on-the-environment-and-climate-change/

61. Silva, quoted in Zimmermann, 'Bolsonaro's War on the Environment and Climate Change'.

62. Jeremy Schulman, 'Every Insane Thing Donald Trump Has Said About Global Warming', *Mother Jones*, available here: https://www.motherjones.com/environment/2016/12/trump-climate-timeline/

63. Stella Schaller and Alexander Carius, 'Convenient Truths – Mapping Climate Agendas of Right-Wing Populist Parties in Europe', Adelphi, 2019, available here: https://www.adelphi.de/en/publication/convenient-truths

64. Patrik Hermansson, 'The Far Right, Europe and Climate Change', HOPE not hate, 2019, available here: https://www.hopenothate.org.uk/magazine/climate-change-far-right/the-far-right-europe-and-climate-change/

65. David Lawrence, 'The Regrowth of Eco-Fascism', HOPE not hate, 2019, available here: https://www.hopenothate.org.uk/magazine/climate-change-far-right/the-regrowth-of-eco-fascism/

66. Lawrence, 'The Regrowth of Eco-Fascism'.

67. Lawrence, 'The Regrowth of Eco-Fascism'.

68. UNHCR Operations Portal: Refugee Situation, available here: https://data2.unhcr.org/en/situations/mediterranean

INDEX

Ashcroft, Michael 40
Atkinson, Graeme 31
Austria 97, 206
Ayling, Alan 53, 56

B
Babri Masjid mosque 224–5
Bailey, Bob 33
Bakri Muhammad, Omar 28, 46,
     68, 70
Banerjee, Sumanta 226
Banks, Arron 38–9
Bannon, Steve 184, 227
Barker, Chris 139–44
Barros e Silva, Fernando de 248
Bartlett, Jamie 89
Beackon, Derek 24–5, 179
Bedford-Turner, Jeremy 179
Belang, Vlaams 110
Belgium 97, 110, 172
beliefs, core far-right 16–17
Bernard, Roman 164
Bharatiya Janata Party (BJP)
     222–3, 224–8
Bianco, Enzo 199
Bin Laden, Osama 69
Birth of a Nation, The (Griffith)
     122
Blackwell, Tracy 6
'Bloc Against Islam' 89
Bloc Identitaire (BI) 203
Bloomsbury Forum 163–4
Bodi, Abel 212
Bokhari, Allum 184
Bolsonaro, Jair 237, 241–8,
     249–50
Borderkeepers of Alabama (BOA)
     115–21, 124–32, 134–7, 138
Bowden, Jonathan 187
Brazil 237, 241–8, 249–50
Breitbart News Network 183–4
Breivik, Anders Behring 11, 50
Brexit 36, 38–41

Brexit Party 109
Brexitland (Sobolewska and Ford)
     39
Brim, Christine 51
Britain First (BF) 57–9, 62
British Citizens Against Muslim
     Extremists 52
British National Party (BNP)
     2010 election 31–5
     anti-black racism 24, 25
     anti-Muslim racism 26, 27–8
     decline 35
     electoral rise 28–9
     first MP 24–5
     HNH campaigns against 8–9,
        10, 21–3, 29–30, 31–4, 36
     modernisation 25–6
     origins 24
     publications 25, 27, 28
     violence 33–4
     voters turning to UKIP 38
Buckby, Jack 91
Busher, Joel 53, 56

C
C-Star, vessel 191, 193–201
Cameron, David 36
Camus, Jean-Yves 16
Carius, Alexander 251
Carlqvist, Ingrid 91, 167
Carroll, Kevin 46, 48, 57
Carter, Rosie 187
Centre for New Community (CNC)
     137–8
Center for Security Policy (CSP)
     148
Champetier, Charles 204–5
Chega 8
China 239
Choudary, Anjem 15, 46, 57, 67–8,
     70, 71, 72
Chowdhury, Mohammed 71
Churchwell, Sarah 122

Index

May, Edward S. 51
Merwe, Ben van der 214
Mignone, Roberto 104–5
migrants *see* refugees and migrants
misogyny 174, 244; *see also* sexism
Miyoshi, Masaki 255
Modi, Narendra
    anti-Muslim legislation 218,
      230–33, 234–5
    anti-Muslim violence 221–2
    fascism 225–6
    Hindutva movement 223
    international networks 221,
      227–8
    Ram Temple Movement 224–5
    rise of 221–2, 226–7
    RSS ties 225
    Twitter account 219
Mohammed, Ibrahim 231–2
Molyneux, Stefan 6
Morawiecki, Mateusz 7
Morgan, David 151, 154–5
Morgan, John 164
Morocco 253–5, 258
Mosley, Sir Oswald 11, 23
Mudde, Cas 16–17, 96, 97, 157,
    159, 223
Mullen, Robbie 11
Murdoch, Simon
    BNP operation 33–4
    Defend Europe operation 194,
      197–8, 199
    far-right and homosexuality
      243
    From Banners to Bullets report
      203
    GI UK operation 210–11, 212,
      214, 215
    GI's attempt to block *Aquarius*
      191–2
    international alt-right report
      181
    Manosphere movement 174

Muslims Against Crusades (MAC)
    45–48, 71
Mutz, Diana 160

N
Naipaul, V.S. 220
Nation Divided, A (HNH) 143
National Action 11
National Democratic Alliance
    (NDA) 227
National Front (NF) 23–4, 25, 27,
    207
National Policy Institute (NPI)
    163–6, 168, 184–5
National Radical Camp (ONR)
    3–4, 5, 6
National Rally (RN)/Front National
    25, 97, 109, 110, 261
National Socialist Underground 10
National Volunteer Organization
    (RSS) 223–4, 225–6
nationalism 24, 124, 140, 171–2,
    183, 185, 204, 222–6, 251–2
Neiwert, David 115, 158–9
neo-fascism 96
Neoreactionary movement 174–5
New Face of Digital Populism, The
    (Demos) 98
New Threat? A (HNH) 212
New York Times 159, 188, 189,
    249
New Zealand 11–12, 202
Ng, Michael 238
Norway 11, 50, 212–13
Nowicki, Andy 164

O
Obama, Barack 127–8, 130, 134,
    158
Observer, The 71, 143, 213–14
O'Kelly, Jeffery 154
online antagonistic communities
    172, 173